Horizons
of the Sacred

A VOLUME IN THE SERIES

Cushwa Center Studies of Catholicism
in Twentieth-Century America
edited by R. Scott Appleby, University of Notre Dame

*Claiming the City: Politics, Faith, and the Power
of Place in St. Paul*
Mary Lethert Wingerd

Horizons
of the Sacred

Mexican Traditions
in U.S. Catholicism

Edited by

TIMOTHY MATOVINA

GARY RIEBE-ESTRELLA, SVD

Cornell University Press / Ithaca and London

First published 2002 by Cornell University Press
First printing, Cornell Paperbacks, 2002

Printed in the United States of America

Library of Congress Cataloging-in-Publication Data

Horizons of the sacred : Mexican traditions in U.S. Catholicism / edited by Timothy Matovina, Gary Riebe-Estrella.
    p. cm. — (Cushwa Center studies of Catholicism in twentieth-century America)
Includes bibliographical references and index.
    ISBN 0-8014-4011-4 (cloth : alk. paper) — ISBN 0-8014-8822-2 (pbk. : alk. paper)
    1. Mexican American Catholics—History.   2. Catholic Church—United States—History.   I. Matovina, Timothy M., 1955–   II. Riebe-Estrella, Gary, 1946–   III. Series.
BX1407.M48 H67 2002
282'.73'0896872—dc21   2002004507

Cornell University Press strives to use environmentally responsible suppliers and materials to the fullest extent possible in the publishing of its books. Such materials include vegetable-based, low-VOC inks and acid-free papers that are recycled, totally chlorine-free, or partly composed of nonwood fibers.

Cloth printing   10 9 8 7 6 5 4 3 2 1

Paperback printing   10 9 8 7 6 5 4 3 2 1

Contents

Preface

This book began with a gracious invitation from Scott Appleby, then director of the Cushwa Center for the Study of American Catholicism at the University of Notre Dame. Scott asked us to participate in the Cushwa Center's larger project on the history of twentieth-century Catholicism in the United States. With generous support from the Lilly Endowment, the project gathered more than forty scholars from across the country to examine twentieth-century U.S. Catholicism in three broad areas: the public presence of Catholics in American life, Catholic women, and the relationship between Catholic practices and Catholic identity. Our charge was to assemble a volume on U.S. Latino religious traditions.

Our first concern was choosing a focus for our exploration. While "Latino Catholicism" may be a convenient term to distinguish the religious world of U.S. Latino Catholics from those of the dominant culture and other ethnic and racial groups in the United States, in fact there is no such thing as a generic Latino Catholicism (nor of a generic African, Asian, European, or Native American Catholicism). Representing more than twenty countries of origin, the Hispanic or Latino population in the United States practices its faith in a variety of ways mirroring its multiple origins. Given this complexity and diversity, we decided to focus on the religious traditions of Mexican American communities in the United States, both because the Mexican-descent population represents some 60 percent of U.S. Latinos and because it is the Latino religious world with which we are most familiar.

We invited contributors who in some fashion practice the type of Mexican American religious traditions we asked them to study. While their practice might be seen as compromising the objectivity of their work, we felt that, given the virtual silence of participants from these religious traditions in many scholarly works, studying these practices as "outsiders" does not result in objectivity and potentially leads to objectivization. As will be clear to readers of this volume, the writers are careful to locate themselves in relation to the practices about which they are writing.

Given the complexities of studying religious traditions and their meanings, we endeavored to enrich the volume by making it as interdisciplinary as possible. Scholars with expertise in religious studies, sociology, Chicana/o studies, critical theory, ethnography, social history, and theology met over the course of two years to develop and write their essays. We are deeply grateful to the contributors for conducting these fascinating and candid conversations in a spirit of cooperation and friendship. To be sure, the various authors reveal differences of method, approach, and interpretation. Nonetheless, our collaboration is evident in the significant disciplinary overlap in the essays.

Two other events in the U.S. Catholicism project contributed to the development of this book. One was consultation with members of the Catholic practices and identity group from the Cushwa project: Joseph Chinnici, Paula Kane, Margaret McGuinness, James O'Toole, and Leslie Tentler. The other was the Cushwa Center's March 2000 national conference, at which we formally presented our papers for comment and critique. Milagros Peña and Robert J. Schreiter, noted scholars in their respective fields of sociology of religion and theology, were invited to respond to our presentations, and a distinguished audience engaged us in further critical conversation about our work. Both meetings were important to the final book. Since a number of these scholars have a vital interest but no extensive expertise in Mexican American Catholicism, their insights helped us to shape this volume not just for experts in the field but also for scholars, students, pastors, church leaders, and others who want to take a deeper look at Latino faith expressions like those of Mexican Americans.

As director of the Cushwa Center, Scott Appleby exceeded all our expectations in his support of this project, from his wise counsel on the initial vision for the volume to his generous efforts in helping us with final editorial matters. Other members of the Cushwa Center team, Barbara Lockwood, Christopher Shannon, John Haas, and Kathleen Sprows Cummings also gave us inspiration and unwavering support throughout the entire project. Jay Dolan and John McGreevy, professors of history at the

University of Notre Dame and fellows of the Cushwa Center, offered insightful comments on key sections of the manuscript. Sheri Englund and her colleagues at Cornell University Press provided outstanding editorial guidance. We are also indebted to the two reviewers for Cornell University Press who offered valuable critique of the manuscript, as well as to José Ramirez for the superb art that adorns the book cover. Ardea Russo and Clifford Green ably assisted in preparing the bibliography and endnotes; generous funding for their assistance came from the Department of Theology and the Institute for Latino Studies at the University of Notre Dame, respectively. Above all, along with our coauthors in this volume, we thank the many leaders and participants in Mexican American religious traditions whose fervor inspired us to examine more deeply their treasured expressions of identity and faith.

TIMOTHY MATOVINA

GARY RIEBE-ESTRELLA, SVD

Horizons
of the Sacred

Timothy Matovina and Gary Riebe-Estrella, SVD

Introduction

THE PARISHIONERS of St. Leander's Church in northern California were in conflict. As the date approached for the December 12 feast of Our Lady of Guadalupe, the revered patroness of the Mexican people, a threat loomed that the annual parish Guadalupe celebration would be canceled. That year December 12 fell on the third Sunday of Advent, the liturgical season that precedes Christmas. Since Catholic liturgical norms state that the Sunday Mass has precedence over feast days, the parish liturgical director had declared that no Mass for Guadalupe could be celebrated. Mexican-descent congregants were distraught and bewildered: how could a parish that called itself Catholic fail to offer their celestial mother proper honor on her feast day? After some confusion and consternation, the pastoral staff agreed to a compromise: a Mass in honor of Guadalupe would be celebrated at 5:00 A.M., early enough not to upset the regular Sunday Mass schedule. Few would come at such an early hour anyway, pastoral leaders reasoned. To their amazement, despite the cold and dark winter morning, by the time the Mass began a standing-room-only crowd of devotees had gathered to acclaim their patroness and fulfill their longstanding sacred tradition.[1]

Such instances of misunderstanding, disagreement, and at times even open conflict are not uncommon as the Hispanic presence in U.S. Catholicism continues to expand rapidly. Of course, not all Hispanic Catholics are newcomers; subjects of the Spanish crown founded the first permanent European settlement in what is now the continental United States at St. Augustine, Florida, in 1565, and in 1598 they established the permanent foundation of Catholicism in what is now the Southwest, at present-day El Paso, Texas. Until the last half-century, however, Hispanics constituted a relatively small and frequently overlooked group among U.S. Catholics. Their numbers and their influence have increased dramatically with an influx of newcomers from such diverse locales as Puerto Rico, Cuba, the Dominican Republic, El Salvador, Guatemala, Nicaragua, Colombia, Peru, Ecuador, and Argentina, along with ongoing Mexican immigration, all swelling the ranks of an established Hispanic population consisting primarily of Mexican-descent Catholics. Hispanic Catholic communities, previously concentrated in New York, the Southwest, and some midwestern cities, now extend from Seattle to Boston, from Miami to Alaska. According to the 2000 Census, Latinos in the United States now number some 35.3 million, fully 12.5 percent of the total population, and constitute the largest minority group in the country. Today Hispanics are also the largest ethnic group among U.S. Catholics, and in the next few decades they will become the majority. This demographic shift presents both an opportunity and a challenge that scholars and church leaders have yet to comprehend or address fully.

The growing presence of Latinas and Latinos and the wide array of Latino rituals, devotions, and sacred imagery have both shaped and been shaped by U.S. Catholicism and the pluralistic U.S. milieu. The essays in this volume examine the worldview underlying the religious traditions of the largest U.S. Latino group, Mexican Americans.[2] The authors of these essays are scholars with expertise in theology, social history, ethnography, critical theory, Chicana/o studies, sociology, and religious studies. All draw on the literature and methodologies of their own disciplines, and on the insights of other disciplines, to address three overarching issues: the challenge of understanding U.S. Catholicism in a way that more fully accounts for and embraces the presence of Mexican Americans and their religious traditions, the influence of U.S. church and society on those traditions, and the contributions that Mexican Americans and their faith expressions offer the wider church and society.

Mexican Americans and the "Remapping" of U.S. Catholicism

Recent general histories of U.S. Catholicism tend to address more adequately the Hispanic Catholic presence and contribution. For instance, most historians now begin the U.S. Catholic story with the Spanish colonial era. Woven into the narrative of noteworthy works like those of James Hennesey, Jay Dolan, and Charles R. Morris are discussions of immigration patterns, demographic shifts, and Latino Catholic leaders, organizations, movements, religious traditions, political involvement, journalism, and social activism. But despite such efforts to integrate Latinos more fully into the U.S. Catholic story, historical treatments often subsume Hispanics into an Americanization paradigm presumed to hold true for all Catholics in the United States. For example, Morris concluded his acclaimed 1997 work with the assertion that there is a "standoff between the tradition of Rome and the tradition of America [the United States]." His claim is based on an understanding of U.S. Catholicism as, in the words of Dolan, a nineteenth- and early twentieth-century "immigrant church" that after World War II had "come of age" as "American."[3]

Some scholars have questioned whether the Americanization paradigm accounts accurately for the experience of European Catholic immigrants and their descendants.[4] Nonetheless, the contention that U.S. Catholics of European descent have become "Americanized" to a significant degree remains an important interpretive lens through which a number of scholars and other observers examine Catholicism in the United States. For example, many analysts hold that the national parish enabled European immigrants and their descendants to integrate into U.S. church and society from a position of strength. By serving as safe havens in a strange new land, these ethnic enclave congregations facilitated a gradual adjustment to U.S. society with the support of an institution that was familiar. In time national parishes gave way to interethnic, territorial parishes in which the children and grandchildren of immigrants integrated into the "middle American" milieu with Catholics of other ethnic backgrounds. In the words of Silvano Tomasi, while facilitating the ongoing Catholic allegiance of numerous immigrants and their descendants, the national parish simultaneously mediated the process of "integration through separation."[5]

Clearly, the notion that U.S. Catholics are immigrants on the road to Americanization does not accurately capture the Mexican American experience. Mexican Catholics in the Southwest during the mid-nineteenth century were not immigrants but enduring communities of faith that survived the U.S. takeover of northern Mexico following the war between the two nations (1846–1848).[6] In the wake of their incorporation into the United States, an activist Mexican laity, at times accompanied by clergy, asserted their Mexican Catholic heritage through collective efforts like the persistent celebration of their longstanding public rituals and devotions. From Texas to California, various Mexican Catholic communities continued to enthusiastically celebrate established local traditions such as pilgrimages, Our Lady of Guadalupe, *los pastores* (a festive proclamation of the shepherds who worshiped the newborn infant Jesus), Holy Week, Corpus Christi, and established patronal feast days. As Bishop Henry Granjon of Tucson noted in 1902 during his first pastoral visit to Las Cruces, New Mexico, many Mexican-descent Catholics in the Southwest "continue[d] to observe their own traditions and customs as they did before the annexation of their lands by the American Union." Among these traditions and customs was *compadrazgo* (literally, "godparentage"), the network of relationships among families that is created through sponsorship in baptisms and other sacramental celebrations. According to Bishop Granjon, in the Southwest "these multiple attachments, mostly between families, maintain the unity of the Mexican population and permit them to resist, to a certain extent, the invasions of the Anglo-Saxon race."[7] Whereas the saga of nineteenth-century European Catholic émigrés is one of seeking a haven in a new land, the story of the first Mexican American Catholics is in large part a tale of faith, struggle, and endurance in their ancestral homeland.

Although there was some previous immigration, particularly from 1890 to 1910, massive Mexican immigration began only after the outbreak of the Mexican Revolution in 1910, just a decade before restrictive U.S. immigration laws vastly reduced the influx of Europeans. Thus, precisely during the era when European immigration declined and descendants of European immigrants were purportedly on their way to a "coming of age" as Americans, Mexican Catholic immigrants were repopulating and revitalizing enduring communities of faith in the Southwest such as San Antonio, as can be seen in Timothy Matovina's essay. At the same time, Mexican immigrants established scores of Mexican Catholic communities in the Southwest and beyond, particularly in midwestern locales like Chicago, examined in this volume by Karen Mary Davalos.

As the work of historian Roberto Treviño demonstrates, like European immigrants a number of Mexican American Catholics learn English, move into the middle class and "mainstream" U.S. society, and, in many cases, subsequently practice their faith in more heterogeneous, English-speaking parishes. Often a decline in their practice of Mexican Catholic traditions accompanies their participation in these parishes.[8] Like Treviño's insightful analysis, the essays in this volume indicate that sharp distinctions between "traditional" Mexican immigrants and culture and more "assimilated" Mexican Americans do not accurately reflect the complex responses of Mexican-descent residents to the U.S. milieu. To be sure, some newly arrived immigrants and more-established Mexican Americans at times conflict over perceived cultural differences. However, the frequent travel of Mexican immigrants and some Mexican Americans back and forth across the U.S.-Mexico border complicates attempts to assess their collective identities, much less facilely divide them into distinct groups that have either "lost" or "retained" the Spanish language and their Mexican heritage. The four case studies that follow examine how, like European Catholic immigrants of earlier generations, Mexican-descent residents selectively engage their heritage and the U.S. context to transform their identities, faith expressions, and strategies for social activism.

Perhaps largely as a result of ongoing immigration and more consistent contact with their homeland than that of European émigrés, Mexican-descent Catholics in the United States today tend to live in urban clusters and frequently exert efforts to retain their language and culture. All these factors increase the chances that, despite transformations in their religious traditions as they adapt to the U.S. context, a significant number of Mexican-descent Catholics will continue to celebrate those traditions in some form for the foreseeable future.[9]

An expanding Mexican-descent population is part of larger demographic shifts within U.S. Catholicism. The U.S. Catholic Church is no longer an overwhelmingly immigrant church, as it was a century ago, but nor is it solely an "Americanized" church. Rather, it is a church run largely by middle-class, European-descent Catholics with growing numbers of Mexican, other Hispanic, Asian, and some African immigrants, along with sizable contingents of native-born Mexican American, other Latino, and African American Catholics and some Native Americans. Depictions of U.S. Catholicism as an immigrant church that has come of age do not adequately account for the seismic shift in the demographic profile of contemporary U.S. Catholicism.

The rituals, devotions, and faith expressions of U.S. Catholics since the Second Vatican Council reflect divergent trajectories between Mexican American Catholics and the descendants of European immigrant Catholics. By all accounts, among "American" Catholics practices like preconciliar forms of Marian and Eucharistic devotion have faded considerably since the Council. To be sure, as Joseph Chinnici and Angelyn Dries have shown, contemporary Euro-American Catholics have also reoriented previous forms of devotion into expressions of collective and personal prayer like retreats, scripture reading, contemplative prayer, and Charismatic prayer groups. In many instances these prayer forms are intended to update and renew preconciliar piety and its practices.[10] Nonetheless, unlike their Euro-American Catholic counterparts, many Mexican Americans and Mexican immigrants have continued and in some cases even expanded longstanding ritual and devotional traditions, albeit in somewhat altered forms, such as the annual *Via Crucis* (Way of the Cross) in Chicago's Pilsen neighborhood.[11]

As compared to the practices of European Americans, the religious practices of Mexican Americans (what many theologians call their popular religion or popular Catholicism) reflect a divergent view of Vatican II teaching on the relationship between popular piety and liturgy (the official prayer of the church such as the seven sacraments). In their reflections on the relationship between liturgy and popular piety, many liturgists emphasize Vatican II's *Constitution on the Sacred Liturgy*, which directs that devotions be derived from the liturgy and not be construed as superseding it. Since Vatican II, the liturgical renewal in the United States has also accentuated the need for Catholics' "full and active participation" in the liturgy, especially the Eucharist, as mandated by the Council. Often this call to accentuate participation in the liturgy entails an attempt to reorient devotional piety to a stronger liturgical piety. Mexican American and other Hispanic liturgists, however, emphasize that the Council encouraged culturally conditioned expressions of faith like those that many Mexican Americans practice and treasure. As Juan Sosa bemoaned in a 1979 essay, "The Council especially attempted to thwart efforts to do without all these [popular] devotions and to reduce them exclusively to the liturgy. Yet unfortunately this became the attitude and the actions of many church leaders." Mexican American liturgists like Rosa María Icaza and Arturo Pérez echo Sosa's sentiments, citing conciliar documents like the *Decree on the Missionary Activity of the Church*, which exhorts local churches to borrow "from the customs and traditions of their people" and teaches that these churches, "adorned with their own traditions, will have their own place in the ecclesiastical communion."[12] Thus, divergent trajectories in ritual and devotional practices reflect an implicit (and at times explicit) theological debate about the teaching of Vatican II on the relationship between liturgy and popular piety.

Pastoral ministry with Mexican Americans frequently reflects this theological debate, particularly when Mexican American devotees engage priests and lay leaders of other ethnic backgrounds.[13] As the essays that follow show, pastoral ministers respond in diverse ways to Mexican American expressions of faith; their responses are frequently shaped by the particular faith expression that they address in a given pastoral situation. Some pastoral ministers try to incorporate devotions like those to Our Lady of Guadalupe into parish life and even into sacramental celebrations, often attempting to engage these devotions (which, in the case of Guadalupe, is an official liturgical feast) as a means to augment participation in parish and sacramental life. Others engage traditions like the Via Crucis as a means to call Mexicans and Mexican Americans (and others) to live gospel and church teachings on social justice. Sometimes cel-

ebrations like the *Día de los Muertos* (Day of the Dead) make more visible
or even accentuate the separation and tensions between church officials
and Catholic liturgy, on the one hand, and Chicano/a community leaders
and ritual traditions. A number of pastoral ministers condemn practices
like those associated with the healing tradition of *curanderismo* as inimi-
cal to Catholic faith and the Catholic tradition; in this case the key issue
is the theological understanding of healing and divine providence that
the practices embody.

Pastoral responses to Mexican American religious traditions are concrete manifestations of the encounter or, perhaps more accurately, collision between "American" and Latino Catholicism in the United States.
These pastoral responses reveal that the "remapping" of U.S. Catholicism entails not only integrating Mexican Americans (and other Hispanics) into U.S. Catholic historiography, but also engaging them as full
members of the U.S. Catholic Church. This challenge will require both
scholars and U.S. Catholic leaders to rethink major paradigms such as the
unilateral Americanization of an immigrant church, as well as the significance and meaning of Vatican II for contemporary U.S. Catholicism.

For pastoral ministers and theologians, the challenges may be even
greater. As the various essays in this volume collectively demonstrate,
Mexican American religious traditions are shaped by their indigenous
heritage as well as the formative influence of Spanish and later U.S.
Catholicism. Given these multiple influences, some who minister to Mexican Americans wonder how Catholic these traditions really are. Yet the
history of Catholicism itself demonstrates that doctrines and religious
practices have developed over time and have been reshaped repeatedly
as the Catholicism of the Roman Empire encountered new and different
cultures in its expansion through Western Europe, Africa, Asia, and the
Americas. In light of that history, Orlando Espín's analysis brings this volume to a close with a crucial theological and pastoral question: what criteria can we use to understand and assess Mexican American religious
traditions, whether the commonly accepted ones like devotion to Guadalupe and the Via Crucis or the ones less well received by Catholic officials
such as Día de los Muertos and curanderismo, as authentic expressions
and developments of the Catholic Tradition? Given the complexity of this
question, it is not surprising that his analysis, here presented in broad
strokes for the nonspecialist in theology, provides no definitive answer.
Nonetheless, his work complements other recent studies on continuity
and development in the Catholic Tradition, offering valuable guidance on
the criteria pastoral leaders can use to appreciate, critique, and celebrate
the religious traditions of Mexican Americans.[14]

The *Segundo Mestizaje*

Although Mexican American religious traditions are in some ways distinct from those of Euro-American Catholics, the U.S. milieu has also shaped Mexican American Catholicism and its expressions. The influence of U.S. Catholicism and the wider society on Mexican Americans and their religious traditions is part of a centuries-long historical process of *mestizaje,* a term that Virgilio Elizondo introduced among theologians and scholars to denote the mixing of two elements (cultures, religious systems, races) in such a way that a new element (a new culture, a new religious system, a new race) is created. According to Elizondo, in order to understand Mexican American religious traditions it is necessary to understand the two conquests Mexican Americans have endured: the Spanish conquest of the indigenous peoples in the territories that became New Spain (and later Mexico) and the U.S. conquest of what is now the Southwest. The effects of the second conquest continue in the pressure put on Mexican Americans to assimilate, to abandon the Mexican way for the American way. Despite this pressure, he perceives in his people a mestizo identity that is neither Mexican nor North American, neither Spanish nor indigenous, but a dynamic mixture of all these root cultures.[15]

Elizondo and other scholars contend that Mexican American life and religion are shaped in significant and ongoing ways by the *segundo* (second) mestizaje, their dramatic encounter and clash with the pluralistic U.S. milieu and a majority-culture Catholicism steeped in European (especially Irish-German) roots.[16] Mexican American scholars, activists, and other observers frequently point out, for example, that as a bicultural people they have the tremendous advantage of being formed by the richness of both parent cultures; as Elizondo puts it, the "birth out of the two great traditions allows for . . . the forging of a new existence, a new creation." However, unlike studies of the first mestizaje between the Mesoamerican religious imagination and that of the *conquistadores* of sixteenth-century Catholic Spain, most treatments of Mexican American faith expressions do not focus on a dynamic "mixing" of Mexican and U.S. religious symbols and traditions. Rather, they frequently contend that Mexican religious traditions continue in the United States, claiming that these traditions function as, in the words of Ricardo Ramírez, "a defense and protest against the demands of the dominant culture."[17]

Several essays in this volume are consistent with the assertion that Mexican American religious traditions not only express collective identity and cultural pride, but also fortify struggles for justice and resistance to assimilatory pressures. Public processions with the *morena* (brown-skinned) image of Our Lady of Guadalupe symbolically reversed the ethnic prejudice Mexican-descent devotees endured in San Antonio. In the Via Crucis through Chicago's Pilsen area, lay leaders taking the place of Jesus, Mary, and other key figures help their community to reclaim their neighborhood in ritual terms and to struggle for dignity and justice in the face of debilitating discrimination and poverty. Similarly, the Chicano movement, which began in the 1960s, encompassed the development of rituals that in part serve to counteract a racist U.S. ethos. In the main this is a movement of cultural retrieval. That is, Chicanos seek "to activate and articulate an identity through an appeal to the glories of past indigenous civilizations."[18] As the annual Día de los Muertos celebration in East Los Angeles illustrates, this attempt to recover indigenous heritage includes retrieving religious traditions and practices from those civilizations. The conscious engagement of indigenous sacred traditions as part of the Chicano identity and struggle for justice reflects the influence of cultural prejudice on ritual practices that Chicanos cultivate in the U.S. milieu.

Clearly, the notion that religious traditions are a form of resistance and an expression of group solidarity demonstrates that continuing these traditions in the United States shapes to some degree their meaning and function, since social conditions in Mexico do not provide a context for these traditions to serve as a "protest" against the "dominant culture." However, if a segundo mestizaje is indeed under way, the unanswered question is how contact with U.S. Catholicism and society is not only buttressing Mexican American resolve to maintain their group identity and treasured expressions of faith, but also transforming (both consciously and unconsciously) Mexican American Catholics and their religious practices and worldview.

The following pages offer some initial insights into this vital question. For example, the juxtaposition of indigenous, Mexican, and North American heroes, symbols, and music reveals that, at least on the level of material culture, the segundo mestizaje is well under way. At the annual Día de los Muertos commemoration in Los Angeles, participants and onlookers encounter both Nahua *danzantes* and Vietnam veterans, remembrances of César Chávez and Robert F. Kennedy, Chicano *abuelos* (grandparents) and an altar with indigenous *ofrendas* (offerings) dedicated to mother Earth, *tlatzotzompantli* (skull racks) and Chicano participants and onlookers dressed in the fashions of contemporary southern California, Our Lady of Guadalupe and a remembrance of AIDS victims, a crucifix and the Nahua mother Earth goddess Coatlicue, mariachi and rock music. Similarly, *botanicas* (herbal and religious goods stores) in East Los Angeles and elsewhere display traditional herbal remedies and everyday products common at neighborhood markets like shampoo and toothpaste, icons well known in U.S. Catholicism like the Sacred Heart of Jesus and popular Mexican healers like El Niño Fidencio, and sacred images representing the Aztec, Christian, and other religious traditions. Some younger Chicanas and Chicanos even wonder if the symbols and rituals associated with traditions like the Día de los Muertos celebration are "un-American," reflecting the influence of the majority culture and the general U.S. milieu on Chicano identity formation and Chicanos' attitudes toward their indigenous and Mexican roots.

Another significant element of the segundo mestizaje is the encounter between Mexican Americans and non-Mexican Catholic leaders in the United States. In some cases Spanish priests like those at San Fernando Cathedral in San Antonio have linked their parishioners' understanding of Guadalupan devotion with the necessity of receiving the sacraments worthily. In other instances North American, post–Vatican II clergy who have learned Spanish and sought to identify with the life and struggle of their parishioners, such as the activist priests in Chicago's Pilsen neighborhood, have made more explicit for Mexican-descent devotees the inherent social justice themes of the Via Crucis. Clergy who discourage traditions such as Día de los Muertos or curanderismo influence Mexican American attitudes about whether or not these traditions are authentically Catholic, although clearly many Mexican Americans continue these traditions despite (and sometimes in response to) church leaders' attempts to discourage or prohibit them. For good and for ill, Mexican Americans' understanding and practice of ritual and devotion are swayed by the pastoral efforts of priests and lay leaders in the United States.

Urbanization is yet another element in the religious dimensions of the segundo mestizaje. For example, as thousands of devotees process in the annual Via Crucis through the streets of Pilsen, symbolically connecting the suffering of Jesus and his mother to contemporary social ills like overcrowded housing, gang violence, city neglect of public services, absentee landlords, crowded schools, and drug addiction, the adaptation of an honored Mexican Catholic tradition to an urban U.S. landscape is visibly evident. Similarly, the healing art of curanderismo as practiced in a Los Angeles botanica involves the relocation of traditional healing practices from home to urban storefront and the varied implications this relocation has for the shape and meaning of those practices. The influences on the contemporary urban practice of curanderismo encompass diverse sources such as indigenous healing beliefs, Spanish and U.S. Catholicism, North American religion generally, capitalism, and modernity, illuminating how multiple factors in the U.S. urban milieu influence Mexican-descent practitioners as they reconfigure and redefine their religious traditions.

Although examining urbanization, contact with U.S. Catholic leaders, material culture, and ethnic prejudice offers some initial insights into the

influence of the segundo mestizaje on Mexican American religious traditions, clearly much further research is needed to discern these influences
more fully. Whereas the first mestizaje has been some five centuries in the
making, the segundo mestizaje is just barely under way; hence any attempt to explore it is inherently provisional and incomplete. As a result,
another element evident in this volume and other recent works that probe
the understanding of mestizaje is that of ambiguity. Some earlier studies
of mestizaje presumed that the outcome of such a mixing is a synthesis.
While some synthesis undoubtedly takes place, the resulting symbolic
world also contains elements that are specific to each of the originating
cosmologies. Because of the dissimilarities present in the worlds that
come together, a complete synthesis is not possible; rather, the new symbolic world is made up of synthesis and interstices. As Jorge Gracia
writes:

> In the mix produced by *mestizaje* we find elements from the original com-
> ponents which remain largely the same, even though they are not in fact
> separable; elements from the original components which remain largely
> the same and are separable; elements from the original components which
> have been modified but are still recognizable as having belonged to the
> original components; elements which have been so consolidated and
> changed that they cannot be recognized as having belonged to the original
> components but whose origins can be traced to them, and finally, elements
> which are new products resulting from the mix.[19]

To accentuate further the notion of ambiguity, some analyses of mestizo
religious cosmologies employ the Nahua word *nepantla*, which literally
means "middle place."[20] People who live in-between, in nepantla, find
themselves moving between these variously fashioned elements in a cultural or religious world whose identity is characterized precisely by its
lack of holism. That is, nepantla describes a world composed of differences that are not forced into coherence but rather remain on discrete
planes. However, for the nepantla person, his or her world is not a mul-
tiplicity of discrete worlds of meaning, but rather is a single world that
has been and is created out of the intersection of *parts* from a variety of
originally discrete worlds. It is a "borderlands" world where meanings,
perspectives, and cosmologies, either in their entirety or in parts that have
survived, collide; the primary characteristic of this new worldview is to
be found precisely in the colliding.[21]

Moreover, this "borderlands" reality should not be construed as static.
Rather, additional worlds of meaning or cosmologies may come into collision with the still interacting original mestizaje in such a way as to com-

plexify the elements of this world "in between." These additional "colli-sions" give that world new shaping, often masking even further the orig-inating elements that survive, as well as their interrelationship. Local variations of religious traditions and their meaning further complicate the analysis and preclude any conclusive definition of a mestizo (or other) religious worldview. In probing Mexican American religious traditions in the context of the segundo mestizaje, the essays in this volume are con-sistent with other contemporary scholarship that seeks to illuminate the complexities and even the ambiguities and inconsistencies of religious traditions and their meanings.[22]

The Symbolic World of Mexican American Religion

Clearly, the U.S. context has influenced Mexican American Catholicism and its expressions. But the converse is also true: Mexican Americans have shaped and contributed to U.S. Catholicism and the wider society. In their 1983 pastoral letter on Hispanic ministry, for example, the U.S. Catholic bishops noted that Mexican Americans and other Hispanics exemplify values that uplift church and society, such as respect for the dignity of each person, profound love for family life, a deep sense of com-munity, an appreciation of life as a precious gift from God, and pervasive and authentic devotion to Mary, the mother of God.[23]

The following essays make clear that Mexican Americans' contributions also include their vibrant worship and treasured expressions of faith. This volume complements previous investigations of Mexican American reli-gious traditions by not only describing those traditions but also probing more deeply into the symbolic worldview that underlies them.[24] Roberto Goizueta's essay most clearly delineates the significant contribution that the symbolic worldview embodied in Mexican American religion—what Goizueta calls Mexican American "theological anthropology"—offers the wider church and society. He argues that despite the influence of the U.S. milieu, this symbolic worldview can serve as a healthy corrective for modern dichotomies such as the individual and community, the materi-al and the spiritual, public and private, life and death. Given the frequent claims of scholars, religious leaders, and other observers that contempo-rary U.S. culture is plagued with misguided values like excessive individ-ualism, consumerism, the relegation of religion to the private or domestic sphere, and the denial of death, Goizueta's essay poses a provocative chal-lenge for both U.S. churches and U.S. society.[25]

As he himself points out, Goizueta's analysis of the symbolic world-view underneath Mexican American religious traditions is consistent with some findings in the four case studies that precede it. Although these studies focus on particular communities and thus do not reflect how traditions like Guadalupan devotion, the Via Crucis, the Día de los Muertos, and curanderismo are practiced among *all* Mexican Americans, collectively the case studies provide thick description and contextualized interpretations that complement Goizueta's more overarching analysis.[26] For example, Luis León's essay reveals that the *curandera* Hortencia and her clients see her work as healing not merely the body or merely the soul, but the whole person within the entire social fabric of their lives. Their sense that sickness stems from a lack of harmony between body and soul, as well as between a person and the network of relationships that sustains them, reflects Goizueta's material/spiritual and individual/community dichotomies. Similarly, in their examination of Día de los Muertos in Los Angeles, Lara Medina and Gilbert Cadena show in vivid detail how contemporary Chicanas and Chicanos ritually engage and even publicly cavort with symbols of death; in the process these ritual participants celebrate their ongoing relationship with their beloved deceased and subvert any notion that death marks a definitive split and departure from life in this world. Like Karen Mary Davalos's study of the Via Crucis in Chicago and Timothy Matovina's exploration of Guadalupan devotion in San Antonio, Medina and Cadena's essay also shows how Mexican American devotees enact religious traditions like processions, prayers of intercession, and making altars in the public spaces of urban life, thus blurring alleged distinctions between private and public domains.

The case studies in this volume further clarify, amplify, and enhance Goizueta's broad theological sketch of the symbolic worldview of Mexican American religion. One key insight is that this worldview has, as renowned Chicana author Gloria Anzaldúa puts it, a "tolerance for contradictions [and] ambiguity."[27] Given the complexity and dynamism of mestizo and other worldviews, as well as local variations in rituals and devotions and their meanings, it is not surprising to find ambiguities and even contradictions in the underlying meaning of Mexican American religious traditions. For example, as Luis León observes, clients of the curandera Hortencia state that curanderismo is contrary to the teachings of the Catholic Church; nonetheless, they also express a strong sense of their own identity as Catholics despite their visits to a curandera. Additionally, whereas Mexican émigrés in San Antonio expressed an identity rooted in Catholicism and Mexican nationalism through their Guadalupan devotion, subsequent Chicana and Chicano organizers of the Día de los Muertos in Los Angeles proudly express an identity based primarily on an indigenous heritage that predates the Mexican nation and Iberian Catholics' conquest and evangelization of their ancestors. Practitioners of the

Via Crucis in Chicago contest the "architecture of domination" rooted in modern capitalism, while the relocation of curanderismo to an East Los Angeles storefront botanica evidences some degree of accommodation to the capitalistic marketplace. The ambiguities and divergent meanings of religious practices in and between particular communities reflect a symbolic worldview that is elastic, malleable, and constantly evolving. As Luis León's essay so aptly concludes, the practices that mediate this worldview are a form of "religious poetics," a fluid tradition that devotees can adapt to changing circumstances in their continuing efforts to commune with and enlist the assistance of heavenly powers and beings.

The "tolerance for contradictions and ambiguity" reflected in Mexican American religious traditions is most clearly evident in how these traditions can both reinforce and transcend social hierarchies within Mexican American communities themselves. These social constructs include hierarchies that favor economic and social elites and even preference "in-group" members of parishes.[28] Ambiguous and even contradictory meanings mediated in these religious traditions are especially conspicuous with regard to social hierarchies based on gender. Previous studies have revealed the ways in which Mexican American religious traditions contest the oppression of women in church and society. For example, Ana María Díaz-Stevens has argued that despite the patriarchy of institutional Catholicism and Latin American societies, Latino Catholicism has a "matriarchal core," in that Latina women have consistently exercised autonomous authority in the devotional life of their people. Focusing more specifically on contemporary Mexican American women, Jeanette Rodriguez examines their engagement of devotion to Our Lady of Guadalupe as a source of empowerment.[29] Like these previous works, the case studies here reveal the pronounced role of women as empowered leaders and participants in Mexican American religious traditions. But they also reveal that at times these traditions provide divine sanction for patriarchy within Mexican American communities themselves. Thus while Guadalupan celebrations at San Antonio enabled women to assume public leadership roles and even occasioned women's demands for equal treatment from male parish leaders, that same devotion also reinforced presumptions of a limiting domestic role for women. Similarly, in the annual Pilsen Via Crucis women exercise significant leadership and pronounce their vital concerns in public prayer. But they also confront patriarchal constraints in their occasional conflicts with male organizers and in their efforts to express in ritual terms their own notions of womanhood and motherhood through key Via Crucis figures like Mary, the women of Jerusalem, and Veronica.

Another insight about the symbolic worldview of Mexican American religious traditions is the notion that these traditions transcend time, space, and, as Goizueta puts it, the "real" and the merely "imagined."[30] One leader in the Pilsen Via Crucis summed up the intersection of yesterday and today: "Christ suffered way back two thousand years ago, but he's still suffering now. His people are suffering. We're lamenting and wailing. And also we are a joyful people at the same time . . . So this is not a story, this is not a fairy tale. It happened, and it's happening now." This leader and other participants in Mexican American faith expressions like Guadalupan devotion perceive ritual as a powerful means to mediate an encounter with God and other celestial beings that transcends limiting distinctions like those between Pilsen and Calvary, Chicago and Jerusalem, San Antonio and Mexico, our "secular" age and the "sacred" time of Jesus. For Mexican American devotees, their religious traditions are not mere pious reenactments but corporeal encounters with sacred times, places, persons, and events that shape their everyday world and its meaning.

Perhaps the most distinguishing feature of this symbolic worldview is belief in the constant presence of the sacred in daily life, a feature already noted by others.[31] Some Mexican exiles in early twentieth-century San Antonio claimed, for example, that the intervention of celestial powers in human affairs took the form of divine retribution, in this case God's punishment of the war-stricken Mexican people for their lack of Guadalupan devotion and their widespread infidelity to divine mandates. In all four case studies here, Mexican American devotees constructed altars on which they juxtaposed symbols and images expressing their conviction that the sacred is immanent and ever-present.[32] Furthermore, public processions that spill out onto city streets and plazas, such as those for Our Lady of Guadalupe, the Via Crucis, and Día de los Muertos, remind both participants and onlookers that the sacred is present even in the midst of the racism, poverty, violence, and alienation of modern urban life. Several essays also illuminate devotees' belief in the intervention of celestial beings in human affairs, such as the healing power of Guadalupe, the curandera Hortencia and her clients' invocation to the saints (both "official" and unofficial) for heavenly assistance, and the *milagritos* (little miracles) that Via Crucis participants attribute to the power of prayer and a loving God who responds to it generously.

In the end, of course, given the complexity and dynamism of mestizo and other worldviews, the various analyses presented in this volume cannot offer a comprehensive, definitive articulation of the worldview that underlies Mexican American religious traditions. Nonetheless, through the interplay between thick description and theoretical analysis in the individual essays and in the volume as a whole, this book offers a prolonged gaze at the world of Mexican American religious traditions in all its complexity, intricacy, and ambiguity. Our collective hope is that the insights provided will enable students, scholars, church leaders, pastoral ministers, and others to more fully understand and engage Mexican Americans, their religious traditions, and their significant contribution to U.S. Catholicism and the wider society.

Timothy Matovina

Companion in Exile

Guadalupan Devotion at San Fernando Cathedral, San Antonio, Texas, 1900–1940

JOSEFINA RODRÍGUEZ has worshiped at San Fernando Cathedral for most of her ninety years. Of her innumerable visits to San Fernando for prayer, one stands out most clearly in her mind: the day her son, Alex, left for the Korean War. As on so many occasions before and since, on that day Josefina first prayed before the main altar and then proceeded to the side altar of Our Lady of Guadalupe, *La Virgen Morena* (the Brown Virgin), who chose the Mexican people as her own. Josefina's gratitude to Guadalupe for her son's safe return a few years later connects her both to this celestial protectress and to San Fernando as the sacred place where her plea for help was heard.[1]

Josefina is one of many Guadalupan devotees I met at San Fernando while I was a parishioner there from 1992 to 1995. Since moving from San Antonio I have returned to San Fernando every year for key celebrations of the annual liturgical cycle like the Guadalupe feast and for continued conversations with parishioners like Josefina. These parishioners' passionate recollections of the San Fernando of their youth prompted me to investigate devotional and congregational life at the parish during the first decades of the twentieth century, when thousands of Mexican émigrés like Josefina resettled in San Antonio.

Josefina and numerous other émigrés had arrived in San Antonio by 1931, the four hundredth anniversary of Guadalupe's reported apparitions to Juan Diego, an indigenous convert to Christianity. San Fernando's Guadalupe feast that year was arguably the most extensive Guadalupe celebration since the parish's founding two centuries earlier. A November 29 parish bulletin announcement reminded cathedral congregants that the forthcoming celebrations in honor of their patroness should be days of enthusiastic devotion "for all those who feel Mexican blood run through their veins, as well as for native Tejanos [Texans of Mexican descent]." In a local newspaper article the following week, a priest assigned to San Antonio opined that devotees at San Fernando and surrounding parishes "will vie with their countymen across the Rio Grande in doing honor to their queen and patroness." To commemorate the quadricentennial San Fernando parishioners held a novena (nine days of services) that included a daily sung Mass offered "for the persecuted church in Mexico." Parishioners also donated a replica of the image of La Virgen Morena, which was blessed and enshrined in the cathedral on Sunday, December 6. On December 11, the eve of the feast, a large public procession wound through the streets and plazas around the cathedral. For the feast itself, large crowds attended the five scheduled Masses, another evening public procession, and the closing service of the novena. One parish society reported that the congregation celebrated the novena and feast with "extraordinary solemnity"; San Fernando clergy stated that the huge crowds and devotional fervor expressed in the religious services were a fitting tribute to Guadalupe for the countless favors she had granted "her chosen people, the beautiful Mexican nation." Prominent among the participants at the Guadalupe celebrations was the local ordinary (bishop in charge of the diocese), Arthur J. Drossaerts; his experience at such celebrations led him to describe the Guadalupan devotion of Mexican-descent Catholics as "deeply ingrained in their soul."[2]

The enthusiastic celebrations at San Fernando in 1931 embodied a parish tradition of Guadalupan devotion ever since the parish's foundation in 1731; in 1755 a group of town officials declared that "now and forever we shall celebrate the feast of Blessed Mary of Guadalupe."[3] At the same time, the fervent 1931 Guadalupe celebrations illuminate the enhancement and revitalization of a centuries-old parish tradition by the devotees who migrated to San Antonio during and after the Mexican Revolution (1910–1917).

During the first four decades of the twentieth century, the Guadalupan devotion of San Fernando parishioners expressed diverse meanings— ethnic solidarity, patriotism, resistance to racism, a justification for social hierarchy, conflicting views of women's role in familial and public life, and a plea for celestial protection and healing. In their ritual exchanges with *la morenita*, their brown-skinned celestial guardian, the faithful sought

San Fernando Cathedral, c. 1910. Courtesy the San Antonio Express-News Collection, University of Texas Institute of Texan Cultures, San Antonio.

solace and hope and shaped their response to the changing conditions in their lives and in the urban landscape around them. Thus the diverse meanings of their Guadalupan devotion cannot be understood without an examination of the shifting urban and congregational context in which parishioners enacted rituals and devotions, particularly those in honor of Guadalupe.

The Urban Context: Immigrants, Municipal Growth, and Social Conflict

Demographic changes in San Antonio facilitated the exuberant devotion evident in the 1931 Guadalupe celebrations. Migration from south of the border continued after Texas's split from Mexico in 1836 and increased during the last decades of the nineteenth century as expanded rail transportation expedited travel and resettlement. The immigrant flow accelerated further after the outbreak of the Mexican Revolution in 1910. Intermittent periods of relative calm followed the enactment of the 1917 Mexican constitution, but spontaneous violence erupted once again in central and western Mexico when President Plutarco Elías Calles (1924–1928) enforced anticlerical articles of that constitution. The resulting guerrilla war, known as the Cristero Rebellion (1926–1929), drove even more émigrés north to the United States, many fleeing religious persecution. During the 1930s the Great Depression and an accompanying wave of nativist fever led to the repatriation of numerous Mexicans and the illegal deportation of many Tejanos, native-born citizens of the United States who increasingly identified themselves as "Mexican Americans." Mexican president Lázaro Cárdenas reconciled with Catholic church officials in 1936, opening the door for some Mexicans to return home. Despite these developments, the previous influx of Mexican nationals had already augmented San Antonio's Mexican-descent population significantly. The San Antonio Public Service Company reported that in 1900 San Antonio had 13,722 Mexican-descent residents, just over a fourth of the total population. For 1940, the same source revealed that some 103,000 Mexican-descent residents accounted for more than 40 percent of the city's population.[4]

Among other changes in San Antonio's urban landscape, the city's expanding population increased the number of churches. San Antonio had more than thirty Catholic parishes in 1940, a threefold increase over four decades. In 1900 San Fernando was the only Catholic parish in which Mexican Americans and Mexicans formed the majority; by 1940 at least ten more parishes served predominantly Mexican-descent congregations. The number of Protestant churches also grew rapidly, as did Protestant outreach by Baptists, Presbyterians, Methodists, and Lutherans to Spanish-speaking residents.[5]

During these decades the San Fernando congregation more than doubled, and its composition changed from predominantly Tejano to predominantly Mexican. In a 1901 parish census, Texas-born Mexicans accounted for more than two-thirds of the 4,041 parishioners, with an additional 26.6 percent born in Mexico. By the following decade, Mexican immigrants outnumbered their Tejano co-religionists. Annual parish reports from 1911 to 1940 indicate that the combined total of Tejano and Mexican worshipers was at least ten thousand; a 1930 newspaper article stated that San Fernando had more Mexican members than any other parish in San Antonio. By 1940 the cathedral was so renowned as a home for Mexican-descent faithful that one scholar noted: "All Mexican people who do not belong to any other Mexican parish by right belong to San Fernando parish."[6]

The growth of the San Fernando congregation was accompanied by its increased prestige within the institutional structures of the Roman Catholic Church. In 1926 Pope Pius XI established the archdiocese and province of San Antonio. Bishop Drossaerts, the local ordinary since 1918, served as the first archbishop of San Antonio (1926–1940) and metropolitan of the ecclesiastical province. San Fernando thus became a metropolitan cathedral, adding further prominence to this center of Spanish-speaking Catholicism.

As successive waves of Mexican immigrants joined Mexican Americans in San Antonio, Anglo-Americans, who tended to lump people from both sides of the border into a single "Mexican" ethnic group, became more hostile toward the growing Mexican-descent population. By the 1920s Anglo-American students formed "Stop Speaking Spanish" clubs at public schools to ensure the enforcement of the Texas legislature's 1918 mandate for English-only instruction. A local Spanish newspaper reported in 1923 that "youths of our race have been villainously attacked by some individuals who ran at them in automobiles" and further charged that local authorities arrested the victims rather than those who assaulted them. In San Antonio's predominantly Anglo-American northside neighborhoods, real estate covenants precluded Mexican home ownership and exacerbated residential segregation in the city. When organizers like Emma Tenayuca led thousands of Mexican-descent pecan shellers to walk off their jobs after management announced a wage reduction in 1938, police dispersed the pickets with tear gas and clubs. Despite public statements of disapproval by state and federal officials, the San Antonio police chief persisted in his refusal to allow picketing. In other instances, Spanish-speaking Catholics met hostility and rejection at the doors of their own church. Older parishioners recall that their people attended San Fernando because they were rebuffed at Anglo-American parishes and told to attend the "Mexican church" where they "belonged." Robert E. Lucey, the second archbishop of San Antonio, claimed the history of Mexicans in Texas was primarily "the story of many Anglo Americans who have shown stupidity, ignorance, and malice in treating their Mexican brethren with injustice, discrimination, and disdain."[7]

The great majority of San Antonians of Mexican heritage experienced not only hostility but also poverty and lack of representation in city affairs. To be sure, some Mexican-descent residents benefited from San Antonio's economic boom during World War I and the 1920s, as the establishment of Kelly Field, Brooks Field, and Randolph Field expanded

Mexican workers in a San Antonio tailoring company, c. 1910s. Courtesy University of Texas Institute of Texan Cultures, San Antonio.

an already extensive network of military installations. The growth of tourism provided Mexican-descent residents with some additional economic opportunities. The city's first public library, automobiles, radio stations, movie theaters, and motor buses were visible signs of success and progress, as were various new multistory buildings that sprouted up in the downtown streets near San Fernando Cathedral. But despite these developments, the emergence of a Mexican American middle class, and the presence of some wealthy Mexican émigrés, a 1929 report indicated that almost 90 percent of Mexican-descent residents were in the city's poorest economic class. Most of these residents lived in the *barrio* (neighborhood) just west of the cathedral and the downtown area. Father Carmelo Tranchese, a Jesuit priest assigned to a westside parish in 1932, described the barrio as "simply terrible. Those long rows of miserable huts in the Mexican Quarter, that exhausting heat, that resigned poverty painted on the faces of the Mexicans . . . I am familiar with the slums of San Francisco, New York, London, Paris, and Naples, but those of San Antonio are the worst of all." Economic disparity was accompanied by limited political influence; from 1900 to 1940 citizens of Mexican heritage held less than 4 percent of city council posts.[8]

The debilitating influence of racism and poverty on Mexican-descent residents' sense of dignity and personhood was strikingly evident in Spanish-language newspaper advertisements for color-altering cream that could "whiten" the skin in "three days." This product purportedly relieved users from the "humiliation of dark and ugly skin." Implicitly drawing a connection between dark skin, poverty, and social status, the ad went on to declare that people with white skin "have greater success in business, love, [and] society."[9]

Despite such signs that Spanish-speaking San Antonians internalized the prevalent racist ideology (at least partially), in some instances Mexican-descent residents struggled to promote their interests and to combat prejudice and oppressive social relations. Armed with the rights of citizenship, Mexican Americans at times led these efforts. A 1908 U.S. government report stated that in San Antonio "There is usually a Mexican member—an American-born citizen of Mexican descent—on the school board to represent the Spanish-speaking people of the city." As more immigrants arrived and Anglo-Mexican ethnic tensions mounted, however, some Mexican Americans found it politically expedient to distinguish themselves from their Mexican counterparts. In a book published in San Antonio in 1933, World War I veteran J. Luz Saenz stated that although Mexican Americans were honorable citizens who had "contributed with their blood" to the U.S. cause, their "worst war" was not against the Germans in Europe but against injustice here "in the bosom of our native land." Organizations like El Orden Hijos de América (The Order of the Sons of America) and the more prominent League of United Latin American Citizens (LULAC), both of which established active chapters in San Antonio in the 1920s, restricted their membership to U.S. citizens of Mexican or Spanish descent. These organizations were primarily attempts by a nascent Mexican American middle class to promote "Americanization," good citizenship, and the use of the English language. Nonetheless, groups like LULAC focused considerable attention on issues like school reform, increased Mexican American representation for juries and other public duties, an end to discrimination, and, in general, their people's rights and advancement.[10]

Newcomers from Mexico also combated racism and discrimination. In 1916 the immigrant editors of La Prensa, the most prominent among some two dozen Spanish-language newspapers in San Antonio, published a series of articles on public education that persuaded the school board in nearby Austin to end segregated education for Mexican-descent children.

Fourteen years later a *La Prensa* editorial complained bitterly that a "campaign dominated and controlled by the Anglo-Saxon element of America" was using the new medium of film to "project [their] racial superiority" and stereotypically portray "the villain" as "a Mexican with long mustache, wide sombrero, and a pistol in his belt." He called on Spanish-speaking artists to combat these racist depictions by making movies that more accurately represented their people. In 1920 another San Antonio newspaper, *El Imparcial de Texas*, defended two Mexicans condemned to death in U.S. courts. *El Imparcial* had been founded by Mexican émigré Francisco A. Chapa, a noted figure in the state Democratic party, who as editor often aired his political views in its pages. One *Imparcial* editorial presented a stinging rebuttal to negative pronouncements on Mexicans' character by former governor of Texas James Ferguson, denouncing Ferguson's conception of an allegedly "inferior race" as a "clamorous injustice." Though focused primarily on ethnic and economic solidarity among Mexican immigrants, *mutualistas* (mutual aid societies) in San Antonio, which doubled in number to some twenty-five during the first decades of the twentieth century, also acted in the public arena to promote the concerns of their members and the wider Mexican-descent population. For example, local mutualistas engaged in struggles to desegregate swimming clubs and movie theaters, ban films that depicted Mexicans in derogatory and stereotypical ways, and defend the rights of compatriots incarcerated in U.S. prisons.[11]

Separate efforts to combat racism reflected antipathies and some tensions between Mexican immigrants and native Mexican Americans. In his landmark 1926–27 study of Mexican immigrants, Manuel Gamio concluded that the differences between the two groups were "purely superficial" and that they were drawn together by their common language, low social status, needs, ideals, and tendency to intermarry, as well as their common plight of enduring Anglo-American prejudice. Nonetheless, he noted that "Mexicans who are American citizens . . . sometimes speak slightingly of the immigrants (possibly because the immigrants are their competitors in wages and jobs), and say that the immigrants should stay in Mexico." He also observed that the immigrant "considers the American of Mexican origin as a man without a country. . . . He criticizes, as well, certain details of American material culture, above all the 'Americanized' Mexican women."[12]

Not surprisingly, differences between Mexicans and Mexican Americans were also evident in the immigrants' greater concern about events in Mexico. Although the editors of *La Prensa* fought against educational discrimination and racist movies in the United States, for example, their expressed purpose was "to serve Mexico and Mexicans and to honor our native land whenever we have the opportunity to do so." During the decades following the establishment of *La Prensa* in 1913, the paper's extensive coverage of events in Mexico reflected this goal, clearly overshadowing the treatment of local news. Mutualistas also fostered Mexican nationalism, particularly through their organization of patriotic celebrations like those for Mexican Independence Day. While Mexican Americans also commemorated Mexican independence, immigrant nationalism was so pronounced that Gamio concluded: "Love of country sometimes goes so far that very often altars are made for saints and flag or [national] hero, or both, giving patriotism thus an almost religious quality."[13]

The most influential voice in shaping Mexican national consciousness in San Antonio was *La Prensa*. Founded by émigré Ignacio E. Lozano, *La Prensa* was run by Mexican elites who developed and propagated the ideology of *El México de Afuera* (literally, "Mexico abroad"). This mentality did not depict Mexicans in the United States primarily as immigrants seeking economic opportunities or other personal gain. Rather, it portrayed the newcomers as exiles who fled repressive conditions at home in order to preserve their national patrimony and await the opportune moment to return and initiate national reconstruction. The concept of El México de Afuera involved dedication to a nationalistic spirit, Mexican national heroes, the Spanish language, Mexican citizenship, and a Catholic faith rooted in devotion to Mexico's national patroness, Our Lady of Guadalupe. *La Prensa*'s view of the exiles and their world resonated with many readers; its circulation extended well beyond San Antonio's city limits and, significantly, peaked at over 32,000 in 1930, just after many exiles had left Mexico during the Cristero Rebellion.[14]

La Prensa also promoted "traditional" roles and values for women, advocating both domesticity and the importance of chastity and "proper" behavior among single women. Catholic leaders reinforced such convictions, particularly with regard to young women; in a 1926 pastoral letter Bishop (soon-to-be archbishop) Drossaerts decried the "unchaperoned automobile parties . . . indecent dances, suggestive moving pictures, and . . . immodesty in dress" among young women and called on them to embrace "Mary Immaculate" as "the ideal of maidenly modesty and purity." The conflicts between daughters and their Mexican-born parents illuminate the tensions that erupted when young women tried to assert their own vision of feminine decorum. One of the interviewees in Gamio's study, an immigrant mother in San Antonio, avowed that she "doesn't like the American customs in the matter of the liberty and way of behaving of the young women of this country—customs and ways of being by which her daughters have been influenced and which greatly concern her." One of the greatest sources of tension in immigrant families was the disparity between parents' expectations for feminine propriety and their daughters' desire for the greater freedom they saw their peers enjoying. Chicana scholar Vicki Ruiz has shown that such disputes cannot be explained simply as the exercise of male dominance nor as merely an indication of young women's acquiescence in U.S. cultural norms. Rather, these conflicts emerged in the contest between parents, who contended that "family honor" was linked to their children's behavior, and daughters, who took initiatives to free themselves from parental and other social constraints.[15]

The Parish Context: Congregational Leadership and Devotional Piety

During the first decades of the twentieth century, exiled Mexican bishops and clergy assisted at San Fernando and influenced the life and devotion of the cathedral congregation. Their presence and influence were particularly evident during the Mexican Revolution and the Cristero Rebellion. For example, in 1914 five Mexican archbishops and eight bishops resided in San Antonio, awaiting a change in the political climate so they could return to their dioceses. Though not formally assigned to the cathedral, exiled bishops and priests were the first Mexican clergy to offer consistent service at San Fernando since the U.S. annexation of Texas in 1845. Apparently the San Fernando congregation appreciated their presence, as parish records frequently indicate a large attendance at *misiones* (parish missions) and other services led by the exiled clergy. When Bishop Maximino Ruiz of Chiapas preached at the *triduum* (three services) to Our Lady of Guadalupe in 1915, the parish chronicler for that year noted that "there was a great assemblage of faithful at all of the rites during these days." He also went on to praise the congregation's "fervor and pious sentiments" during the triduum services.[16]

New cathedral clergy also energetically promoted the spiritual growth of the congregation. In 1902 priests and brothers of the Missionary Sons of the Immaculate Heart of Mary, or Claretians, began seventy-six years of service at the cathedral. Significantly, unlike the mostly French diocesan clergy whom they replaced, the Claretians were largely of Spanish origin and thus were native Spanish-speakers.[17]

Claretians assigned to the cathedral congregation reported that Mexican-descent Catholics suffered from "religious ignorance" and required "much attention" to keep them "constant in the practice of their religious duties; otherwise, Protestants who are zealous here will get them." Today older parishioners recollect that the Spanish clergy were occasionally im-

San Fernando Cathedral amidst the growing urban landscape on San Antonio's Main Plaza, 1927. Courtesy University of Texas Institute of Texan Cultures, San Antonio.

patient and overbearing with their Mexican and Mexican American congregants. However, the same parishioners recall the tireless dedication of the Claretians in vitalizing San Fernando's sacramental and devotional life. Extant primary sources confirm the priests' extensive ministrations in preaching and leading devotional services and in enriching the devotional space of the cathedral by procuring more than a dozen new statues as well as new stations of the cross, stained-glass windows, and a *nacimiento* (crib scene) for the Christmas season.[18]

Parishioners also launched and sustained efforts to ensure that their own sacred images were prominently displayed at the cathedral. Some parishioners acted on their own to procure new images, as María Jackson did in 1930, when she donated a new statue of St. Anthony in honor of her deceased mother, Francisca Luna. In other cases members of pious societies acted collectively, as during 1931, when members of the Asociación Nacional de los Vasallos de Cristo Rey (National Association of the Vassals of Christ the King), which Mexican exiles organized in both women's and men's sections at San Fernando in 1925, worked with their Claretian spiritual director to procure a *Cristo Rey* (Christ the King) statue. Despite the economic woes of the early Depression years, they raised $150 in less than five months. This image was blessed at San Fernando in January 1932, just three years after the end of the Cristero Rebellion in which Mexican Catholics fought under the banner of Cristo Rey and declared him and Our Lady of Guadalupe the only legitimate rulers of their nation.[19]

The procurement of images of the Immaculate Heart of Mary and Our Lady of Guadalupe in the early 1930s illuminates a process of negotiation between clergy and laity. In April 1931 the Claretians launched a campaign for donations to purchase a statue of their religious congregation's primary patroness, the Immaculate Heart of Mary. By the following week only twenty dollars had been collected, and over the next five weeks there was little improvement. The Claretians put the project on hold for six months, renewing their plea for donations on November 15, as the parish prepared for the four hundredth anniversary of the Guadalupe apparitions. Again, however, the response to their appeal was minimal; over the following month they received a mere $16. It took another two years to raise enough money for the statue. Significantly, in the midst of the first two faltering fund drives for the Immaculate Heart statue, congregants presented the parish with both the Cristo Rey statue and a Guadalupe *cuadro* (picture). Parish records mention no collections or other fundraising activities for the Guadalupe image, which devotees apparently secured on their own to mark Guadalupe's quadricentennial. According to the parish bulletin, a group of unnamed *padrinos* and *madrinas* (donors or "sponsors") presented the image for blessing and enshrinement at the cathedral during the novena of Guadalupe celebrations held that year.[20]

Parishioners exerted their strongest leadership and influence at San Fernando through the numerous pious societies that they established and developed. Extant records reveal that nine parish societies and associations functioned at the cathedral in the late 1890s. In 1930 there were at least eighteen such organizations. As elsewhere in the United States and throughout Latin America, pious societies at San Fernando served multiple purposes. Their explicit purpose was primarily religious, with membership requirements for observing codes of conduct, practicing specific devotions, and participating in sacramental celebrations like corporate communion (the group reception of communion by the members of a parish organization). In addition, these associations provided social networks and activities, communal support during time of illness or other critical need, the consolation of collective presence and prayer at funerals for deceased members, and a fundraising source for the parish. Moreover, as Edmundo Rodríguez has noted in a study of Hispanic church movements, in the face of growing urbanization pious societies enabled congregations like San Fernando to engender "a sense of belonging to

Entrance procession for Mass during the Christmas season at San Fernando, c. early 1950s. The Guadalupe image that devotees presented and dedicated at the parish in 1931 is enshrined prominently at the right edge of the sanctuary. Courtesy Esther Rodríguez.

human-size communities" despite the congregation's increasingly unwieldy size. However, in almost all cases the "communities" formed in pious societies were exclusively for members of a particular age group and gender.[21]

From the outset the Claretians praised the pious societies as the "principal supporters of the cathedral's worship life." They sought to animate and guide these societies by providing them with spiritual directors, endorsing association activities in bulletin announcements, and attending society-sponsored events, all as part of an effort to strengthen parishioners' faith and allegiance to the church. They enforced their conviction on worthy reception of the sacraments by requiring that members of parish associations be married in the church.[22]

Claretians' participation in the pious societies afforded parishioners their most frequent opportunities to interact with the pastors and spiritual directors and to influence decisions that shaped parish life. One clear example of lay initiative was the founding of the Asociación Nacional de los Vasallos de Cristo Rey. In August 1925 Mexican émigré Félix V. García and a group of compatriots organized the first parish-based women's and men's sections of the Vasallos. This exile association addressed the violence and political upheaval in their native Mexico by fostering the revival of religious practice among Mexicans in the belief that this was "the most effective means to achieve the national reconstruction of our country." Members were to recite their commitment formula daily and proclaim it publicly at society events: "For the honor and glory of the Sacred Heart of Jesus, perpetual king of Mexico, I submit myself voluntarily as his vassal, promising to promote his interests and work until death to extend his sovereignty in my native land, always under the mantle of my holiest mother of Guadalupe, queen of the Mexican people." Both the society banner and the member medallion reinforced their dedication to the "true" king and queen of Mexico: the Sacred Heart of Jesus appeared on one side of these insignia and Our Lady of Guadalupe on the other side. After establishing their pious society, the San Fernando Vasallas and Vasallos organized a monthly *Hora Santa Nacional* (National Holy Hour) and an annual Cristo Rey novena and feast-day celebration, leading the cathedral parish in intercessory prayer for their beleaguered homeland.[23]

Although lay leaders in organizations like the Vasallos addressed the specific concerns of Mexican exiles, pious societies at San Fernando also facilitated Tejano-Mexican interaction and collective initiatives. The growing number of parish societies and associations provided ample opportunity for Mexican and Mexican American congregants to interact at monthly corporate communions, devotional services, meetings, social gatherings, and joint fundraising efforts for cathedral projects such as the 1930 construction of a new San Fernando School. Significantly, although parish records from this era reveal various conflicts among members of pious societies, there is no indication of the tensions that occasionally marked social relations between Mexicans and Mexican Americans.

In several cases immigrants and native Mexican Americans worked collaboratively within a single parish association. One of these, the Hijas de María (Daughters of Mary), founded in the late nineteenth century, was comprised of unmarried young women. The San Fernando Claretians saw this pious society as a potent defense against "the dangers that surround and assault [young women]," as well as a source of spiritual life that helped them preserve "the incomparable beauty . . . of [their] chastity." For the young women themselves, this organization also provided numerous opportunities for social gatherings that their parish priests publicly endorsed as "most wholesome amusement[s]" and as "occasion[s] in which parishioners get to know one another and interact as family members, taking on the parish's interests as their own." Given the disagreements over social activities that observers noted between young Mexican-descent women and their immigrant parents, the Hijas no doubt valued highly this endorsement from San Fernando clergy. To be sure, the Hijas were among the most active devotional groups in the cathedral congregation, as is evidenced by their leadership in annual parish Marian devotions like those to honor the feast of the Immaculate Conception (December 8), the Assumption (August 15), and the month of May (which in Catholic devotion is dedicated to Mary). But parish records also reveal that the Hijas far surpassed all other pious societies in organizing plays, concerts, parties, dinners, picnics, booths for parish festivals, and other fundraising events. Unlike most other parish groups, they did not limit the site of their social and fundraising activities to the cathedral, but held several events at social centers such as the Beethoven Hall and the San Pedro Park Auditorium. In their first annual variety show, held at the outset of the triduum for Our Lady of Guadalupe in 1923, the Hijas played to a full house of about a thousand at the Ursuline Academy; the local press reported the event as "a brilliant artistic, social, and financial success." While the popularity of their events and their status as one of the largest pious societies in the cathedral congregation necessitated these more ample gathering spaces, clearly the Hijas worked to ensure that their association fulfilled both their religious and social needs.[24]

Women's initiatives and extensive participation in pious societies like the Hijas de María and the Vasallas (the female counterpart of the Vasallos) are consistent with today's analyses of these organizations. For example, Yolanda Tarango contends that church volunteer work and associations "provided an opportunity for women to work in an area outside of the home at a time when patriarchal structures did not allow other spaces for women to develop." She claims that for many Latinas, church activities afforded "the *only* arena in which they could legitimately, if indirectly, engage in developing themselves."[25]

Though frequently successful in shaping and enacting a distinct organizational vision, female and male leadership efforts in groups like the Hijas and Vasallos were not always marked by harmony. After a contentious meeting about low attendance and inadequate recruitment of new members, in June 1928 Macario Guzmán, the president of the Vasallos, quit the organization. In other instances controversy arose between groups, as for the 1927 Guadalupe celebration, when the Vasallas successfully contested their male counterparts' presumed prerogative of carrying the society banner in all association events and processions.[26]

Despite instances of conflict, lay initiatives to foster devotional piety, particularly through pious societies, complemented the Claretian pastoral strategy of augmenting Catholic faith and allegiance through devotional activities. This common emphasis on an expansive network of devotions enabled lay leaders to help shape and enlarge San Fernando's annual calendar of liturgical and devotional celebrations. By 1930 San Fernando held novenas, triduums, and feast-day celebrations nearly every week of the year. Parishioners often spilled out into the city plazas and streets in processions for celebrations like *el Santo Entierro* (the entombment service for Jesus on Good Friday), the entrance rite of the Mass at which young children received their first communion, Christ the King, and Our Lady of Guadalupe.[27]

The Symbolic World of Guadalupan Devotion

The extensive and ardent devotional piety of the San Fernando congregation encompassed a resurgence of its public Guadalupan devotion. With the support of Spanish Claretians and exiled Mexican clergy, along with the frequent symbolic presence of San Antonio's bishop or (after 1926) archbishop, the growing San Fernando congregation expanded their annual Guadalupe celebrations and revivified their tradition of acclaiming their patroness in public ritual. An annual triduum with solemn feast-day rites began in 1914, extending the practice of holding services solely on the feast day. By the following decade, Guadalupe processions were held on two nights: the procession of roses on December 11 (to commemorate the roses gathered by Juan Diego as a sign from Guadalupe) and the procession of lights on December 12. Devotees bore roses and candles in these respective processions; members of pious societies were prominent as they walked in unison under their society banners, wearing their society uniforms or medallions. The processions were part of the annual Guadalupe triduum, which now included daily Masses as well as evening services like the rosary, various other prayers, sermons, Guadalupan and other Marian hymns, benediction of the Blessed Sacrament, the distribution of commemorative holy cards, and the panegyric, an oration extolling the honors of the community's Guadalupan patroness. In some years parishioners further expanded these festivities with an all-night vigil service before the Guadalupe feast, a corporate communion of all pious societies, and/or a dramatic reenactment of the apparitions to Juan Diego. They also organized social events to accompany religious services. San Fernando's fervent Guadalupe celebrations drew huge crowds and

Our Lady of Guadalupe procession flowing out of San Fernando Cathedral, 1933. The Mexican flag and Guadalupe image are above the main entrance of the cathedral. Members of the Hijas de María (Daughters of Mary) are dressed in white and processing behind their society banner. Courtesy the San Antonio Light Collection, University of Texas Institute of Texan Cultures, San Antonio.

on several occasions even attracted groups of pilgrims who walked as far as thirty miles to the cathedral from Poteet and other nearby towns.[28]

The primary reason for this resurgence of Guadalupan devotion and public ritual was the participation of exiled Mexicans at the cathedral. San Fernando's first recorded Guadalupe triduum in 1914 followed closely upon the mass exodus at the outset of the Mexican Revolution; more than a hundred exiled bishops and clergy, along with hundreds of Mexican faithful, attended the Guadalupe feast-day celebration that year. Similarly, the reanimation of religious processions through the city streets and plazas coincided with the Cristero Rebellion, an era when numerous exiled bishops, priests, and lay Catholics formed part of the San Fernando congregation. The congregation frequently offered Mass and other prayers for the peace and well-being of Mexico. Significantly, in the late 1920s and early 1930s participants in the Guadalupe processions bore torches decorated with the green, white, and red colors of the Mexican flag, while members of the various parish associations marched under their respective banners and Mexican flags. Devotees also decorated the cathedral for the Guadalupe feast in the Mexican tricolors. Although all pious societies participated in Guadalupe celebrations, the most conspicuous group and the attendants of the Guadalupe image in feast-day processions were the Vasallos de Cristo Rey, which had a pronounced exile identity and forged a strong link between religious devotion and the national reconstruction of Mexico. Clearly, Mexican exiles, who founded newspapers and organizations in San Antonio to express and reinforce their national allegiance, also demonstrated that allegiance through their enthusiastic devotion to their national patroness. Perhaps fear and anger at the upheaval in their homeland and their own displacement intensified the exiles' intercessory prayer to the celestial guardian of their people.

The juxtaposition of religious and national symbols embodied the famous words of Mexican thinker Ignacio Altamirano, which La Prensa reprinted several times during this period: "The day that the cult of the Indian Virgin [of Guadalupe] disappears, the Mexican nationality will also disappear."[29] Essayists in La Prensa frequently echoed these sentiments. One writer confessed that although he had become a religious skeptic as an adult, in exile the celebration of Guadalupe's feast engulfed his "entire soul . . . in a prayer of grand and sorrowful memory" and transported him and others "a little bit closer to our beloved, lost homeland." Mexican prelates in exile in San Antonio also highlighted the intrinsic connection between Guadalupe and the Mexican nation in their public addresses and statements. In a 1914 sermon for the Guadalupe feast at San Fernando, for example, Archbishop Francisco Plancarte y Navarette of Linares reportedly urged "the people of Mexico to return to an adoration and supplication of Our Lady of Guadalupe as a means of obtaining peace in their country." Two decades later Archbishop Leopoldo Ruiz y Flores, the ordinary of Morelia and the pope's apostolic delegate to Mexico, issued a press release from San Antonio on Guadalupe's feast day, assuring his fellow exiles that Guadalupe "will save Mexico from the claws of atheism, the plague of materialism, and the hate of Bolshevik socialism." Similarly, Claretians assigned to San Fernando assured their flock that "if Mexico is faithful to the Virgin [of Guadalupe] . . . there will be days of peace and prosperity for the Mexican people." Clearly, a sense of protest—sometimes implicit, sometimes explicit—against political and religious conditions in Mexico was present in the San Fernando congregation's supplications to Our Lady of Guadalupe.[30]

Conversely, some exile commentators used the feast day to claim that Mexico's social upheaval was a divine punishment for national infidelity to the covenant God had enacted with the Mexican people through Our Lady of Guadalupe. Just as the "Virgin of Guadalupe rose up terrifyingly" to champion Mexican independence and castigate Spanish subjects who refused to fulfill "the civilizing mission that had been entrusted to them," so too this loving mother now permitted, in the words of one exiled priest, "tribulations" among "the Mexican people who had not shown themselves suitably fervent" in their faith and devotion. Another exiled clergyman contended that the Mexican government had brought a "severe and just punishment" down from heaven by its misguided efforts to banish God from schools, persecute the church, profane sacred temples, and mock the clergy in press reports that fomented paganism. To remedy the horrific conditions in Mexico, he called his compatriots to a spiritual renewal that included the rich sharing their goods with the poor, a return to mutual love as the basis of social life, parental insistence on religious instruction in their children's schools, greater respect for the things of God, and the clergy's diligence in fulfilling their duties of propagating Christian doctrine and consoling the afflicted. Such proclamations added the theme of covenant renewal to San Fernando's multivocal commemorations of Guadalupe.[31]

For the editors of *La Prensa* and other elite exiles who propagated the ideology of El México de Afuera, Guadalupe represented even more than a national symbol and a special protectress of the Mexican people. These enthusiasts, many of whom worshiped at San Fernando, did not merely claim that they remained Mexicans because they retained their language, culture, religious and patriotic spirit, longing for the homeland, and Mexican citizenship. Rather, they boldly professed that they were the "true" Mexicans, since they embodied these core elements of Mexican nationality more faithfully than their compatriots who remained at home. Indeed, as literary critic Juan Bruce-Novoa has observed, these exiles pointed to conditions in their homeland as a betrayal of the Mexican Revolution and contended "that they were right and justified in choosing exile, because exile was the only place the true Mexican could morally exist." In 1940 exile Federico Allen Hinojosa wrote from San Antonio that members of El México de Afuera distinguished themselves by maintaining "their unbreakable religious spirit, their firmly-grounded Catholicism that reflected especially in their love and veneration of the Virgin of Guadalupe." This statement echoed sentiments previously expressed in *La Prensa*. Moreover, according to Hinojosa, not only did exiles retain the faith and devotion that their counterparts in Mexico had lost; they even achieved "a reconquest of the lost lands" that the United States had taken from Mexico. This reconquest entailed a physical repopulating of the former Mexican territories, but was at its core "vigorously spiritual." Thus, from the México de Afuera perspective, while Mexicans at home despoiled the national heritage and patrimony, the exiles' propagation of Guadalupan devotion in the United States was an integral part of their success in keeping Mexico alive and even recreating it in conquered territories.[32]

The fervent piety of newly arrived Mexican patriots enhanced the devotion of a faith community that had been functioning for two centuries. Some religious and cultural traditions had weakened as San Antonio's Mexican-descent residents were numerically overwhelmed during the latter decades of the 1800s,[33] but ongoing feasts like Guadalupe presented the newcomers with familiar symbols and rituals. These common symbols and rituals, particularly the celebration of Mexico's national patroness, united the émigrés in worship with San Fernando parishioners, who, like their exiled counterparts, had a longstanding tradition of devotion rooted in their religious and cultural heritage. Like San Fernando's pious societies, the cathedral congregation's Guadalupe celebrations fostered ethnic cohesion and blurred the distinctions between Mexican-descent devotees from either side of the border.

As Mexican immigrants streamed into San Antonio during the first decades of the twentieth century, their conviction that Guadalupe had elected the Mexican people as her "chosen race" contrasted sharply with Tejanos' experience of being relegated to secondary status during U.S. territorial expansion. Mexican editorialists in La Prensa expressed their solidarity with people of Mexican ancestry born "in distant lands that were at one time Mexican." One writer opined that although Mexicans born in the United States might be "enmeshed in the contradictory intermingling of Anglo-Saxon education and Latino thought" and consequently lose touch with their ancestral heritage, in spirit they remained Mexican because they had not forgotten how to "pray in Spanish and worship the Virgin of Guadalupe." Another essayist contended that the consequences of the U.S. war with Mexico would have been "100 times" worse if the "invader" had not made the fatal error of negotiating peace terms at a site near the basilica of Our Lady of Guadalupe, who consequently protected her children's dignity and won them an unexpected diplomatic victory! One immigrant women's group, the Club Mexicano de Bellas Artes (Mexican Fine Arts Club), gathered annually during the Guadalupe triduum at San Fernando to offer a Mass and further their objectives of conserving "Mexican traditions and customs . . . [and] the Castilian language."[34] The immigrants' esteem for their heritage and confidence in their dignity as Guadalupe's favored daughters and sons provided an impetus for Mexican Americans to renew their own ethnic pride and sense of dignity as the children of a heavenly mother. In an era of rising ethnic prejudice in San Antonio, Mexican émigrés' assurance of their celestial election and rich cultural patrimony fortified both Mexican Americans and the immigrants in their resistance to discrimination.

Seen in this light, San Fernando's Guadalupe celebrations engendered a sacred realm in which cathedral congregants were valued and respected, symbolically reversing the racism they encountered in the world around them. While Mexican-descent residents continued to struggle for equal rights in schools, courtrooms, and the work place, at San Fernando they instilled in one another a sense of dignity and pride as children of a loving mother. While racism in movies and other areas of social life was so strident that even Spanish-language newspapers advertised "whitening" cream, Mexican-descent devotees acclaimed the brown-skinned morenita, displayed her image in public processions, and enshrined the image prominently in the cathedral. While their representation on government bodies like the city council was minimal, San Fernando congregants exercised leadership in their many pious societies, organizing communal events like the annual Guadalupe triduum and processions. While the Spanish language was officially banned in public schools, Guadalupan devotees marched through the city plazas and streets singing the praises of their patroness in their native tongue. While the threat of repatriation hovered ominously, especially during the Depression, familiar devotions like those to Guadalupe made San Fernando a spiritual home that provided solace and reassurance. While frequently rebuffed at Anglo-American parishes, San Fernando congregants celebrated their patroness's feast in the company of archbishops, bishops, and priests whose presence confirmed the value of their language, cultural heritage, and religious traditions. Consciously or not, San Fernando's reanimated Guadalupe rituals counteracted the hostility and rejection that parishioners often met in the wider church and society. As one devotee remarked in acclaiming Guadalupe's compassion for the poor and downtrodden: "Because the Virgin is Indian and brown-skinned and wanted to be born in the asperity of [Juan Diego's] rough cloak—just like Christ wanted to be born in the humility of a stable—she is identified with a suffering, mocked, deceived, victimized people." Another enthusiast opined that la morenita was nothing less than a "symbol" of "our race" and contended that "if it had been a Virgin with blue eyes and blonde hair that appeared to Juan Diego, it is possible that she would have received a fervent devotion, but never as intense, as intimate, nor as trusting as that which the multitudes offer at the feet of the miraculous 'Guadalupita.'"[35]

The ethnic solidarity evident in Guadalupan devotion did not preclude some differentiation between worshipers. One Claretian parish chronicler noted in 1926 that "the most prominent Mexican families attended this [Guadalupe] triduum by invitation"; although there is no indication that the rich received any special recognition or other prerogatives in worship services and other festivities.[36] While the Vasallos de Cristo Rey did not exclude Mexican American members, their frequent prominence in Guadalupe celebrations reflected a predominant focus on Mexico. Even more strikingly, like pious societies and spiritual exercises such as Lenten missions, Guadalupe processions generally divided devotees into separate groups, with children leading the entourage, followed by young women, older women, and then the men. This arrangement was consistent with the sense of decorum and order expressed in *La Prensa* and Archbishop Drossaerts's pastoral letter on feminine modesty, as well as the Claretians' vision for the Hijas de María and other parish associations. Thus the high point of the Guadalupe celebration symbolically represented and reinforced a hierarchical vision of the world, with assigned roles and "places" based on age and gender.

Chicana scholar Juanita Luna Lawhn contends that *La Prensa*'s prominent reference to Guadalupe as a virgin accentuated the editors' conviction that "the ideal woman was the sexually pure woman." Although no *La Prensa* editorials on Guadalupe during the period under study explicitly treat the subject of virginity, the longstanding Catholic association of Mary with what theologian Elizabeth Johnson calls the "male projection of idealized femininity" clearly influenced the Claretian vision of the Daughters of Mary and, more generally, the San Fernando clergy's promotion of Marian devotion. Significantly, Beatriz Blanco, the only woman credited with publishing a Guadalupan reflection in *La Prensa* during this period, was also the only editorialist who opined that Guadalupe "personif[ies our] native land, religion, and home." She went on to warn that "whoever tries to destroy the Guadalupan Virgin will have committed a crime" against "the sacred laws of the home, love and unity, the foundations of the family." These statements say at least as much about *La Prensa*'s editorial policies as they do about women's perspectives on Guadalupe, illuminating the invocation of Guadalupe's authority to buttress an insistent endorsement of female domesticity.[37]

Guadalupe's importance in the lives of Mexican-descent women and their families is confirmed by their private devotion and by the presence of Guadalupe images in their homes, where "the feast day of the patroness of Mexico was observed by religious and civil exercises." At San Fernando, women's initiatives extended beyond their traditional role as leaders of familial piety to leadership in the congregation, and even to demands for parity with their male counterparts. For example, Elena Lanzuri, who had previously led the choir at the Guadalupe Basilica in

Mexico City, directed a group of more than fifty singers at San Fernando in a 1935 celebration of Guadalupe's feast; young women from the Hijas de María planned social gatherings in conjunction with the Guadalupe feast; and various women's groups, most notably the Vasallas de Cristo Rey, participated in the preparation of Guadalupe celebrations and walked together in Guadalupe processions. Beginning in 1927 the Vasallas took turns with the Vasallos in carrying the society banner for events like the Guadalupe procession, a ritual action that reflected their equal (and often greater) contribution of hard work and financial support for Guadalupan festivities.[38]

The primary basis of Guadalupan devotion for many Mexican-descent residents was their steadfast conviction that Guadalupe "continues to perform miracles." Their fervent appeals for Guadalupe's celestial aid led local clergy to denounce some forms of devotion as superstitious, such as the praying of forty-six rosaries for the forty-six stars on Our Lady of Guadalupe's mantle. Nonetheless, advertisements in local Spanish-language newspapers appealed to devotees' strong faith in Guadalupe as a protectress and healer. One ad for "Te Guadalupano Purgante" (Guadalupe Purgative Tea) described Guadalupe as the "queen of the infirmed," extolling the powers of this tea made from "herbs, flowers, tree bark, seeds, [and] leaves . . . that grow in the environs of Tepeyac, where Our Lady of Guadalupe appeared."[39]

Not surprisingly, San Fernando Claretians tended to perceive Guadalupan devotion as a Mexican expression of Marian piety. While the San Fernando clergy joined with lay devotional writers in calling Guadalupe "la morenita," they more frequently identified her with titles like "Nuestra Santísima Madre" (Our Most Blessed Mother) or "la Santísima Virgen" (the Most Blessed Virgin). Perceiving Mexicans and Mexican Americans as lax Catholics and easy prey for Protestant proselytizers, the Claretians strove to link the vast force of Guadalupan devotion with Catholic identity and full participation in the church's sacramental life. One parish bulletin announcement proclaimed that "it is not enough that the [Guadalupe] image occupies a preferential place in your home and that you invoke her with devotion in all your perils; you must also proclaim your love for Mary in public," and thus all the faithful should honor her by "approaching the eucharistic banquet with souls purified through a sincere confession" during parish Guadalupe celebrations. When some devotees failed to participate in the sacraments and other church services for the Guadalupe feast, the San Fernando clergy decried the "unpardonable indifference" in hearts so devoid of devotion and patriotism that they "palpitate not a drop of blood for the Virgin of Guadalupe nor for Mexico."[40]

Conclusion

Clearly, Guadalupan devotion at San Fernando was far more than an expression of Marian devotion. It encompassed patriotism and political protest, divine retribution and covenant renewal, ethnic solidarity and the resistance of a victimized people, spiritual reconquest and reinforcement of social hierarchy, a model of feminine virginity and domesticity and an inspiration for women to be active in the public arena and demand equality, a plea for miraculous intervention and an inducement for greater participation in the church's sacramental life. Despite attempts to engage Guadalupan devotion as a justification for existing social relations, at San Fernando Guadalupe commemorations also provided a ritual arena for Mexicans and Mexican Americans to forge and celebrate an alternative world, one in which painful realities like exile and racism could be redefined and reimagined. A brown-skinned "exile" herself, Guadalupe was a treasured companion whose faithful encountered her most intensely in the midst of the displacement, discrimination, degradation, and other difficulties they endured. Fortified by her presence, these faithful confronted their plight by symbolically proclaiming in Guadalupan devotion that exiles were the "true" Mexicans, that despised Mexican-descent residents were a chosen people, and that devotees of la morenita were heirs to the dignity she personified.

Today Guadalupan devotion at San Fernando continues to evolve in both its expressions and its meanings, as newly arrived immigrants and a new generation of devotees, many the children and grandchildren of earlier Mexican émigrés, adapt to life in the United States and shape their devotional piety accordingly. But the sense of dignity celebrated by early twentieth-century Mexican émigrés remains a living legacy in San Fernando's Guadalupan devotion. One current devotee is Patti Elizondo, the daughter of Mexican immigrants, a generation removed from those who fled Mexico during the tumultuous years of the Mexican Revolution and its aftermath. A broadcaster and television documentary producer, Patti is a highly trained, bilingual professional who could easily blend into any of San Antonio's more suburban, northside parishes. Yet she faithfully attends San Fernando, where she serves as a lector and participates fervently in the annual Guadalupe celebrations. Patti finds in these Guadalupe celebrations an opportunity to acclaim her celestial mother, awaken her "sense of community," and "feel the nationalistic pride to be of the same ethnic extraction as the *morenita* . . . to indulge in the splendor of my rich culture and its infinitely delicate expressions of religious fervor."[41] It is this inspiration that leads Patti and other San Fernando parishioners to continue the evolution of their congregation's Guadalupan devotion and its vital significance.

Karen Mary Davalos

"The Real Way of Praying"

The Via Crucis, *Mexicano* Sacred Space, and the Architecture of Domination

"IT IS NOT A PLAY. The Via Crucis [Living Way of the Cross] is a reenactment of a historical event, but it is not a play."[1] The young man spoke with emphatic certainty and clarity. "We are reliving that moment, which is actually happening now." Not pausing to consider the theological significance of making present the crucifixion of Christ, he continued to speak in two temporal moments. "I was a Roman soldier, and I whip Jesus, and this is my sin. He is carrying the Cross, and it is the weight of our sins, but he is acting this out for our sins today. We say forgive us for what we did then—in the past when Jesus was actually put to death—and for what we are doing now, as I whip him." It became increasingly difficult to determine if the young man was referring to Jesus or to the person representing Jesus. "It is a testimony that I am a Catholic, but we are not actually preaching. We are teaching and praying."

My retelling of this young man's story maps a multifocal argument of the body and space. As his words suggest, the Via Crucis has sensual, collective, spiritual, and transcendental dimensions, but it does not separate those dimensions from the physical realities of life. In the predominantly *Mexicano* area of Chicago, the Via Crucis is a multidimensional event that contributes to the sacralization of the Pilsen neighborhood. Moreover, it is a corporeal experience in a particular place that connects with other places and times. Accordingly, any ethnographic analysis that attempts to capture this temporal and spatial blending must fuse ethnography, history, and critical cultural studies into a theology that is also a politically grounded concept of culture. There is nothing exotic or alien here, no romantic rendering of a colorful and fantastic religious practice, no detached social scientist, only an interdisciplinary exploration of how people live with and against forms of domination, and thus manage to be American and Mexican, European and indigenous all at once.[2] I hope for a scumbled effect in which the unrelenting beauty of the Via Crucis is made explicit within a wash of subordinating powers that are both external and internal to Pilsen.[3]

The significance of domination becomes clear through the physical realities. It is the shape and size of domination that consistently moves people and reminds them of everyday manifestations of racial supremacy, capitalism, and patriarchy. In Chicago, the daily experience of inequality is apparent in the difference between weekly and irregular garbage pickup, clean alleys and those overrun by rats, or full use of the parish facilities and church services in the basement. In the annual enactment of the Via Crucis in Pilsen, the crowd cannot repress these experiences as it maneuvers around broken glass, uncovered manholes, and potholes in the street. These material barriers, physical dangers, and social inequalities constitute the architecture of domination.

I argue, however, that domination—as material and concrete as it may be—has not produced a fixed social space or identity.[4] While participants' physical bodies engage and experience domination, the Via Crucis has become a practice through which struggle is performed. At the same time, the collective practice includes forms of manipulation and legitimation. Thus an expression of a new social community (or, of knowledge about collective emancipation) is complicated by its own repression and ambiguity.

Before I fully engage the topic, I offer an explanation about Pilsen and my use of the word *community*. Pilsen is by no means a homogeneous place. Its residents embody diverse cultural practices, communication styles, and beliefs that can be found in Chicago, Mexico, and many other parts of the continent. But through the Via Crucis, Pilsen residents challenge an essentialist understanding of human experience and offer a deterritorial or transnational claim to space. It is a public event in which Mexicanos momentarily position themselves as the center—displacing a "minority" or "alien" status and the sanctioned racialized landscape of Chicago.

For a grasp of the landscape and how Mexicanos transform it, I address five topics. First, I examine the history of Mexicans and Mexican Americans in Chicago and the ways in which continuing geographic movement has strengthened a transcultural sense of belonging and communal relationships. Second, I examine the origins of the Via Crucis and its use as social protest and an alternative vision for the neighborhood. Third, I describe the event ethnographically and explore it as a site of negotiation. In the fourth section I analyze how the Via Crucis transforms the physical and human community. I end with a legend about the park in Pilsen that epitomizes Mexicanos' interrogation of how the city imagines them, through spirituality, cultural identity, and collective action. Each section incorporates a history of the urban plans and policies that produced an architecture of domination.

Movement and Homespace

The immigrant and settlement history of Chicago's Mexicano population explains the connection between the architecture of domination, capital, and immigration. Large-scale Mexican immigration to Chicago began after the outbreak of the Mexican Revolution, in 1910 and later, in response to industrial expansion and a demand for low-wage laborers.[5] This migration pattern was repeated after World War II and during the 1950s and early 1960s. Recruited by steel and railroad companies or traveling along well-paved routes of seasonal employment in agriculture, Mexicans (usually young men) came originally from the urban centers of Guanajuato, Michoacán, and Jalisco to work on railroads and in steel mills, meatpacking houses, and automotive factories. Conforming to established patterns of working-class residential segregation, Mexicans settled near employment centers: employees of the stockyards and packinghouses settled in the Back of the Yards, those at Illinois Steel and Wisconsin Steel in the Calumet region moved into Chicago's South Side, and the railroad workers settled in the Hull House area on the Near West Side. These areas developed into the most significant Mexican communities in Chicago.

The invasion of the labor market into domestic life continued into the 1930s, and national repatriation programs, economic turbulence, and racism nearly devastated these neighborhoods. According to historian Juan García, "The Mexican population in Chicago numbered about 21,000 in 1930; by 1938 it was less than 16,000."[6] Although most Mexicans left voluntarily, many were forced out of their jobs by a 1931 Illinois statute that provided preferential treatment to U.S. citizens in public works projects or by employers' practice of giving jobs to "whites." Unemployed Mexicans were denied public assistance or received relief and a train ticket to Mexico. Others, to avoid exposure and deportation sanctioned by the Deportation Act of 1929, did not apply for public assistance, turning instead to their mutual aid societies. Even aside from the number of

U.S. citizens of Mexican descent who voluntarily or involuntarily left the country in the 1930s, a significant number of Mexicans were repatriated from the Midwest.[7]

In the 1950s market interests supported migration to the Midwest and helped to restore Mexican communities in Chicago. When the Bracero Program was expanded to include laborers for nonagricultural midwestern industries, the Mexican population in Chicago grew, reaching 24,000 by 1950. These immigrants, however, arrived in a city altered by deindustrialization, machine politics, and white flight. Employment in food, retail, communication, and hotel service—sectors of the economy characterized by low wages, rapid turnover, part-time labor, and few opportunities for advancement—was increasing, while jobs in manufacturing—the traditional occupations of Mexicans and blacks in Chicago—were in decline. During his twenty-one-year tenure as mayor (1955–1976), Richard Daley developed the infrastructure of the city with a 1958 blueprint that facilitated Chicago's shift from heavy industry and railway to a management- and service-oriented economy, an economy that has structural disadvantages for workers struggling to accumulate capital. At the same time, Daley's concentration of private investment in the Loop had a negative effect on the infrastructure of working-class neighborhoods. As public funds were funneled into private corporations, Chicago's poor and nonwhite residents experienced a decrease in services and physical improvements.[8]

Yet while fashioning a life of movement, Mexicanos continued to establish Chicago as their destination. In the late 1960s and the 1970s, Mexicanos came to Chicago as a result of 1965 U.S. immigration laws that made it easier for immigrants from Mexico and from elsewhere in Latin America to enter the United States. Community-based organizations and activism increased as a result of the swelling population and leadership.[9] But they had to do so in the face of massive displacement from their established community in the Near West Side.

As part of an urban renewal project that carved out another space for white privilege, in 1961 the Chicago Land Clearance Commission announced plans to build a new university in the Near West Side, the area directly north of Pilsen. The announcement shocked and angered the residents of the Near West Side, who had been actively involved for over ten years in a campaign for neighborhood improvement. The University of Illinois at Chicago (formerly Chicago Circle) was financed through urban renewal programs but offered few direct advantages to the poor and working-class Italian, Greek, black, and Mexican residents. The project displaced the Jane Addams Hull House, the settlement house for the area, and demolished approximately fourteen thousand housing units. By the time the university opened in 1965, the Near West Side had become a neighborhood of upper-middle-class homes, office buildings, and educational institutions.[10]

Although no official record describes what happened to the nine thousand Mexicanos forced to leave the Hull House area, Louise Año Nuevo Kerr estimates that nearly half moved to Pilsen, a neighborhood with a concentration of industrial zones, railroad yards, and absentee landlords—none of which materially or spiritually benefits local residents. Together with immigrants from Mexico and migrants from southwestern and midwestern states, the "refugees" from the Near West Side dramatically changed the landscape of Pilsen. By 1970, twenty-six thousand Mexicanos accounted for 55 percent of Pilsen's total population, and the area emerged as a Mexican "port of entry."[11]

With displacement fresh in their memory, the new Pilsen residents began to make claims in their neighborhood. Throughout the 1970s Mexicanos obtained federal grants for "an alternative college program, supplementary educational programs, recreational programs, a bilingual library, a social service program, a contracting and skill-training agency, a methadone-maintenance clinic, a drug program for youth, and a health clinic."[12] Many of the federally funded agencies are still located on 18th Street, including the Spanish Coalition for Jobs, Inc., a job- and skill-training organization; Casa Aztlán, a multipurpose arts center that offers courses in English-language skills; and Asociación Pro Derechos Obreros (APO), a group that fights for workers' rights. Thus the Via Crucis was just one of many collective actions that aimed to displace the history and architecture of domination that made Pilsen a port of entry.

By the time I came to Chicago, in 1989, the experience of movement, dispersal, and marginalization had become a pattern for Mexicano households. Although all the women and men I met there have legal standing in the United States and have been raised in Chicago and educated in U.S. public or Catholic schools, they have diverse ties to Mexico and the United States as a homeplace. Several families provided firsthand accounts of seasonal migration, railroad strikes, or applying for amnesty. Ongoing movement was the most common experience. Many people consistently travel to Mexico, spending their summer or winter vacations there among family or in their own homes. Even during their school years, young women and men might spend up to six months in Mexico. Mothers deliberately plan a trip to Mexico during a child's first few years so that the youngster can learn to speak Spanish. Family members from Mexico also "vacation" in Chicago, and some of these vacations can become very long, involving work and in some cases relocation. The length of the visit often depends on the job market, upcoming family celebrations, and emotional ties. Some parents who are U.S. citizens may have a succession of children born alternately in the United States and Mexico. Dispersion, travel, and transnationalism describe these Mexicanos' experiences better than linear accounts of assimilation and resistance.

Justice and Grace: Via Crucis as Social Prayer and Action

The congregation of St. Vitus organized the first Via Crucis in 1977.[13] From the beginning the event conveyed Mexican Catholic sensibilities, social commentary on local injustices, dramatic reversals of power and authority, the sacralization of space, and acts of cultural recovery. Of these components, a vision of justice and grace was clearly articulated in the first procession and recitation of the Stations of the Cross. James Colleran, then pastor of St. Vitus, was a worker-priest who strenuously acted against social injustice. He welcomed organizers, undocumented families, and union activists into the parish facilities. Together they initiated worker strikes, boycotts of a supermarket with poor hiring practices, demonstrations against municipal neglect, a protest rally and campaign against the Chicago Transit Authority for employment inequity, and confrontations with the U.S. Immigration and Naturalization Service during attempted illegal detentions of Mexicanos. For the congregation of St. Vitus, the Via Crucis was one of many socially committed actions they used to create a better life, to unite the neighborhood, and to maintain lay leadership in the parish. Yet this time they expressed their new vision of Pilsen through an explicitly spiritual practice and performance.

Like other community struggles organized by the St. Vitus congregation, the social drama of the Via Crucis emerged as a response to suffering and sorrow. On Christmas Eve 1976 a fire swept through an apartment building two blocks from the church where a children's party was in progress. When firefighters arrived, adults were dropping children from third-floor windows. Unable to communicate in Spanish, the firefighters did not realize that other children were still trapped in the building on 17th Street. Ten children and two mothers died in the flames.[14] According to Robert H. Stark, a priest and activist who described the first Via Crucis, "News spread throughout the Pilsen barrio," and "by midnight Mass many people still in shock packed the small St. Vitus church."[15] All the victims were members of St. Vitus parish. Parishioners gathered at the church for an impromptu vigil that became an organizing meeting. Working with volunteers from other parishes and with the Red Cross, the St. Vitus congregation led efforts to comfort, house, and administer to the needs of the victims' families. After the funerals Pilsen residents held a community meeting demanding the attention of the media and city officials. Joined by St. Pius V and other Pilsen churches, St. Vitus parishioners argued that city neglect of public services, overcrowded housing, lack of Spanish-speaking firefighters, and absentee landlords had fueled the disaster. These charges were sounded again when five more people of Mexican descent died in a fire on New Year's Day.[16]

It was another, older fire, the Great Chicago Fire of 1871, that produced the living conditions to which Pilsen residents referred. Their experiences of poor housing reflected a century-old city policy even more attuned to class privileges and distinctions. After the Great Chicago Fire, to secure regrowth of the new central business districts and continued protection against another conflagration, the City Council permitted only brick and stone buildings "in and adjacent to the downtown area." This ordinance forced the poor and working class, who could not afford the more expensive building materials, to relocate to the industrial districts, where another ordinance, allowing for "'temporary' wooden structures for emergency housing," was virtually ignored. Many of the substandard and extralegal wooden buildings occupied by blacks and Mexicanos in Pilsen, South Lawndale, Little Village, and the Near South Side are vestiges of this nonenforcement.[17]

Aware that the neighborhood's dilapidated condition was the result of longstanding neglect, St. Vitus parishioners organized Pilsen's first Via Crucis the following Good Friday with attention to their current situation. By turning to this Catholic devotion, they communicated multiple messages to Pilsen and the city, including a call to cultural heritage and faith, an act of solidarity, collective remembrance of the people who had died in the fires, and a moment of consciousness-raising about conditions in Pilsen. James Colleran asked Claudia Aguirre and a few other parishioners to coordinate the event with the seven other parishes in the area.[18] According to Claudia the first event "was not organized [and did not have] a very strong plan," but she recalled that "many people [were] involved," and, for her, their actions spoke "more about their faith and religion than anything else." More than two thousand people joined the first procession, "expressing," as Claudia noted, "their hopes and their, *our* way of believing" by walking together and with Jesus from parish to parish, praying the Stations of the Cross, and reflecting on the neighborhood's tragedy and its substandard living conditions.[19]

The sites at which Claudia (as the mother of Christ) and others performed the Stations of the Cross reveal the power of faith, unity, and the ability to analyze daily experience. St. Vitus coordinators decided to enact the crucifixion stations in public locations and to express their communal suffering with that of Christ. Starting at Providence of God Church and moving westward, the procession stopped in or near each parish to pray the conventional meditations of the Stations of the Cross and reflect on commentaries. Although the route was somewhat determined by the location of each parish, the coordinators frequently chose specific places that had meaning to the community, often connecting each station to a particular issue or event. For example, the crowd prayed the fourth station, in which Jesus encounters his mother, at the Guadalupe Grotto in the side yard of St. Procopius Church. The incorporation of Guadalupe is significant, since she is the mestiza mother and holds special meaning for Mexicans. The working together of Christ's life with that of Pilsen was dramatically enacted after the thirteenth station, in which Jesus is taken down from the Cross. The procession paused in front of the burned-out apartment buildings on 17th Street and reflected on the deaths, symbolically linking Christ's pain with the community's. The integration of collective resistance and a pastoral message in which Christ's or his mother's suffering is present became an important element and message of subsequent processions.

Since 1977 the Via Crucis has become a communitywide ritual that draws people from throughout the city and the Midwest.[20] Hundreds of Mexicanos and other Latinos make a pilgrimage from Chicago's North Side or southwestern suburbs. Since 1991 the media have reported annual attendance at more than ten thousand. Some local residents estimate that the number is closer to fifty thousand, given the size of Pilsen's Mexicano population. The crowd itself has become a symbol of the event and people comment on its size, strength, and security for "the undocumented, who normally remain hidden."[21] During the procession through public space, Pilsen residents and other Mexicanos forge a relationship as a community, speak in a nearly unified voice against forms of oppression, and transcend space and time from Mexico to Jerusalem, Mexico to the United States, Chicago to Calvary.

Negotiating the Sacred and the Profane: Scripture, Pilsen, and Womanhood

Notwithstanding the symbolic meaning of the procession, the events that precede and conclude the public pilgrimage reveal something about the struggle for authority in the community and the tension over the notion of social construction. Ironically, the size of the crowd makes it difficult for people to witness these points of contention. Approximately two hundred people can observe the first part of the event, which strictly follows the text of the Bible for the Last Supper, the Agony in the Garden of

Gethsemane, and the first two Stations of the Cross (Christ Condemned and Christ Made to Bear His Cross). Since approximately 1982, these scenes have been presented in the auditorium of Providence of God, a parish that sits nearly beneath a highway offramp at the eastern edge of Pilsen. Likewise, the last station is not witnessed by many people, even though it is enacted inside St. Adalbert, a large Roman basilica in which the original Polish congregation's statue of Our Lady of Czestochowa shares space with Our Lady of Guadalupe and Our Lady of San Juan de los Lagos.[22] The scenes that take place in both buildings are subjects of intense debate among laity, clergy, *veteranos* (experienced elders), and a younger set of coordinators.

For example, the dramatic presentation in the auditorium demonstrates a rereading of official Catholicism, which dictates that the Last Supper be celebrated on Holy Thursday. In order to make a seamless connection between the Last Supper, the Agony in the Garden, and the trial, crucifixion, and entombment of Christ, the coordinators enact on Good Friday the Last Supper and the other events preceding his condemnation. This emphasizes and defines Jesus in relationship to others, as a member of a community, and thus makes more significant his abandonment by the community. Although the symbolic repositioning between the laity and the institutional church is somewhat repressed for most of the audience because they cannot see it, the Via Crucis itself captures this negotiation through the fact that it is a popular religious event organized for and by Mexican and Mexican American parishioners.

The other debate partially hidden from the audience is an ongoing conflict within the coordinating committee.[23] Elder members of the committee believe that scripture and religious images are divine intervention, whereas another group views them more as social constructions. Antonio Covarrubias, a coordinator at Providence of God who has been involved with the Via Crucis since 1982, believes that scripture determines how people speak, move, and dress, including the material and color of Jesus' clothes, chalice, and cross. It has been his goal to present the Last Supper, the Agony in the Garden of Gethsemane, and the first two Stations of the Cross as they appear in his collection of religious pictures and the Bible. "I have a picture that identifies how you walk the first station, the second station, the third station. Each act has a picture, and there is the picture and then the scripture. [But] five years ago they modernized it, and with time they have stopped using sacred scripture and put in other things. It is okay for them but not for us."[24] Antonio and other veteranos still control the larger narrative in Providence of God, since it is presented without commentary.

Some of this conflict came to a head in 1993, when Patricia Luz, the lead coordinator from St. Procopius, challenged the guidelines by which Mary was selected. Previously the core committee had required that a young woman enact the part of Mary. Some coordinators, including Antonio, argued that Scripture, specifically Luke 1:26–27, indicates that Mary looked young. Patricia recalled the conflict and her own interpretation:

> Because that was the concept supposedly of a Mary. When she had Jesus she was a teenager, sixteen years old. So [the person selected for] Mary would always be a young woman. No older than twenty, eighteen. I didn't like that. . . . [I would ask] "But how old was she when Jesus died? . . . But what did she look like when that sword pierced her heart when she saw her son die? What do women look like when their sons die?" . . . They're not teenagers. They're not teenagers. A woman has a child when she's fifteen, sixteen. Okay, so [now] she's about thirty-two, thirty-five. Her son is fifteen, sixteen in a gang. He gets killed. She may look young, but at that time there's a transformation. That sorrow and that anguish and that grief—everything just seems to turn you.

Drawing on both the experience of Mary and the reality of motherhood in Pilsen, Patricia created a unified perspective for women experiencing "sorrow, anguish, and grief." She tacked back and forth between Jerusalem and Pilsen, creating a subject-position for Mexicanas that dwells in all temporal and spatial domains. Thus, not only did Patricia convince the core committee to reconsider their guidelines by demonstrating that Mary must have grown older by the time Jesus was put on the Cross; she offered a theological explanation that underscored the position that the past and present come together in Pilsen. It is this theology that is emphasized and practiced throughout the Via Crucis.

In fact the women with whom I spoke consistently talked about seeing themselves through Mary's suffering. Although the Via Crucis commemorates the death of Jesus, women find particular meaning for their lives as mothers because Pilsen's enactment of the Passion offers them a culturally familiar form and face for their prayers. This association with Mary as a Mexicana allows them to engage the Passion narrative intimately and see themselves in Mary's actions and emotions. Their interpretation of and relationship to the Passion narrative offer insight into the making of Pilsen, Mexican Catholicism, and womanhood itself.

Coordinators, participants, and observers all speak about the centrality of Mary and identify with her hardships and maternity. Others add that the women of Jerusalem, and to a lesser extent Veronica, become the conduit by which they define family and their role in the community, as well as their faith and participation in the church.[25] The participants who had represented the women of Jerusalem and Mary articulated a theological connection between the sacred and the everyday. They identified with Mary, who mourned for her son, and with the women of Jerusalem, who cried for Christ. They found additional meaning in Jesus' instructions to the women of Jerusalem, and several participants interpreted Christ's words as advice about their own lives as mothers who must watch their children endure the difficulties of structural inequalities. These women were specific in naming the conditions of their neighborhood—*racismo e injusticia*—that forced them to keep a careful eye on their children. Many women told me that the Via Crucis gave them strength, knowing that Mary and her contemporaries also felt helpless and could not stop Christ's pain. "The Via Crucis is something we live in the barrio," a coordinator told a reporter. "The Virgin Mary cried for her son and now the mothers cry for their sons who use drugs and are in gangs. It's real."[26]

Although the experiences of womanhood that do not depend on motherhood are repressed by the association between Mary as mother and their own lives in Pilsen, women's empathy for Mary and her contemporaries makes sacred their daily rituals of nurturing and caring for others. Similarly, the celebratory image of motherhood makes heterosexuality and patriarchy the norm, yet within this definition of womanhood, their claims validate the mundane work of caring for children: watching after them, teaching them right from wrong, worrying about their safety, supplementing their education so that they can have more opportunities than their parents, wiping their runny noses, holding them when the school bully makes them cry, or teaching them to have pride in their cultural heritage—to name a few of the ways mothers weave a relationship with their children.

Certainly, the Via Crucis itself provides women with religious and cultural lessons for their children. All spoke about the Via Crucis as an occasion to teach their children about Jesus' life and death and about *nuestra cultura*. As with other rituals in which women embody intersecting identities, the Via Crucis demonstrates how culture, faith, and gender overlap for women of Mexican descent.[27] It is a spiritual event that takes its form and meaning from Mexican culture and history; the Via Crucis is a heritage they want to share with their children. Some women are certain that an authentic Via Crucis is found only in Mexico, while others do not question the *mexicanidad* of the event. Nonetheless, all articulate the difficulties of living in a city in which everyone—the media, *los blancos,* the school system, and even the church—attempts to diminish, deny, or negate Mexican culture. Living under these conditions, they recognize the importance of taking children to see the procession and to see Christ or Mary as an example for their own lives. However, this production of collective identity is not merely a celebration of cultural nationalism.

Women in Pilsen teach their children about their heritage as an act of defiance against a social code that subordinates their Mexican culture.

Whereas participants and observers interpret the actions of Mary and the women of Jerusalem as a shared maternal experience, the connection to Veronica is less clear. Though women do not elaborate on Veronica's significance, her actions literally correspond with their own. It is the subaltern Veronica who embodies resistance. In the sixth station, Veronica pushes past the Roman soldiers surrounding Jesus and cleans his face. It is important to infer Veronica's symbolic role in Pilsen even though she is not "thickly described." I suspect that Veronica's agency in the face of military might resonates with the lives of Pilsen's female leaders and the female coordinators of the Via Crucis. Indeed, Mexicanas have been central to Pilsen's grassroots organizing efforts. Socially and doctrinally restricted from holding public or clerical office, they work in community-based organizations or parish councils in order to voice their concerns and make changes in the community. In fact many of the social services that Pilsen receives were engineered by Mexicanas who founded organizations such as the Spanish Coalition for Jobs, Inc., Pilsen Neighbors Community Council, Alivio Medical Center, Mujeres Latinas en Acción, and El Hogar del Niño. Perhaps women are ambivalent about Veronica because she complicates their notion of motherhood. She is not present as a mother, though her gesture fits within a nurturing model. Nevertheless, Veronica is defiant and transgresses the boundaries of male rule; and it is this perspective that Mexicanas may verbally repress, although their actions perform this transgression very clearly.

Transformation on 18th Street: Body, Spirit, and Power

Through its response to the social codes, such as patriarchy and white privilege, that limit its residents' lives, Pilsen transforms itself into a Mexicano community through space, body, prayer, song, and crafted reflections about power, inequality, and faith.

Camera crews, photojournalists, Latino worshipers, the Hispanic representative from the archdiocese, and the participants enacting the Stations of the Cross press for space and fresh air in the overheated auditorium. When Jesus is given his cross, the crowd breathes a collective sigh of relief at the prospect of moving outside into the cool air. As people exit, volunteers hand out song sheets, and everyone joins a throng already assembled on the street. Once the auditorium is cleared, approximately eighty ushers control the group that will swell on Pilsen's main street and engulf pedestrian traffic.[28] To keep the crowd from swallowing up the

The procession near Providence of God, 1998. Camera crews are temporarily allowed inside the roped-off area to photograph Christ and the procession. Used by permission of the author.

men and women who participate in Jesus' walk to Calvary, the ushers establish a playing area in the street with a circle of rope. Within the roped-off playing area, the carefully selected parishioners continue to enact the final hours of Jesus' life, as narrated in the Stations of the Cross. The west-moving crowd will speak as one voice in a combination of prayer, song, and reflections until they reach a small mound in Harrison Park. For two hours all traffic stops, most businesses close, and people put down their work and watch from a window or a door while a massive crowd takes back the streets.

In general the text for the procession comes from the Passion narrative. A narrator, also carefully selected each year by the core committee, reads a reflection or commentary for each station and invites the people to join in with responsorial prayers and songs—most of which are in vernacular

The apostles walking in the procession, 1998. The Sears Tower is visible in the background. Used by permission of the author.

Spanish. Since the mid-1990s the event has included abridged reflections in English to acknowledge the presence of Latino youth and the small but growing number of non-Latinos who may not speak Spanish. Naming the unnamed and mundane experiences of everyday life, the reflections are information for the crowd about living conditions in Pilsen. They are also affirmations that Christ is present in the neighborhood and suffering from poverty, undocumented status, sickness, unemployment, and imprisonment.[29] By naming sources of domination, the reflections become a method of subversion and resistance that is grounded in faith and community solidarity.

Originally the Stations of the Cross were enacted inside the Catholic churches that line 18th Street, since seven are located on or very near this major thoroughfare. People would either wait at their parish to join the procession, or they would follow the procession into each building, and the narrator would lead them in prayer and song from the pulpit. But since the mid-1980s all stations have been recited at points along 18th Street that serve as symbolic or literal places of social injustice, struggle, violence, or solidarity. Some locations are community landmarks, such as the local branch library named for martyred political activist Rudy Lozano, who was murdered in his home allegedly because of his efforts to unionize laborers and because he had testified against several tortilla factories on the West Side of Chicago for bringing people from Mexico to work as indentured slaves.[30] At the same time, the library itself marks a victory for the neighborhood and symbolizes their efforts to improve and take part in the education offered to their children. Moreover, the Mesoamerican motif decorating the building suggests that quality education includes indigenous forms of knowledge. Whereas the library evokes both empowerment and opposition to that empowerment, other sites have been selected because they are notorious landmarks of recurring violence perpetrated by residents themselves. The intersection of 18th Street and Racine Avenue is, according to the narrator's reflection in 1995, "the site of much gang violence. Here youth attack other youths with knives, bats, and guns. They fight for the sale of drugs, they fight for money, for pride."[31] Other locations have become landmarks as a result of repeated pilgrimages, such as the small hill in Harrison Park. Whether

Residents standing at their door and on the front porch to watch the procession, 1998. Used by permission of the author.

Rudy Lozano Branch of the Chicago Public Library, 1994. At left is the Mesoamerican motif that circles the building. Used by permission of the author.

representations of communal pride or shame, the meditations and songs are recited publicly and in unison at the places that people inhabit every day and thus define these places as part of their spiritual topography.

For some observers who attend the procession annually, memory of the event punctuates everyday life throughout the year, so that passing each landmark causes them to remember the Via Crucis, its message and vision. Indeed, observers consistently state that the event is a symbol of unity and solidarity within Pilsen. They are most attached to the size and diversity of the crowd, although they also note the harmonious atmosphere during the procession. For them, the throng of Mexicanos and Mexicanas walking, praying, and singing in unison is an act of solidarity that strengthens the community and makes it a special place.

Building on the sacralization of space in Pilsen, in the early 1980s women from St. Pius V initiated the practice of making temporary altars at the sites of the eighth and ninth stations. Women related by kin and social networks take items from their homes to create two elaborate altars. These and other, similar altars are the ephemeral but sacred landmarks on Pilsen's streets. *Altarcitos,* home altars, are part of a rich tradition of devotional art, such as yard shrines, *nichos, capillas* (chapels), roadside crosses, street murals, tattoos, and graveyard art, that create a topogra-

A Station of the Cross located in front
of a grocery store on 18th Street, 1998.
Used by permission of the author.

phy of the relationship with the sacred.[32] Home altars are a site at which
Mexican Catholics, usually women, ensure an affiliation between ordinary experience and divine grace. They are intimate and private spaces
for familial and sacred communication, worship, homage, and faith. They
are often filled with images of deceased family members, candles, flowers, prayer cards, statues, and other religious images; many of these objects are considered family heirlooms. The style of accumulation and
layering is characteristic of Mexican Catholic altarcitos.[33] As a domestic
representation of intimate knowledge and the sacred, altars map emotions, family relationships, and spirituality.[34] Moved into public view, the
altar takes on additional meaning. Not only do the collectively produced
altars articulate the blurring of boundaries between "the divine and the
human, the spiritual and the material,"[35] but they make explicit a communal claim for the sacred, acknowledge the multiple forms and rela-

tionships people have with Christ and his mother, and offer a collective memory and relationship to the divine.

Several families produced the two altars I photographed in 1998. Combining their private icons and images in a collective shrine, the women of St. Pius have challenged the distinctions between public and private domains. They have enacted a new condition for public space and declared it as part of their own intimate concerns and daily experience. By diminishing the boundary between public and private matters, these women make issues—such as domestic violence and the undereducation and malnutrition of their children—and prayers about these experiences into public concerns. Moreover, they make these claims through sacred relationships, which are often multiple, redundant, and layered.

It is not surprising that the women of St. Pius and the core committee voice and claim sacred space on 18th Street and outside church buildings.

Altar created for the Eighth Station of the Cross, 1998. The bricoleur style of accumulation and layers is prominent. Used by permission of the author.

Altar created for the Ninth Station of the Cross near Laflin at 18th Street, 1998. Multiple images and icons of Mary and Guadalupe are used. Used by permission of the author.

Although the women and the core committee may not have the same motivation for publicly performing their faith, in both cases their movement to public space makes sense because collective devotion to the Catholic institution has been problematic for Chicago's Mexicanos. Before the 1960s, local clergy ordered Mexican Catholics to the basement for worship. Others directed them to the nearby St. Francis of Assisi parish, a Mexican national parish established in 1925.[36] Even the parishioners who spoke with pride about a storefront chapel in the Back of the Yards that was devoted to Spanish-speaking worshipers questioned the insufficient facilities of the Immaculate Heart of Mary chapel in comparison with other national parishes in the city.[37] They were aware that los blancos received preferential treatment, and they could not reconcile this fact with Catholic doctrine, let alone Jesus' teachings. Mexicanos remembered well that the Catholic institutions of Pilsen had been participants in racialization and segregation. The ambivalent relationship between the archdiocese and Mexicano worshipers again became part of public debate in the early 1990s, when the archdiocese closed or consolidated dozens of parishes and schools with Mexicano congregations. Unconvinced by the archdiocese's reasons for church closures, many Mexicanos spoke openly to me about a history of racism in the Catholic Church, connecting a history of preferential treatment of los blancos to the recent events. By moving the Via Crucis into the streets of Pilsen, the residents make their faith public, insisting on their visibility and unmediated spirituality. The route reverses and displaces clerical authority by asserting that the divine is no longer found exclusively inside a church building, although at least one veterano was more comfortable encountering it inside a church.[38]

But it is likely that something more than geography has made 18th Street the place where Mexicanos walk and pray in unison with Christ to invoke sacred ground. Eighteenth Street runs east–west through the center of Pilsen, with significant intersections at Blue Island, Ashland Avenue, and the Chicago/Alton railroad tracks. No other space in Pilsen functions like this street, more commonly known as *El Dieciocho* (18th Street). The street and the neighborhood are united at the cognitive level in that people often use the names interchangeably. Perhaps its symbolic power derives from the fact that the street does not have separate zones for home and work or residential and commercial usage: everything is on 18th Street. People eat, drink, shop, pray, study, play, and conduct business there. From one door to the next and frequently from one level to the next, zones change. Restaurants, ma-and-pa grocery stores, photography studios, law offices, churches, medical clinics, *panaderías* (bakeries), *tortillerías, taquerías,* clothing stores, liquor stores, the public library, and several community-based organizations line the street, along with apartment buildings and single-family homes. Demographically dense and culturally specific, 18th Street is the visible embodiment of this Mexicano community. The Passion of Christ in enacted on this street, a space filled with social and cultural activity.

For Patricia, an awareness of the overlapping communal activities on 18th Street and of the insufficient services provided to Pilsen makes the Stations of the Cross a vehicle for voicing injustice and struggle and experiencing grace.

> Christ suffered way back two thousand years ago, but he's still suffering now. His people are suffering. We're lamenting and wailing. And also we are a joyful people at the same time. . . . So what we try to do is incorporate some of that. So this is not a story, this is not a fairy tale. It happened, and it's happening now. . . . We must be Christlike. He fought [against] injustices. We should also fight [against] injustices, to make our life and our world a better place to live. . . . And in order to do that we have to bring these things to focus, to mind. And what we did is [connect] where Jesus meets his mother; we picked this spot, the El Rey Tortillería or the school,

and the theme we use there is Mary laments for her son who will be put to death. And here a lot of women lament for their sons who are killed because of the craziness of the gangs. Or they lament that their children are not fed properly. They do not receive the nourishment that they should receive. They do not receive the nourishment of the education [system]. They are discriminated against because they are poor.[39]

Patricia's words suggest that by praying the fourth Station of the Cross at a public place symbolic of youth violence, malnutrition, or insufficient education, Mexicanas are reminded that Mary also grieved over her child. In addition, the shared experiences make relevant and legitimate the call for change, the vision for "a better place to live." Furthermore, by practicing this relationship between mother and son Pilsen residents literally see themselves in the moreno bodies that walk and weep as Jesus and Mary. Indeed, the spiritual transformation of Pilsen is crystallized in the moment that mestizos and mestizas give bodily form to Christ and his mother while other mestizos and mestizas pray for their new vision of their community.

Some participants believe that the sacralization of Pilsen has helped produce significant changes on 18th Street. One young man, Jorge, who at different times has represented Jesus, a thief, and a disciple, spoke about the transformation he attributes to the Via Crucis. "I think one of the reflections . . . has meant a lot and we have gotten a great result. . . . The taverns around here . . . they're all gone. We have only two on 18th Street. Before, it was like every block there was a bar. And I remember as we stopped, I don't how many years [ago]—we had stopped in front of these taverns and prayed for the alcoholics. . . . And almost all the bars are gone from here [now]."[40] Jorge's remarks indicate that prayer *in the street* has changed Pilsen. He did not state that the aim of the procession is to create results, but he spoke of the power of the call for action and the request for divine intervention that originates from the residents themselves as they come forward in a massive crowd and demand attention, whether to city hall's indiscriminate granting of liquor permits in poor neighborhoods, to local gerrymandering of voting blocs that disfranchises Mexicano residents, or to municipal favoritism of big business. From this perspective, the procession is an act of civil disobedience or social protest. In the words of one of the first coordinators, Claudia, it is "the real way of praying," because it is "the opportunity to reflect and analyze how we are living and the things we have to [do] in order to have a better life."[41]

Another coordinator, Dolores Yáñez, also believed that the Via Crucis had transformed Pilsen, but she was less romantic about the long-term changes. From her perspective, some of the problems related to gangs are ongoing. "It's always gangs and drugs, because that problem we just can't seem to get rid of in Pilsen."[42]

Although Dolores's comment about gangs may sound fatalistic, her vision of Pilsen was optimistic and positive. For instance, she was clear about the major transformations in Pilsen that have emerged from progressive political activism. "I think in general Pilsen has become a different place to me. 'Cause I've seen the changes that are taking place. The changes that the Resurrection [Project] is causing, and I find that to be inspiring."[43] As she continued, Dolores explained that these changes and struggles are part of a longstanding battle. The current form of the struggle was a threatened immediate displacement. Action was occurring on two interconnected fronts, and not surprisingly the coordinators of the Via Crucis are part of these efforts.

In 1998 Pilsen residents fought against the implementation of Tax Increment Financing, a redevelopment program offering tax-free and low-interest loans to developers whose projects used public services. Developers are often exempt from paying taxes to local school boards, and such an exemption would further disadvantage Pilsen youth, who already attend overcrowded schools. Pilsen residents, often working through their parish leaders, organized protests and demonstrations in the neighborhood and in the civic center. In an effort to stall the gentrification that would remove them from their neighborhood, some residents publicly announced their claim to a home and a neighborhood by posting signs declaring, "¡Esta Casa NO Está Por Venta! / This house is NOT for sale!"

This public statement is part of a larger effort to save Pilsen housing for low-income Mexicano residents. The Resurrection Project, also known as Pilsen Resurrection Development Corporation, is an organization devoted to creating homeownership among people of Mexican descent and other Latinos. It works with banks to secure loans for residents who do not have a record of savings, and it also functions as a developer, building low-cost single-family homes. In October 1998 the Resurrection Project celebrated the construction of its first hundred homes.

Dolores placed the current work of the Resurrection Project and the older protest against the University of Illinois at Chicago on a continuum. After describing the various fronts on which Pilsen residents must fight to keep their homes, she offered the following explanation: "It's been that way for many years now, and people have been trying to . . . squeeze us out, squeeze us out. Well, they squeezed us out of Roosevelt and Halsted over by St. Francis [of Assisi when they built the university]. We came here [to Pilsen]. And now they want to squeeze us out of here. Don't move us from here. You can't move us from here."[44] Her memory of being "squeezed out" by the University of Illinois at Chicago in the 1960s may also include events of the late 1970s and early 1980s, when the city was planning to convert the deteriorated industrial factories of Pilsen into attractive, middle-income loft apartments for the professionals who worked at the university and hospitals immediately north of the neighborhood. Pilsen housing had been shrinking at the rate of 100 units per year, the result of absentee landlords and city neglect. Mexicanos had been in danger of being "squeezed out" because they could not afford new apartments; 23 percent of them were living below the poverty line. Although Pilsen residents mounted a successful protest in the 1980s, they lost to city developers in the 1990s.[45] The expansion of the university permanently removed Pilsen residents and shut down the underground economy at Maxwell Street, which supplemented the incomes of working-class Mexicano families. In these circumstances it is not surprising that residents would use the Via Crucis as a vehicle to protest the urban-renewal plans that displace and disfranchise them.

One such instance of action occurred in 1991, when the reflection for the ninth station addressed Pilsen's lack of public services. At this station Jesus falls for the third time, and the reflection equated the weight of living in a poor, neglected community with the weight of Christ's cross and his abandonment. Recalling the poor housing, insufficient street lighting, unpaved alleys, the dangerous sidewalks, lack of sanitation, and abandoned buildings, the reflection mounted a critique of city policy. Moreover, by citing the structural forms of inequality, the reflection subverted a cultural or biological explanation for these conditions (such as Mexicans are lazy, dirty, and immoral) and pointed to the real factors in the deteriorated condition of their neighborhood. Identifying Christ's ordeal with their own, Pilsen residents sanctify their claims for neighborhood improvements.

Some reflections directly address the reasons for Pilsen's decay. The third station, in which Jesus falls for the first time, is typically recited in front of a place of employment, and the crowd is asked to pray for the suffering workers who face economic and human injustice. Linking Jesus' pain to that of the workers, the reflection calls attention to an employer or corporation that ignores the plight of workers. It invokes the sacred to legitimate class struggle. Naming the sources of oppression, such as absentee landlords and ruthless employers, is an important strategy in community empowerment. In 1994 the crowd stopped in front of El Rey Tortillería to pray for the employees working in unhealthy conditions. The reflection brought a previously hidden issue to public attention and helped force the owners of El Rey to change their practices.

Naming and breaking the silence that surrounds and maintains the architecture of domination is central to the Via Crucis. The reflections and sites of each station are part of a larger effort to make residents aware of obscured social facts and hold others accountable for their actions. Indeed, the procession even bears witness to inequalities created in the 1800s. The vaulted sidewalks and streets are the result of a nineteenth-century public project to improve the drainage and sewer system. At a time when Chicago faced rapid expansion, city planners realized they were in a quagmire. In 1855 and 1856 the downtown buildings were elevated out of the mud and given new drainage systems. Municipal concern didn't reach Pilsen until 1875, but in that working-class Irish, German, Czech, and Polish neighborhood, the "vaulted streets and sidewalks were installed eight to ten feet above the original levels, leaving the first floors of many homes below street level."[46] The so-called improvement project has had long-term effects on Pilsen property values, among the lowest in the city, a fact that makes it difficult to accumulate the necessary assets for higher education. In addition, the improvement project is literally full of holes, which range from the size of a child's foot to the size of a compact car. The holes are real threats to people's physical safety, and during the procession everyone must continuously take account of these hazards.

However, though physically taxing, the architecture of domination does not obliterate spiritual devotion and a vision for change. Even during a procession in which thousands of people must maneuver around potholes and cracks, people are also attuned to their spirituality and faith. Patricia recalled the *milagros* she witnessed during the procession.

> You see certain things. I call them my little milagros, my little miracles. Men stopping, taking off their hats. They would stop, and all of a sudden they sobered up for a few seconds. They see what is going by, make the sign of the cross. Or they bow their heads. Just standing there, to me, was a sign of respect. They knew something good was happening. . . . Things of that nature, you know. Gangbangers. . . . There's a little bit more respect by the way they carry themselves or just [by] their silence . . . when we would pass by. . . . we'd pass by and you'd see them bow their heads. Just little things like that make me feel more sensitive to their surroundings, to what is actually going on, to what is happening. And you see how this evangelization touches them. My little milagros, that's what I call them.[47]

Patricia has observed the power that collective prayer can have on people. Gang members and drunks are moved to participate in this communal act and its public claim to a culturally specific form of spirituality. Such a transformation in people makes the larger transformation in Pilsen seem real, tangible, and permanent. At the same time, the milagros offer inspiration to those who elect to do battle with the city or those who some-times express discouragement about the everyday struggles. Several orga-nizers and participants spoke to me about their renewed faith when they witness these milagros. They often add that the public demonstration of Pilsen's humanity may also inspire other people.

The milagros are signifiers of the power of the Via Crucis. Albeit mo-mentarily and in silence, the Via Crucis displaces the culture of fear and violence in Pilsen and extends the space of the sacred even into gang ter-ritory. Stations have been recited at places where a gang-style homicide occurred, at the home of a family actively working to end the cycle of gang violence, and at a known gang hangout. Moreover, although the recitations name gang violence and sites of gang activity, they have not faced gang retaliation, even though these public actions are locally known as a sign of disrespect to a gang. With the unwritten code to not harm coordinators and participants being constantly negotiated, the Via Crucis has made it possible for people to talk openly about illegal drug traffic, violence, and youth homicide. Like most inner-city, suburban, and rural communities, Pilsen has active criminal gangs. Unlike most subur-ban and rural communities, however, Pilsen annually brings these issues to public attention, using prayer and song to initiate change.

Through the Via Crucis, Mexicanos and Mexicanas in Pilsen create and make present their cultural and spiritual identities in the actual spaces of their daily lives. They live within, react against, and transform the phys-ical realities of their existence. They bring to consciousness a critique of their own condition, including patriarchy, racial privilege, and material domination, and thereby demonstrate that public space is not only phys-ically determined but also culturally constructed.[48] It is the public enact-ment of faith—the procession, the commentaries, the altars, and the milagros—that illuminates the sacredness of Pilsen.

This process of making and taking space counteracts an authoritative practice that reinforces the architecture of domination, an aspect of what Helán Page and R. Brooke Thomas refer to as "white public space." For Page and Thomas, white public space is not a particular physical location but the public domain in which strategies, institutions, public relations performances, sensory experiences, and other tactics "routinely, discur-sively and sometimes coercively privilege European Americans over nonwhites." It is a domain in which white privilege and whiteness are protected, though not to the exclusion of all nonwhite people. Nonwhites are recruited to compete with one another for white approval and to "seek [the] rewards and privileges of whiteness for themselves at the expense of other racialized populations." Thus, although membership is denied, nonwhites inhabit the domain because its success depends on their promotion of it and of whiteness. Whiteness is a contingent identity that implies a certain orientation and the acquisition of a right to race privilege. To inhabit white public space ideologically, people deploy whiteness in order to shore up "resources, power, and opportunity."[49]

It is useful to extend the concept of white public space to include general and specific locations or sites in which the physical architecture of domination creates the vigorous success of Americans with access to whiteness. Racialization and its articulation in public space are concurrent with class interests, patriarchy, and other master narratives of domination.[50] White public space recruits heterosexuals, professionals, men, and "whites" into full membership and excludes laborers, meat packers, assembly-line workers, janitors, domestic servants, and women. Domestic workers and other service providers enter white public space on a temporary, contingent basis: their wages are not life-sustaining, capital accumulation is improbable, advancement and other options are controlled by those with access to whiteness, occupancy is dictated by markets that change when labor costs are higher than racial and gender norms permit, and physical distance is structured. All these processes are at work in Chicago, a city in which southern and eastern Europeans gained access to whiteness at the expense of African Americans and Latinos, who later negotiated their temporary membership in white public space.

In Chicago white privilege ensures that some people receive street repairs, social services, comprehensive police and fire protection, quality education, and other opportunities that encourage asset accumulation. It is a form of domination that maintains housing and employment segregation, secures the control of religious and secular institutions, promotes English monolingualism and Mock Spanish, concentrates investment in private corporations, and sanctions an unregulated (nonunion), low-wage workforce upon which middle-class prosperity relies.[51] Clearly, white public space has tangible effects on people's lives, specifically on their corporeal bodies.

However, as several Pilsen residents point out, the Via Crucis challenges the social codes of white privilege, particularly the architecture of domination. It names the forms and sources of power and offers an alternative vision of the community. This transformation of Pilsen, generated through spiritual/cultural devotion, makes its position explicit not only in terms of the profane and the sacred, but also in terms of the divide between the unnamed/illegitimate/undocumented and the named/authoritative/documented. Woven within the claim to sacred space is a critique of the forms of domination that function to silence Mexicanos and

Mexicanas. The ritual dramatically claims the neighborhood as theirs despite a social code that pushes them to the margins. The act itself is a counterdiscourse to white public space, since it acknowledges a cultural heritage that is otherwise without power. The Via Crucis articulates a vision of equality and justice.

The event does not, however, support all forms of equality, namely the challenge to patriarchy. This ambivalent vision for women demonstrates a betweenness that border theorists have come to recognize as the norm.[52] This interpretive paradigm finds that mestizos and mestizas alike have lived for centuries within and against the dominant society, absorbing and rejecting various aspects of the authoritative cultures of which they are a part.

The profound lived reality present in, and made possible through, the sensual and spiritual practice of the Via Crucis does not remove people from their daily physical realities. It is prayer grounded in experience. The Via Crucis crystallizes experience within the spaces people inhabit every day and helps to establish a sacred realm for Mexicanos, lo cotidiano (the everyday).

The Hill

One last image symbolizes how and why Mexicanos challenge the institutions that continuously attempt to alter and shorten their daily lives. Its site is the final stations of the Via Crucis, but it offers no closure to the possibilities in Pilsen.

Since its inception, the procession has ended at a hill in Harrison Park, also known among Latinos as Parque Zapata (Zapata Park). Here three men are raised on crosses while soldiers enact the final scenes in Jesus' life. The spectators gather near the hill, although less than a third are able to hear or see these crucifixion stations. Those able to witness the death of their moreno Christ almost always gasp at the moment when the body goes limp. Although the park is the largest open space in the neighborhood, it cannot accommodate the huge crowd, the hundreds of strollers, the dozens of peddlers, and the media. Even after Christ and the thieves have been removed from their crosses, people continue to face the hill and to pray in silence. The crosses themselves remain on the hill for about an hour, and people who were unable to witness the crucifixion scene approach the spot to conclude their pilgrimage. Some are still weeping. The hour may be punctuated by laughter and roaming children, but the mood is solemn as group after group, family after family, makes its way to the temporary fences surrounding the hill, signs the cross, and prays quietly.

The hill is a powerful focus of shared experience, community empowerment, and spirituality. Nearly everyone I met in Chicago attests to its power, and so does the public record. In the 1980s the Chicago Park Department attempted to flatten the hill, claiming that it was sinking anyway and was taking up space that could be used for baseball fields. Although local residents enjoy the park's two baseball fields and could use another, hundreds of Mexicanos came out to protest against the department's plan. The protesters claimed that the place was sacred ground to them. In fact some people make the sign of the cross whenever they pass by. After a year-long struggle the Chicago Park Department dropped its plans. Today the hill is reportedly no longer sinking.[53]

Lara Medina and Gilbert R. Cadena

Días de los Muertos

Public Ritual, Community Renewal, and Popular Religion in Los Angeles

We can't forget our dead; because of them we are here. We have to keep fighting.

I T W A S A G O O D Y E A R to honor the dead in Los Angeles. According to one Latino newspaper, "Los Angeles must be the United States' Day of the Dead capital. . . . Angelenos take this day seriously—so seriously that many spend the whole month of October making sugar skulls and altars."[1]

The several hundred people gathering on the sunny morning of November 1, 1998, at the intersection of "Five Corners," in East Los Angeles, are living testimony to this claim. Many are in full *calavera* (literally, "skull," but referring to the entire skeleton) attire, the predominant icon for Días de los Muertos, or Days of the Dead. Adults and children enthusiastically line up to have their faces painted to represent the skeleton within. Others mingle with anticipation while waiting to join the mile-long procession soon to begin. Many carry bouquets of bright orange *cempoaxóchitl* (marigolds), the traditional flowers for the *ofrendas* (altars for the dead); the bright color and pungent smell will attract the spirits of departed loved ones. Others attentively watch a theatrical performance on the north side of the small plaza, portraying a son speaking with the spirit of his dead mother. Words of forgiveness help reconcile a lifetime plagued by drugs and violence.

The beat of the Aztec drums notifies the crowd that the procession is about to begin. *Danzantes* (Aztec dancers) wearing feathered headdresses and beaded ceremonial clothing offer prayers of thanksgiving to the four cardinal directions with the scent of *copal* (holy incense) rising to the heavens. Individuals, couples, and families quickly maneuver into line to be-

Many carry bouquets of bright orange *cempoaxóchitl*, or marigolds, as offerings for the dead. Photo by Lara Medina.

gin the short trek down Cesar Chavez Avenue to Self Help Graphics, a Chicano community art center. Banners publicize the collective sentiments: "¿Cuantas más masacres?" (How many more massacres?) refers to the recent killing of forty Zapatistas in Actael, Mexico, and "Vivan los muertos" stresses the enduring presence of the dead. An oversized papiermâché calavera on a flatbed truck brings up the end of the parade. The living proceed to honor their dead. Death does not have the last word, here in East Los Angeles.

Three miles away, at Dolores Mission Parish, two hundred Mexicanos and Chicanos spanning several generations gather for Mass. The bilingual crowd listens attentively as Father Ted delivers a homily in English, urging those present to remember the "saints of today and the saints of history, persons who model holy living." For a community afflicted by gang violence and poverty, such models emerge from the numerous base communities that have formed in this three-square-mile neighborhood. The small, simple church building exhibits the communities' central icons—a Salvadoran cross of liberation, la Madre Dolorosa, and Mary with her child walking the streets of Los Angeles. But today an ofrenda shares the sacred space. On the left side of the sanctuary in a newly constructed alcove, the four-tiered altar displays photographs of the deceased, *pan de muertos* (sweet bread shaped into stylized skulls or human figures), *papel picado* (decoratively cut tissue paper), calavera masks, and, of course, marigolds. Many of the photographs are of young men lost to gang violence. A drawing of a homeless woman with a child dying of hunger shares the altar with popular heroes of justice, Oscar Romero, César Chávez, and Mother Teresa.

After the service the parishioners gather at the altar to pray while some share photographs and stories of loved ones. A "Book of Names" circulates with an invitation to write in its pages the names of those remembered. The next day, All Souls Day, at the evening Mass, Father Greg places this book on the main altar and invites more additions, then ceremoniously carries the book to the ofrenda and blesses both. Clearly, the memories occupy a sacred place in the community of Dolores Mission.

Here we examine the spiritual and political significance of Días de los Muertos in the lives of "unchurched and churched" Chicanos and Mexicanos in East Los Angeles. Although many Chicano families have hon-

The living proceed to honor their dead. Photo by Gilbert Cadena.

An oversized papier-mâché calavera marks the end of the parade. Photo by Gilbert Cadena.

ored their dead for generations, until the 1970s ritual practices tended to be private in nature, centered upon home altars and family visits to cemeteries. The increasingly public celebration of the Days of the Dead over the past three decades signals its ever broader social impact. We use the plural form, *Días,* to emphasize the numerous days of preparation, as well as the several days that participants actually spend honoring and communing with their dead. As a third-generation Chicana and Chicano we have shared in the expansion of these celebrations in Los Angeles and San Francisco for the last twenty years. The order of the ritual components may vary from place to place, but the components themselves remain essentially the same. Our work at several universities in Southern California introduced the tradition to several campus communities in the early 1990s. The exuberant response affirms that the tradition reflects both the rich spirituality and the political sensibilities of Chicanas/os.

The annual communal and public ritual celebrations for the dead renew and enlarge a collective historical memory that gives life to past, present, and future generations. The public nature of the ritual and its underlying Mesoamerican Indigenous worldview, which values the interconnectedness of life, defy mainstream attempts to silence a culture and

Parishioners gather at the altar to pray or to share their photographs and stories of loved ones. Photo by Robert Dolan.

a spirituality "forged in the struggle against domination."[2] In the following pages we explore several general questions: How do secular cultural centers and Catholic parishes commemorate Días de los Muertos? How are urbanized Chicanos/as transforming a traditional Mexican ritual? Does Días de los Muertos contribute to popular religion, popular culture, and spirituality?

This ethnography focuses on the collaborative effort between Self Help Graphics (SHG) and Proyecto Pastoral at Dolores Mission Parish in their 1998 celebration of Días de los Muertos. Although SHG has celebrated the tradition since 1972, 1998 marked the first time that artists and cultural workers collaborated with a Catholic parish. Other participants included the Getty Research Institute, which contributed substantial funding, and the Aztlán Cultural Arts Foundation, which offered workshop space. The Getty funds paid several professional Chicana and Chicano artists to teach Días de los Muertos art to eastside residents. Workshops at the Aztlán Cultural Arts Foundation, in Lincoln Heights, and at Dolores Mission, in Boyle Heights, both predominantly Latino communities, attracted hundreds of adults and children over a ten-week period. These workshops produced papel picado, calavera masks, ofrendas, floats, murals, props, and drama, all essential elements of a public Días de los Muertos celebration. Artists also worked with Catholic priests and lay leaders during the preparations for Días de los Muertos at Dolores Mission, and a communitywide celebration took place at SHG.

According to Tomás Benítez, the director of SHG, the collaborative project sought to promote both artist participation and community empowerment, and in doing so to shed light on how community production of art affects a sense of neighborhood ownership, citizenship, and a capacity to be active agents of change.[3] We recognized the project as a rich source for exploring community, art, religion, and Chicano/a culture all at once.

Traditions for the Dead in Mexico and Spain

Traditions of honoring the dead among both the Nahua, the dominant cultural group in central Mexico at the time of the Spanish conquest, and Spanish Catholics at the same time help illuminate both the continuity and the reinvention of the tradition among Chicanas/os. The Nahua ritual of honoring the dead centered on special food and flower offerings, overnight graveside visits with music and dance, elaborate ceremonies, processions, and communal feasting. Extensive public rituals took place during at least six months of the eighteen-month calendar year; several days of each twenty-day month were devoted to honoring the dead. Two of the most important months for public ritual were the ninth, Tlaxcochimaco (August 5–24 of the Gregorian calendar), when the *Miccail-huitontli,* or "Feast of the Little Dead" (children), took place; and the tenth month, Xocohuetzi (August 25–September 14), which included the *Hueymiccaytlhuitl,* or the "Feast of the Adult Dead."[4]

In Nahua belief, the dead joined the realm of the deity under whose protection fell the circumstances of their death. For example, people who died by drowning entered the realm of the rain god, Tlaloc, and were honored during the thirteenth month, dedicated to deities associated with water. The dead acted as intermediaries between the living and supernatural beings, and the feasts honoring the gods included the honoring of their dead servants as a means to appease or achieve the protection of the deities.[5] Death caused by old age or certain illnesses necessitated a four-year journey to Mictlan, or Place of the Dead, and offerings were meant to assist in their journey.

Sixteenth-century Spanish Catholic rituals honoring the dead shared some characteristics with those of Indigenous Mexico. Influenced by Roman practices, Christians made graveside meal offerings, and by the ninth century Masses for the dead were common practice.[6] According to most sources, Pope Boniface IV established the feast of All Saints Day in the seventh century, Gregory III moved this holy day from May to November 1 in the ninth century, and in the eleventh century the observance of All Souls Day was established on November 2 as a means to assist the souls in purgatory during their time of purification.[7] By the time of Spain's occupation of Mexico, Todos los Santos (All Saints) combined the two feasts, and Spanish Catholics honored the dead not only with Masses but also with food and flower offerings at home and in cemeteries. Skull imagery represented the dead, and All Souls bread was given to the poor.[8] Communion between the living and the dead took the form of mutual assistance.

The ritual importance of honoring the dead was far greater in Indigenous than in Catholic practice. Spanish Catholic tradition includes nine-day novenas for the souls in purgatory immediately following a death, and annual commemoration of a death. In contrast, Indigenous practice involved long periods of preparation for the numerous days honoring the dead. Nevertheless, belief in an afterlife and the ability and responsibility to commune with the dead offered points of intersection between the two belief systems.

Syncretism is the term most often used to describe the fusion of distinct religious systems into a new one. Many scholars acknowledge the limitations of this term, which implies a blending of two or more separate and "pure" religious systems, resulting in a new and unique form. The term suggests simple historical contexts and static religions, and ignores power relations involving physical and spiritual violence. To make sense out of Christianity, the Indigenous peoples of Mesoamerica had to appropriate Christian rites and symbols in a way that would enable them to maintain balance and harmony with their drastically changing world. Indigenous Mesoamericans had to decide how the religious systems could work together and what aspects of each enabled communication with transcendent powers.[9] The Spanish Christians would condense all the celebrations connected with Días de los Muertos into November 2, along with the accompanying feast of Todos los Santos on November 1, but Indigenous sensibilities and practices honoring the dead survived in spite of Christian attempts to dominate the tradition.

The celebration of the dead varies in many parts of Mexico today. Its different expressions reflect the nature of Indigenous practices at the time of the conquest, the degree to which particular regions engaged in syncretism throughout the colonial period, and more recent cultural variables. For example, in Oaxaca, Mexico, private and public altars, cemetery visits and festivals, public theater, and the creation of sand paintings are predominant ritual elements. In Chiapas processions claim a central place, while in the state of Guerrero "living" tombs with life-size coffins are constructed and family members perform the parts of angels and skeletons.[10] The style and elaborateness of the offerings vary depending on family income and the influence of Indigenous and / or Catholic ways.

Días de los Muertos and Self Help Graphics

Self Help Graphics, the first and primary Chicano/a community arts center and gallery in Los Angeles, has played an important role in reintroducing Days of the Dead to Chicanas/os in Los Angeles and to the larger U.S. population. Begun in the early 1970s with the help of Franciscan Sister Karen Bocallero, Self Help Graphics has provided opportunities for Chicano and Chicana artists to exhibit and further develop their work. Originally operating in a garage in East Los Angeles, a handful of artists dedicated themselves to making art that reflected the rich cultural values and spirit of resistance of the Chicano movement. By 1978 the expanding group relocated to a storefront site on Brooklyn (now Cesar Chavez) and Gage Avenues. SHG gradually emerged as the leading visual arts organization producing and exhibiting Chicana/o art and culture. Initial projects included the Barrio Mobil Arts Studio, which provided art education to thousands of local children by bringing artists and programs directly to the schools. Since the early 1980s the Printmaking Atelier, Professional Artists Workshop Program, and the Exhibition Print Program have enabled hundreds of artists to create and exhibit their work locally, nationally, and internationally. Through touring exhibits such as Across the Street: Self Help Graphics and Chicano Art in Los Angeles (1995–1997) and Chicano Expressions (1995–1997) in Europe, Africa, and Mexico, SHG is recognized as an international ambassador of Chicano/a art and culture. In 1996 SHG presented its first international Days of the Dead exhibit and celebration at the Glasgow Print Studio in Scotland.

Self Help Graphics began celebrating Days of the Dead in 1972. According to art historian Sybil Venegas, "Sister Karen credits Mexican artists Carlos Bueno and Antonio Ibañez with suggesting that El Día de los Muertos be celebrated as a collective, public art project aimed at cultural reclamation, self-determination and definition."[11] The first celebration was on a small scale, involving primarily local artists and including a procession from the local cemetery, the building of an ofrenda, and the sharing of food among participants.[12] By 1976 participants numbered several thousand. "The festivities included a cemetery Mass, a street parade, altar and art exhibits."[13] Fathers Gary Riebe-Estrella and Juan Romero presided at several of the liturgical celebrations until 1979, when the archdiocese announced that Catholic liturgies in the nearby Protestant Evergreen Cemetery could not be approved.[14] This action and the artists' increasing integration of Indigenous beliefs and practices into the event created a separation between the church and Days of the Dead at SHG. SHG has since sponsored Los Angeles' largest Días de los Muertos celebration without church involvement.

Preparations at Self Help Graphics and the Aztlán Cultural Arts Foundation

During 1998 Chicano communities of East Los Angeles began preparing for their dead in late August with artist-led workshops at SHG. Presentations by altarmaker Ofelia Esparza and photographer Anne Murdy introduced the project on the evening of August 31. By early September a series of eight free art workshops opened at the Aztlán Cultural Center, on the north side of downtown Los Angeles. Six additional workshops were offered at Dolores Mission and Self Help Graphics during September and October.

Located in the old Los Angeles County prison building, the Aztlán Cultural Arts Foundation uses the first floor of a large three-story building for workshop space, a performance stage, an exhibition gallery, offices, storage, and a small store. On this sunny Saturday morning a core of community artists prepares for the day's activities. Every room is dedicated to a specific project. At the entrance volunteers collect registration forms while face painters create calaveras on the faces of young children. One room offers more calavera making: two artists cut skull shapes from cardboard squares, and children and adults transform the lifeless shapes with paint, sequins, feathers, and glitter into imaginative renditions of the dead. By the end of the day at least forty colorful masks await use in the procession on November 1. Displayed near the room's corner shrine to Guadalupe, they seem to absorb her blessings.

In the next room busy hands produce papier-mâché masks. Strips of paper are dipped in a thick paste solution and layered over preconstructed molds. A family collaborates in creating an oversized calavera. By the end of the day more than a dozen masks wait to be decorated in the weeks ahead.

Designs for a portable mural take shape in another part of the building. Five murals will be used as backdrops for the performance stage at SHG. The largest will commemorate the twenty-fifth anniversary of Días de los Muertos at Self Help Graphics. The design evolves over three weeks, with local youngsters offering ideas and sketches. A young man suggests a "yin/yang" symbol formed by two serpents, one representing death and the other life. Below this symbol of duality, the artists configure a procession of the living who bring offerings to a traditional ofrenda. It will hold photographs of the dead whose lives have intersected with the development of SHG.[15] Bold colors add depth to the intricate mural design that reflect the spirits of the artists and the communities they serve. Over the next two months many more adults, teenagers, and children will participate in the production of this "ceremony of memory" and community renewal.[16]

Preparations at Proyecto Pastoral, Dolores Mission Parish

Proyecto Pastoral, established at Dolores Mission in 1986 as a Jesuit community service project to the five thousand residents of Boyle Heights and the Pico-Aliso housing projects, is best known for Homeboy Industries, a job-training program designed by Father Greg Boyle to help "at risk youth." Proyecto's many other projects include a women's childcare cooperative, preschool teacher training, teen leadership training, support to the homeless, and food distribution to needy families.

Proyecto Pastoral provided an essential link to grassroots community involvement in the collaborative effort with SHG and the Getty. Olivia Montes and José "Azul" Cortés of Proyecto worked closely with Tomás Benítez of SHG; Josephine Ramirez and Christina Miguel-Mullen of the Getty; Fathers Mike Kennedy, Greg Baumann, and Ted Gabrielli of Dolores Mission; and Chicana/o artists Consuelo Flores, Barbara Carrasco, Ernesto de la Loza, Mita Cuaron, Kathy Gallegos, and others. Youth and parents of Dolores Mission participated enthusiastically in the art workshops.

In mid-October artists lead two Saturday workshops on making sugar skulls, papel picado, and calavera masks in the parish school cafeteria of Dolores Mission. The creative energy flowing in the large workroom relays the same excitement and anticipation one might expect for Christmas preparations. Young children and their mothers station themselves at long tables and make sugar skulls from molds while others paint cardboard skeleton masks. Sequins, feathers, and beads complete an assembly of brightly colored masks to be used in the upcoming procession down Cesar Chavez Avenue. Another group of children folds colored tissue paper into one-inch strips. With scissors, they cut notches to make simplified papel picado. Close by the sound of a wooden mallet can be heard as a group of women learns how to make more-detailed papel picado. Their apprentice hands maneuver cautiously the tools that chisel an intricate design of flowers and calaveras from tracings on a stack of tissue paper. In the far corner reporters and their camera crew from a Spanish-language television station attempt to capture the excitement and significance of the preparations. "This is for our loved ones, for *los muertos*," is the common response to the journalists' questions. As the children and adults crowd around the tables to produce their creative work, adolescents focus intently on a large portable mural in the parking lot outside. The ten-by-eight-foot painted unstretched canvas will be one of the backdrops for the performance area at SHG. Rich colors and strong lines give shape to their church and neighborhood amidst downtown Los Angeles. A male image, possibly a contemporary Christ figure, towers above the skyline, embracing Dolores Mission and the surrounding city.

Mural depicting a contemporary Christ figure, embracing Dolores Mission Parish and the surrounding city. Photo by Gilbert Cadena.

Across the street and inside the church building eight women construct the ofrenda. Several pews hold a diverse array of votive candles,
boxes, photographs, and altar cloths. Socorro, the matriarch of the parish,
watches attentively as several other women prepare an arch of mulberry
branches covered with orange and yellow paper flowers deftly shaped to
resemble marigolds. Ofelia Esparza, a third-generation altarmaker and
professional artist from SHG, ponders the space and table to be used. As
an outsider to the parish community, Ofelia carefully consults with the
"modern temple keepers" before any decisions are made.[17] According to
Ofelia, "It is a process of sharing what my mother taught me . . . and seeing it connect with their own experiences. They all want to help and are
so excited to see their work incorporated into the altar."[18] Three of the
women meticulously lay white tablecloths on the sturdy crates and table
forming the four-tier foundation. Next come small crocheted cloths, followed by photos of loved ones, some glued in small cardboard boxes
painted and decorated to resemble *nichos* (devotional boxes). All vacant
areas are quickly filled with sugar skulls, votive candles, miniature

Women prepare an arch of mulberry branches covered with orange and yellow paper
flowers for the church ofrenda. Photo by Lara Medina.

Festive oversized calaveras create an unavoidable intimacy with death. Photo by Gilbert Cadena.

squash, pan de muertos, and paper calaveras made during the work-shops. Several large vases of marigolds complete the montage of memo-ries. As the women survey their work, they welcome the praise offered by Fathers Mike and Ted and others stopping by to witness their work of art and love. Their sense of accomplishment and pride illuminates this modest worship space. The ofrenda will soon become a site of solemn prayer, of talk with neighbors after Mass, or simply of gazing at the pho-tos and . . . remembering.

Celebration at Self Help Graphics

The program for the day announces what can be expected:

Culture is not static. And in the hands of artists, it is volatile and exciting. The traditions of Mexico are honored and respected, and then added to, modified to accommodate the North American experience of La Raza [the Latino people]. As is Day of the Dead, a custom both secular and religious, sacred and sacrosanct, Christian and pre-Columbian, the modern celebra-tions are old and new, maintaining the most popular customs and prompt-ing the next edge of invention. Day of the Dead has become a paradigm for how local artists contribute to the quality of life in their community, and it has become the ideal vehicle for sharing culture with the larger realm of society.[19]

By noon on November 1 the facilities at Self Help Graphics on the corner of Gage and Cesar Chavez Avenues are clearly marked as sacred space. Led by Mexicana danzantes, the procession of living calaveras makes its way to the parking lot decorated with oversized papier-mâché masks, large, richly painted canvas murals, and a centrally located pyramid-shaped structure. The danzantes bless the event with copal and drumbeats as they circle the pyramid. Then the procession of four hundred disperses to wait with the others as a float depicting Quetzalcoatl, the plumed serpent deity, maneuvers to the middle of the lot while the six-foot calavera on the flatbed truck parks close to the fence. Children's masks, papel picado, and two long tlatzotzompantli decorate the chain-link fence enclosing the parking lot. The tlatzotzompantli resemble the one found in the Templo Mayor in Mexico City. But these skulls, with sunglasses and teeth bared in smiles, reveal their southern Californian roots. The opening prayer, offered by En Lak Ech (You Are My Other I), a group of Chicana poets, emphasizes the spiritual significance of the day ahead:

> We would like to offer you all, in a good way, in a humble way, a prayer song.
>   We would like to honor all those who have passed on, all our ancestors, our grandmothers, and our grandfathers.
>   We want to pray for those who are yet to come and those who are here present with us today.
>   We, En Lak Ech *mujeres* [women], pray to the women and mujeres who have died through violence or through life and struggle. We offer this prayer for you.

The day's schedule includes twenty-seven performances, including more prayer, music, theater, poetry, comedy, and dance. The music—mariachi, Chicano rap, blues, Mexican, rock, salsa, and reggae—reflects the diversity of the crowd. Groups with names like Quetzal, Aztlán Underground, and Quinto Sol represent the Los Angeles music scene, incorporating an Indigenous consciousness.

As the performances get underway, it is evident that political concerns will be heard throughout the day as the community gathers to remember and renew itself for ongoing social struggles. Social criticism informs many of the musical compositions. The lead singer of Aztlán Underground responds to the power of the system toward Chicanos/as:

They gave us a lie
They taught us in their schools, in their media, in their churches.
They perfectly cloned us
It's the invasion of the body snatchers

Kill the materialist lust
Put the money aside
What is the history of the men on the money?
This is not going to keep you free.

We need to honor our ancestors
Don't forget where you came from
Stand up for your children
That's what it is all about.

So they can see a strong brown man, a strong brown woman
And feel proud of who they are.
So we can finally stand up
And take the foot of the oppressor out of this land.

The themes of the performances reflect an Indigenous consciousness: 1, *Nezahualcoyotl* (Aztec sage); 2, La Carpa Tezcatlipoca (a troupe named after an Aztec deity); 3, *Luchando con la Vida* (Struggling with Life); 4, twenty-five years of *Chicanahuatl* (Chicana Indigenous) fashion; and 5, Poem to *Miquitztli* (Death). One performance art group, Indians Teaching Spaniards, urges people to "tak[e] back the streets of Los Angeles" not just this one day but every day, and not just for the dead but for all the living in Los Angeles. En Lak Ech recites poetry, prays, dances, and sings to a captivated audience. Throughout the day people sit, stand, dance, and mingle with family and friends as they soak up these rich cultural expressions.

The gallery space on the first floor of SHG is packed with people viewing the "room altars." These sacred spaces portray intimate lifelike scenes from the homes of those remembered. One of the altarmakers has dedicated a sewing room to her mother. A black Singer sewing machine, a full-length mirror, and a dress form create the center of this ofrenda; an ironing board draped with clothes provides a sense of the activity that once filled the sewing room. Flowers, crochet needles, sewing boxes, crocheted dolls, and bolts of material fill the remaining space, recalling a creative sanctuary from the problems of everyday life or perhaps the workplace of an efficient seamstress. Another room altar displays a 1940s kitchen, one familiar to many Chicanos who grew up with a grandmother who healed others through her cooking. A "dining room altar" adjoins the kitchen, displaying a buffet table filled with photographs, flowers, and food offerings. This "altar within an altar" emphasizes the ofrenda's

Altars diffuse the boundaries between the living and the dead, between the human and the divine. Photo by Lara Medina.

traditional centrality in this family space. A "backyard porch altar" includes potted plants and a swinging chair where the artist's grandparents used to sit. The presence of a shrine to Guadalupe calls to mind the home religious practices embedded in Chicano Catholic culture.

On the second floor of SHG seven more altars line the sides of the hall. Some are sponsored by organizations, others by individuals. The altar dedicated to Mother Earth has a globe at its center accompanied by a map of the Americas. Cornstalks frame the altar along with offerings of pumpkin, squash, and tomatoes. This is the only altar without any Catholic symbols. The artist working on it comments: "Ecologically, the Earth is dying. . . . It is a wakening call to people."

Another altar on the second floor is dedicated to migrant farm workers. Its five levels are filled with a dozen small black-and-red United Farm Worker flags and plenty of orange marigolds. Several black-and-white photos of farm workers fill three of the levels. At the top is a photograph of César Chávez and Senator Robert F. Kennedy after Chávez's 1968 fast. A Guadalupe image occupies the center of the altar, and a crucifix is nailed to the wall above. Red-and-black papel picado frames the altar. Another altar, sponsored by The Wall, an organization for gay Latinos, honors those who have died of AIDS. Photographs, a statue of Guadalupe, teddy bears, and burning sage bless their presence. Space is reserved for people to add names or prayers for others remembered. By the end of the evening, thirty-four names on green-and-white sheets of paper decorate the wall. Pamphlets on AIDS prevention and services for gay Latinos in Los Angeles are freely distributed as part of this ofrenda.

From noon until ten in the evening, several thousand participate in the activities. No alcohol is served, but an espresso stand provides coffee. The aromas of Mexican food—carne asada, tacos, tamales, tostadas, chimichangas, and champurada, a Mexican chocolate drink—fill the air. A half-dozen vending booths sell T-shirts, sugar skulls, books, jewelry, candles, and assorted Días de los Muertos iconography. Participants line up to get their faces painted calavera style. Guitarists roam the area singing "La Llorona," and others serenade the dead. A calavera representing a Vietnam War veteran leads a ragtag procession, announcing their presence with a solemn drumbeat, flute music, and burning sage as they weave in and out of the crowd. In the far corner of the parking lot stands a permanent fifteen-foot mosaic statue of Our Lady of Guadalupe. Neighborhood women clean and maintain this shrine on a regular basis. Many Chicanos and Chicanas who come to SHG identify her as Tonantzin, the Nahua mother goddess. She appears to bless the crowd and the celebration.

The participants in the celebration are diverse. Of those we interviewed, about half identified as Catholic; the rest no longer affiliated with organized religion. One woman shared, "I follow *Indigena* ways; that makes me balanced." All acknowledged the spiritual significance of the day as they offered their respect for the dead. As one informant said, "I honor all my relations who have passed away. I feel their presence even more today. They are always with us, but today they come back to check to see if we still remember them." Despite diverse religious affiliations, the sense of a communal identity pervades the celebration. With a shared purpose of remembering and renewing, many participants acknowledged the value of passing on traditions and affirming cultural, spiritual, and political values. "I love how families with their children are here, teaching them the traditions, and how to honor their elders. Unless we teach them they won't know," said one. Knowing that the tradition helps them resist marginalization adds to the importance of the celebration.

"All we get from the media is that we [Chicanos] are worthless. Our children need to know their traditions so that they will know right from wrong when they hear stereotypes." The rituals of making and exhibiting art, constructing ofrendas, parading in calaveras, and performing from the heart sanctify what is important here in East Los Angeles. As one participant stated, "Remembering and honoring is praying." Through Días de los Muertos, Chicanos and Chicanas find strength and renewal in their struggle to survive and prosper as a people.

Chicanas/os Reclaiming Días de los Muertos

Public rituals rooted in Indigenous Mesoamerican and Mexican Catholic beliefs in communing with the dead have proliferated in the last three decades not only in Los Angeles but in Chicana/o communities throughout the United States. In the United States, the very public ritual Días de los Muertos carries forward the essential elements of the tradition such as the making of elaborate ofrendas, but in addition, as Sybil Venegas points out, "It has become an annual visual arts and performance celebration, combining popular culture, fine art and its own unique iconography. Contemporary, urban, spiritual, bicultural, often political, resting upon an indigenous base while promoting a Chicano aesthetic, with a smattering of North American mass culture, El Día de los Muertos is like no other event in contemporary North American culture."[20] These annual communal celebrations create continuity with ancestral spiritual practices and beliefs. As Mesoamerican populations cyclically asked the hearts of their dead ones to return from the sacred mountains so that new life and new harvest might continue, so, too, Chicanas/os are replenished with new life and new hope when they invite their dead to return.[21] The reinvention of traditional ways to express contemporary concerns renews and (re)centers a people hungry for spiritual nourishment in their continuing struggle for justice. Continuity with ancestral ways, whether conscious or not, heals the wounds incurred by the historical memory of European and Euro-American colonization and challenges ongoing attempts to silence Indigenous and mestizo peoples.

For a historically subordinated population, publicly honoring their ancestors takes on political meaning. The genealogy being honored is Indigenous and of mixed blood. Claiming public space to honor these "others" is "an ultimate act of resistance against cultural domination."[22] And the parading en masse of "others" rejects daily efforts to dismiss their very presence in an increasingly segregated society. Furthermore, publicly communing with the dead contests mainstream fears embedded in Western cultural practices. As a ritual that honors and interacts with the dead in a familial and joyful manner, the tradition challenges a society that silences the dead shortly after a funeral. Western cultures enclose death in gated cemeteries devoid of color and merrymaking. As Father Greg Baumann points out, "In Anglo culture an altar for the dead seems bizarre, because we divorce ourselves from the fact that we die . . . we try to put it off in the corner and only face it when we have to. The Latino culture is not afraid of death . . . when you age you don't have to be ashamed."[23] Días de los Muertos does not replicate patterns of exclusion. With its color, humor, and friendly spirit, the rite invites all people to approach death and the "other" without fear. The silence of death and the pain of exclusion are challenged in the festivity of this public mourning ritual.

Recreating the tradition of Días de los Muertos in new ways expresses a Chicana/o spirituality valuing Indigenous ancestral wisdom, including the interconnectedness of life, death, and all forms of natural beings, balanced dualities, and the sacred in nature. According to one participant, "It represents the duality of life; life and death go hand in hand, side by side." Another said, "Días de los Muertos has become a significant spiritual celebration for Chicanos. Without that sense of who we are, and who our ancestors are, we become a lost culture. Many segments of our society are lost because they don't know their ancestry and they don't understand death." As cultural theorist Laura Pérez puts it, a worldview that diffuses the boundaries between the natural and the supernatural, between the living and the dead, "is a view ultimately at odds with the reigning capitalist culture of extreme exploitation of the planet and human beings, hierarchically ordered according to degrees of difference with respect to the dominant."[24] Chicana/o spirituality expressed through Días de los Muertos supplants Western thought that denies the sacred in nature and creates false dichotomies between complementary opposites, between the living and the dead.

Although the majority of Chicanas/os have been Christianized, there is a concerted effort by many to reinstate and identify with Indigenous ancestral knowledge. Estrangement from Roman Catholicism is due in large part to a historical attempt to assimilate Mexican Americans and Chicanos into a "universal" Euro-American Catholicism, compounded by the absence of native-born Mexican American clergy and by the limitations placed on the authority of women in the ecclesiastical structure. Many Chicanos who have left "the institutional Church," however, continue to identify with symbols that represent the faith, courage, and survival of their Catholic parents and grandparents. Días de los Muertos reflects these allegiances as participants consciously construct a symbol system that contains significant elements of Indigenous spirituality along-side the elements found meaningful in Mexican Catholicism. Icons of saints, madonnas, Guadalupe, and the sacred hearts of Jesus and Mary, among many others, continue to claim a strong presence in visual expressions of Chicana/o consciousness and spirituality. Catholic icons share physical space with Indigenous elements such as earth, water, fire, herbs, symbols of duality, and images of non-Christian deities such as Coatlicue, the Nahua Mother Earth goddess.

This coexistence of Catholic and Mesoamerican symbols reflects an aspect of nepantla spirituality, a spirituality where diverse biological and cultural elements converge, at times in great tension and at other times in cohesion. Nepantla is not syncretism in the traditional sense, but an example of "transculturation," or a continuous encounter of two or more divergent worldviews.[25] The Nahuatl term *nepantla*, meaning "in the middle," was recorded by Friar Bernardino de Sahagún in the sixteenth century. A Dominican friar, Diego Durán, had reprimanded an Indigenous elder for his behavior, which appeared discordant with Christian and Nahua customs and morals. The elder responded, "Father, don't be afraid, for we are still nepantla . . . or, as he later added, 'we are neutral.'"[26] The elder's indecisiveness, or the "trauma of nepantlism," resulted from forced cultural change, producing a psychological and spiritual condition filled with ambiguity, confusion, and conflict. The Indigenous or non-Western self is forced to deny its essential being and become like the conqueror.

The state of nepantla, however, can become a site of transformative struggle and creativity, a state of inherent being and meaning-making.[27] Once the tensions of nepantla are understood and confronted, and the Indigenous self is reclaimed and continuously healed, nepantla becomes a psychological, spiritual, and political space that Chicanas/os and other Latinos/as can appropriate or recast as a site of power.[28] Rather than being limited by confusion or ambiguity, Chicanas/os act as subjects or agents in deciding how diverse religious, cultural, and political systems can or cannot work together. They creatively maneuver the fissures, boundaries, and borders and consciously make choices about what aspects of diverse worldviews nurture the complexity of their spiritual and biological mestizaje, and what for them enables communication with transcendent powers. To those who have seen it expand over the past three decades, Days of the Dead appears as a central expression of nepantla spirituality.

Art expressing a nepantla spirituality reflects the intersection of politics and spirituality for a people committed to justice and self-determination; it is art that expresses joy, pain, and a people's resolve to survive and prosper, not as individuals but as a collective. Since the renaissance of the politically based Chicano art movement, visual and performance art, literature, and music have become key vehicles for reclaiming Chicana/o history, reconstructing an identity, and proclaiming ultimate values. Continuity exists between Chicana/o art and the *flor y canto* (flower and song) tradition among the Nahuas. Poetry, flower, and song were the primary means of communicating with divine forces. This continuity helps explain the importance of art to Chicana/o celebrations of Días de los Muertos.

Art Honoring the Dead

Art as an offering to the dead drives the Chicana/o ritual practice of Días de los Muertos. Whether it be colorful calavera figures, intricately cut paper tissue sheets, elaborate ofrendas, music, or poetry, all with a Chicana/o aesthetic, the art cannot be underestimated in its power to commune between the spiritual and physical realms. The art renews and enlarges the collective historical memory and identity of the group.

Primarily through the work of Chicana/o artists and cultural workers, Días de los Muertos has become one of the most important "politically motivated celebration[s] of Chicano spirituality and cultural heritage." Artists and cultural workers formed an integral part of the Chicano/a movement, a national struggle for civil rights beginning in the 1960s. The movement reclaimed a collective historical memory and shaped a Chicano and Chicana identity around ethnic pride and a "politics of protest" against social injustices. Artists assisted profoundly in this process. Chicana and Chicano artists developed "a new iconography and symbolic language which not only articulated the movement, but became the core of a Chicano cultural renaissance."[29] Reinterpreting and reinventing symbols and metaphors shaped a consciousness of self-determination and resistance to oppression.

A sensibility for folk and everyday practices guided artistic productions that quickly evolved into a distinct style. *Rasquachismo,* the art of combining and transforming everyday and even discarded materials into an elaborate display, characterizes the ability of Chicanas/os to survive and ingeniously create the most out of the least. For Chicana artists a distinctive, domestically oriented *rasquache* style articulates a resistance to prescribed gender roles.[30] Playing with traditional domestic imagery and using symbolic metaphors unveils the silenced issues in women's lives. Chicana/o art not only critiques systems of oppression; it also expresses a spirituality that values change as well as continuity with ancestral wisdom. In Days of the Dead art, rasquachismo is skillfully employed as performance, poetry, song, ofrendas, and the spirited calavera join forces in this festive public mourning ritual.

Ofrendas hold a central role in artistic expressions for the dead. As sacred environments where the visible and invisible forces meet, altars diffuse the boundaries between the living and the dead, between the human and the divine.[31] Consisting of "objects imbued with meaning," altars sustain a reciprocal relationship between the living and the dead.[32] Offerings of food and drink nourish the dead, and in return the dead renew the living. Through photographs, iconography, natural elements, candles, and flowers, altars tell the story of the loved ones remembered in the context of an ancestral lineage. They make public a historical memory, lest we forget a collective past. Altars recover and teach histories absent in mainstream public discourse. These sacred spaces reflect a politicized spirituality unwilling to let a people's history be silenced.

The icon of the skeleton also holds a prominent place in Chicano/a expressions of the tradition. Representing one's own mortality as well as personifying the dead, the calavera creates an unavoidable intimacy with death, an intimacy that is lovable and approachable, yet also grotesque. The grotesque places in front of us physical frailty, the nonglamorous erosion of the body, a reality that the dominant youth-oriented society tries hard to ignore. The outspoken calavera boldly says, This is life; why fear your dead and your own death?

As the center of attention during Days of the Dead, the calavera turns the normal order of things upside down. Calaveras become the central actors as they go about comically depicting the mundane chores and interests of the living. By representing distinct social classes, calaveras "manage to carve out space and time in which the status quo can be examined and questioned, ridiculed, and put into perspective as an arbitrary human construct that serves the interest of only a few."[33] Calaveras perform the toil of a laborer, the chores of a mother, or the leisure activities of the wealthy. Their humor reflects a working-class ability to maintain a sense of dignity amid the burdens they endure. Calaveras challenge the living to ponder the ultimate meaning of our activities.[34]

Reflections

Us Mexicans,
We love our dead,
Love 'em like we do chile,
Like we do guitar wailing

Corridos on drunken nights,
Like we do loud abuelas
Smoking on blue porches . . .

This excerpt from a poem titled "Miquitztli" (Death), by Chicana poet Olga García, captures the love and dedication that many Mexicans and Chicanas/os feel toward their dead. As she reads her poem on the stage at Self Help Graphics it is impossible to ignore the passion and joy in her words, in the colorful personifications of death in the audience, and in the numerous ofrendas sanctifying the dead.

Días de los Muertos provides Chicanos/Latinos opportunities for renewing and enlarging a group identity. The collective memory of past, present, and future generations expands with each annual ritual celebration. Days of the Dead in the United States is a spiritual practice responding to a complex historical process of colonization, displacement from land, language, and religion, class stratification, and efforts to assimilate a distinct ethnic population. Rooted in the ancient traditions of the native peoples of Anahuac, today's central and southern Mexico, Days of the Dead in the United States allows for the transmission of cultural, political, and religious values and continuing adaptation to contemporary needs and concerns.

Days of the Dead provides a site where Catholic and non-Catholic Chicanos and Mexicanos can incorporate a spirituality linking Indigenous, Mexican Catholic, and familial expressions with or without the blessing or support of the church. Some celebrants may build an ofrenda at home and/or go to the family cemetery with gifts of food and drink for their loved ones, then attend a Catholic Mass on Todos los Santos. Many others attend large public ritual celebrations held at cultural centers. Most churches in Los Angeles do not celebrate Días de los Muertos with culturally specific practices, but merely conduct the All Souls Day (November 2) liturgy. A handful of predominantly Mexican and Latino parishes throughout the archdiocese are increasingly incorporating Días de los Muertos traditions into their liturgical calendar. One example is the parish community at La Placita, where following a Mass, clergy lead a night procession through Olvera Street and stop to bless the altars constructed in businesses and restaurants. Other parishes, such as Our Lady of Guadalupe Church, in East Los Angeles, construct ofrendas in their worship space.

Tensions do exist between the archdiocese and individuals celebrating their dead at Catholic cemeteries. Although decorations may be left at gravesites during Christmas and Easter, no items other than flowers may be left during Días de los Muertos. In the San Fernando Valley cemetery maintenance workers posted notices outlining the archdiocese's restrictions.[35] According to Tomás Benítez, director of Self Help Graphics, in recent years local cemeteries have not allowed Self Help Graphics to start the procession from inside the cemetery grounds. The Latino transformation of southern California presents new and critical opportunities to reflect and incorporate Mexican and other Latino culture and traditions or to exacerbate ethnic tensions within the church. Pastoral efforts to understand and incorporate the tradition into the liturgical life of the church assist the goal of ministering meaningfully to a growing Latino population.

For many Chicanas/os, popular religion and art are the primary avenues by which they nourish their spiritual lives. Popular Catholicism, as Orlando Espín writes elsewhere in this volume, reflects a way of knowing and constructing the "real" that is culturally specific. Popular religion is not merely a reaction to the institutional church, but the creation of a tradition by the believers and participants. For Roberto Goizueta, Días de los Muertos is an example of the liberationist notion of a new way of doing theology.

Karen Mary Davalos describes elsewhere in this book how secular space can be made "religious" through public displays of religious ritual. During the processions for the dead Chicanos/Mexicanos both reclaim their right to public space and invoke it as religious space, as César Chávez and the United Farm Workers did in countless marches and processions. The public march claims the streets for the marchers, their ancestors, and future generations. Likewise, the gallery space, general hall, and parking lot at Self Help Graphics exhibit sacred meaning during public religious ritual.

In the Catholic Church, from whose institutional structure Chicano/ Latino leadership has historically been absent, lay-led activities, rituals, and ceremonies provide for popular participation. As the numbers of priests and sisters decline drastically, lay-led rituals serve as models for the church. As in other popular religious activities, women play a significant role in both church and secular celebrations as key organizers. In preparation for both events, women conduct workshops on making altars, murals, calaveras, and papel picado. On the day of the SHG event, they participate fully in all activities. At Dolores Mission, the altar built by women becomes the symbolic center of the community.

The collaboration in 1998 marked the first time a Catholic parish worked with cultural institutions in southern California around a public ritual celebration for the dead. Several hundred people participated over eight weeks of preparation at the art workshops, and six hundred parishioners attended the Todos los Santos services at Dolores Mission. At least four hundred walked in the procession, and several thousand participated in the celebration at Self Help Graphics.

Because of lack of transportation and an unwillingness to leave their "territory," most of the youth at Dolores Mission involved in the workshops did not attend the celebration at Self Help Graphics. They did, however, attend the art workshops and church services and interacted with the ofrenda in the church. Classes from the parish school held a ceremony of memory at the altar. Sister Pat of the parish school invited her students to write brief notes to a deceased member of their family and leave them on the ofrenda. According to Father Ted, the youth of Dolores Mission used to view the celebration as "un-American," as a ritual that only their grandparents and parents from Mexico celebrated. The collaboration with the wider community of artists and cultural workers communicated to them that Days of the Dead is a living tradition claiming a place in North American life.

Few of the participants at the Self Help Graphics celebration attended the two Masses held at Dolores Mission or other churches. A significant social distance persists between Chicanas/os and the Catholic Church. However, many stated that they had an altar at home. One participant said, "It may sound like a contradiction, but for me it is a matter of spirituality as opposed to a religious organization." Another commented, "I gave up on the Catholic Church, but I have an altar in my apartment. Today, I am remembering my mother and brothers. Death is a part of the cycle of life."

Although there was little interaction between the "churched" and "unchurched" on the day of the communal ritual celebrations, the collaborative project between a parish community and secular cultural institutions proved beneficial in many ways. Religious and cultural workers joined in devoting their time to drawing out the wisdom and artistic skills of a struggling community. Adults and youth participated in the making of the ritual, activities that reinforce self-determination and community solidarity. In this context, cultural knowledge becomes sacred knowledge as people engage in the process of identifying what for them holds ultimate value. For Chicanas/os estranged from Catholicism, collaboration with church representatives provided a sense of relief that their traditions were finally being respected. Said one participant, "I remember being chastised for going to Mass and wearing a T-shirt that had a calavera face on it. The priest told me it was a demonic tradition . . . maybe they are finally listening to us." In the process of preparing for the celebration, the cultural and religious participants created a collaborative sacred space at the community and church level, one usually lost in traditional Catholic-Chicana/o relationships. The ritual allowed Catholic and non-Catholic,

Indigenous and non-Indigenous, religious and nonreligious, Chicana/o and non-Chicana/o to participate in a public ritual for the dead. This case study provides merely one example of how Días de los Muertos is institutionalizing its place in the city. Throughout southern California, thousands more reinvented the tradition at colleges and universities, high schools, art galleries, museums, businesses, community centers, and churches.

As Días de los Muertos in Los Angeles shows, the ritual allows for the articulation of popular religion, social criticism, and nepantla spirituality. It is a celebration that strengthens a collective historical memory as ancestors and cultural heroes/heroines are remembered and sanctified. In a society that ignores Chicanas/os as historical actors, the mere act of remembering one's ancestors carries subversive elements. In the process, a community renews itself as it gathers publicly to honor the interconnectedness of life and death. As Chicanas/os revisit and consciously select an Indigenous heritage that supposedly was obliterated by colonialism, they make a political decision as well as a spiritual one. As legislation opposing Latino immigration, affirmative action, and bilingual education shows, it is not advantageous to be Indigenous, Chicano/a, or Mexican in the United States. Yet underlying the political significance lies a rich faith "respecting those who have gone before and celebrating our ability to communicate with them."[36] The poem "Miquitztli" concludes:

> We love our dead
> like fire
> like memory
> like the bouncing reflection of all of us here,
> now,
> *con caras pintadas* [with painted faces],
> *bocas sonriendo* [smiling mouths],
> dancing in front of this smoking mirror,
> waiting for it
> to break.[37]

Luis D. León

"Soy una Curandera y Soy una Católica"

The Poetics of a Mexican Healing Tradition

From specialized healers to more ordinary women . . . who labor privately in their homes, it is such *curanderas* who daily and relatively uncharismatically engage with late capitalism's baleful effects on the mexicano body politic as they continue a struggle with the devil.

DOLORES MULTIPLICADAS has had a hard life.[1] She looks much older than her twenty-four years. "Nothing goes right for me," she gently complains one bright and smoggy fall afternoon at the Sagrado Corazón (Sacred Heart) botanica in East Los Angeles. "I came here to see the señora because I heard she was good." Her story is typical of the many patrons who visit this storefront healing center to see the curandera Hortencia. They come with great expectations, seeking hope, succor, and power. Punctuated by a pair of gunshots, and unfolding to the rhythms of Cesar Chavez Avenue—families laughing, tacos frying, babies crying, stereos blaring, and Cristina pontificating from her electronic pulpit—Dolores's painful story, combining tragedy, comedy, and struggle, finds mystical affirmation in the charismatic presence of Hortencia the healer, Hortencia the clairvoyant, Hortencia the psychic, Hortencia the prophet, and, above all else, Hortencia, by her own profession, the practicing Catholic.

The following study is situated in that paradoxical space—the border that connects yet divides Catholicism and indigenous Mexican ritual, a space between submission and resistance, between hope and despair, between life and death, at the intersections of colonialism, modernity, capitalism, primitivism, the nation, and the self—where desire meets dread, where will meets surrender, where La Virgen de Guadalupe meets the Mesoamerican mother goddess Tonantzin, where Guadalupe and To-

Exterior of Sagrado Corazón. Used by permission of the author.

nantzin meet Malinche, and where all coalesce and become *La Llorona*.[2] The Mexican-derived healing tradition known as curanderismo illuminates the conditions of possibility for poor Chicanas/os and Mexicans to heal themselves and their loved ones, to negotiate the suffering and injustice that is for many the quotidian stuff of life. It provides some answers about the alternatives available to Mexicans and other Latinos attempting to overcome the limitations of the material world, to mend the injuries inflicted upon them by the harsh realities of intense late capitalism. It helps Latina and Latino postmoderns bring order to chaos, and wholeness to broken bodies and souls.

It has long been axiomatic in the study of religion that people make sense of the anomie that is the phenomenal world through myth and ritual, and that myths and rituals are culturally inflected. The practice of curanderismo offers guidance on a long, less-traveled path to uncover the salient idioms and symbols of Mexican American religious experience, charting the ways in which tradition and discourse have been imagined and reimagined, and the material conditions under which such imaginations were rendered possible.

This documentary study maps one site of curanderismo and proposes directions for further investigation. It makes no pretense toward definitive research statements, but offers instead an accurate account of my own limited perceptions. Over the course of twelve months, and with the help of Lara Medina, I have studied one center of faith and healing in East Los Angeles: the Sagrado Corazón botanica. I brought my many years of research on curanderismo to this study. However, during this year-long period I focused on one site; I spoke with and interviewed dozens of the women and men who came to the botanica seeking healing. I listened to their stories, recorded many of them, and in what follows I recount the prominent themes that emerged from these conversations.

The majority of patrons at Sagrado Corazón were reluctant to explain exactly what it was they sought, and they were, understandably, unwilling to submit to longer more personal interviews. I respected people's wishes for privacy, and did not push anyone beyond a first refusal. A study as limited as this can do little more than provide another starting point for future research. Thus, in what follows I provide background material and preliminary assessments based on participant observation, and grounded in on-site conversations or interviews. But the wealth of this study comes from the genius of Hortencia herself. She is thirty-eight years old. Born in Mexico, she has lived in the United States for eight years. She has four children, the youngest born in September of 1999.

Storefront Religion

Certainly public understanding of curanderismo would benefit from sustained case studies that are afforded the opportunity to probe more deeply into the lives of willing patrons.[3] The proliferation of public sites like Sagrado Corazón in Chicano barrios within the last ten to fifteen years opens up opportunities for curandera research heretofore unavailable when curanderismo was mostly restricted to private homes and extended kinship networks.

Lara Medina brought Sagrado Corazón botanica to my attention one afternoon while driving down Cesar Chavez Avenue. Earlier I had visited another more traditional curandera who denied me admission to her healing center, which doubled as her private residence. But all are welcome at Sagrado Corazón. People of many faiths visit this storefront religious center. Hortencia does not ask questions of her clients, except what

Hortencia at her work desk. Used by permission of the author.

they seek. Though the definitive signs identifying the space point to Catholicism, there is no dogmatic text against which believers measure the (in)accuracy of their lives. This public space is encoded by multiple and multivocal religious symbols drawn from Mexican Catholicism, Aztec and Native North American traditions, literally creating a hybrid religious text for which the exact meaning is left to the interpretive faculties of the viewer.

When Lara and I first entered the center, Hortencia was at the counter tending to some paperwork. I introduced myself and Lara and explained why we were there; I identified myself as a college professor who teaches religion, especially religion in Latino communities. Later, in my first private session with her, I elaborated on my project, explaining that my desire was for her to narrate to me, to describe and locate her practice in her own words. She committed her cooperation without much coaxing. I occupied significant periods of her time over the course of one year; we collaborated with each other closely on at least a half-dozen sessions. Most often, I would come in on a day she was seeing other clients; she would tend to me in turn. She read my cards and talked to me as if she were teaching me. She never charged me. At our second meeting I offered to pay her for the time I was taking in one lump sum: three hundred dollars. This was the only time I managed to offend her. She was obviously hurt, but did not react spitefully. She just asked, rhetorically, how she could accept money from me when I was doing a good work. On a number of occasions, while I was sitting in wait for her, Hortencia would enter the waiting room and instruct the clients to talk openly with me, that it was fine to be honest.

At our first meeting, after I introduced myself, Hortencia did not immediately release my hand. Instead, she held it tightly and looked deep into my eyes. "You're a very passionate person," she said to me in Spanish (she never once spoke a word of English to me). "And because of that," she continued, "you have suffered a lot in love." Lucky guess, I thought, and remained a bit skeptical about this place with a cash register and standard fees for services. Nonetheless, I became a believer in this woman: in her charm, her charisma, and most of all her sincerity. I believe that she believes in the integrity of what she is doing, and that she helps people.

Even while I maintained a hermeneutic of suspicion about the place from the beginning, the devotees who called upon Hortencia immediately seemed oddly familiar to me—not for my years of bibliographic research and fieldwork on curanderismo, but because their motivations for being there and their passionate search to encounter and touch the sacred reminded me of the souls who were members of my father's church in East Oakland, La Iglesia de Dios Pentecostal. Like my father's parishioners, and like those attending Catholic Masses in Mexican and other Latino communities, the vast majority of patrons at Sagrado Corazón are women. Women relate to Hortencia not only as an ambassador of the sacred, but as another woman whose experiences of the world are mediated by those things universal to women's embodied experience—especially women who occupy bronze bodies racialized in peculiar ways by North American society.

At this storefront religious center, Hortencia is spiritual guide, muse, mystic, even shamaness, and the clients her followers. In Hortencia's ritual practice, her story, and her religious philosophy—a synthesis of Catholicism and, in her own words, "conscience"—the poetics of religious healing are elaborated and manifested.[4] But it is in that uncanny public space itself, Sagrado Corazón, where the narrative of suffering and the drama of healing forcefully unfold and take place. Thus, after a background on curanderismo, this essay thickly describes the religious ecology of place before weaving the stories together as so many fibers in an organically produced tapestry and local manifestation of the Divine. The narrative turns next to the voice of Hortencia, allowing her perspective to guide the analysis to conclusion.

This narrative, then, is not so much a modernist ethnography that purports to reveal some positive facts based on an experimental design, quantitative data, and a set number of interviews. Instead, I approach this project with a desire to know more about this remarkably persistent phenomenon by conversing with devotees at various levels and by creating, reading, and interpreting religio-cultural texts in social and historical contexts for what they disclose about curanderismo and, of course, the issues that attend and are produced but it. That is, in synthesizing the narratives of the devotees I inscribe a context of religious healing, and in my transcription of key parts of my discussions with Hortencia, I create a text of healing. In the conclusion, I interpret the text and context with the goal of advancing an understanding—a perspective—on religion, North American religions, and especially on Mexican American religious situations and culture.

Deciphering Curanderismo

Curanderismo comes from the Spanish verb *curar,* to heal or to cure. It signifies everything from herbal home remedies to elaborate spiritual, psychic, or symbolic medical operations conducted to unblock clogged arteries and heal diseases such as cancer and AIDS. At its most general, curanderismo is a synthesis of pre-Tridentine Catholicism, Spanish-Moorish medicine, and ancient Mesoamerican medicine and religion.[5] It is a religious and medical nexus articulated in colonialism.

Some hospitals in Latino communities are now conjoining curanderismo practices with conventional medicine.[6] Harmony is possible between religious and conventional healing because of curanderismo's etiology and general philosophy. Though they are faith healers, curanderas believe themselves knowledgeable about human anatomy and physiology and recognize the purely biological maladies that afflict the body. Therefore, curanderas value conventional medicine and routinely refer patients to medical doctors. Yet curanderas are also aware of the high cost of medical care and the financial difficulties visiting a doctor poses to many ethnic Mexicans. Moreover, visiting any U.S. institution, like a hospital, can be a source of great anxiety for undocumented workers in the United States. But mostly curanderas thrive because of their belief that some illnesses affecting the body have supernatural origins, against which medical doctors are powerless. In addition, curanderas provide services such as tarot card readings and spiritual cleansings—*limpias*—that cannot be rendered elsewhere in Mexican American communities.

The traditional foundation of curanderismo is the *don,* or gift. Each healer believes that his or her curing power is a gift that comes directly from God; in some cases this gift is brokered through a helper spirit, which acts in effect as the familiar of the healer. If a person is endowed with the gift of healing, she or he will ultimately need to employ that gift in the service of others or suffer general dissatisfaction in life, lack of fulfillment, and in some cases more severe penalties. This sets up an elaborate system of obligation, gift, and exchange: because the healer has received a gift from God, she or he must in turn give healing to those who seek it, and in return the persons seeking healing must gift the healer and others.

Derived from ancient Nahua cultures, the Mexican healing tradition views the body as composed of both hot and cold properties, and wellness as dependent on maintaining these dichotomous energies in equilibrium. The concept of duality was one of the key organizing factors in Aztec culture. In Aztec thought, the cosmos was divided into various levels of heavens and earth, delineated by complementary dualities: mother and father (corresponding to earth and heavens), female and male, cold and hot, down and up, underworld and heavens, wet and dry, dark and light, night and day, water and fire, and life and death. Many Aztec deities reflected this division, and the highest Aztec god, Ometeotl, was thought to have both feminine and masculine properties. For the Nahuas, the preservation of cosmic order was the highest charge of humanity. Since the body was seen as a microcosm of the cosmos, it too was understood to be divided into complementary dualities.

Just as cosmic disorder was thought to originate in disruptive forces, illness in the body was believed to derive from external stimuli disrupting the body's equilibrium. Healing procedures sought to restore balance not only to the body but to the soul. Today curandera healing techniques are designed to restore balance to the body and soul. The focus on the soul derives from both the Aztecs and Spanish Christians and is a premise sympathetic to *espiritualistas* (Mexican spiritualists) and evangelicals.

The major ailments thought to be responsive to curanderismo are *mal de ojo,* also called *mal ojo* or *ojo* (the evil eye); *bilis* (excessive bile); *muina* (anger sickness); *latido* (palpitation or throb); *envidia, mal puesto, salar,* or *maleficio* (a physical disorder caused by envy); *caida de mollera* (fallen fontanel); *empacho* (indigestion); *mal aire* (upper respiratory illness and colds); *susto* (loss of spirit); *desasombro* (a more severe form of spirit loss); and *espanto* (the most serious form of spirit loss).

Susto is the best-studied malady addressed through curanderismo.

Dating back to pre-Columbian Mesoamerica, susto is ubiquitous through-out the Latino Americas (including North America). From the earliest Nahuatl rendition, *tonalcahualiztli,* or loss of soul, susto was associated with the loss of *tonalli,* the "spiritual force sent by the Aztec god Ometeotl, the sun, and fire into the human body, giving it character, intelligence, and will. Tonalli was concentrated in the head."[7] The Aztecs believed in three vital life forces corresponding to a triad human soul residing in the head, the heart, and the liver. In this way, a human life could remain animated even after the tonalli escaped from one's head.

Generally, susto is considered to be caused by a severe fright, shock, or encounter with a benign natural spiritual entity. Any experience, rela-tionship, or circumstance that causes distress and fear can result in susto. Spirit loss may have a long incubation period, sometimes as long as sev-eral years. Bernardo Ortiz de Motellano has compiled the following symptoms: "restlessness in sleep, listlessness, loss of appetite, weight loss, loss of energy and strength, depression, introversion, paleness, lethargy, and sometimes fever, diarrhea, and vomiting."[8]

Thus, susto is also diagnosed as a loss of vital forces that keep the body in balance. Sudden heat or cold can cause disturbance, as can powerful emotional forces that overwhelm the body and drive away the soul. Di-agnosis of susto typically involves checking the patient's pulse. A patient who has all vital forces in balance will demonstrate a normal pulse, whereas an excess of heat will cause the blood to pulsate more rapidly, and the loss of heat, or of tonalli, will slow the pulse rate.

Susto is cured by administering a limpia while calling the soul back to the body. Limpia, or cleansing, is perhaps the most widely practices cu-randera healing technique. It consists in sweeping the body with a sym-bolic object, usually held in the left hand of the healer. A limpia is thought to absorb negative energy from the body, driving evil forces into the rit-ual object used for the sweeping. The most commonly used ritual tool is an egg, a lemon, or a bunch of herbs bound together with a string. Some healers conduct limpias by systematically passing a large crucifix over the body of the supplicant while praying or reciting a Catholic narrative. Cus-tomarily, the object used to perform the cleansing is ceremoniously de-stroyed; most often it is burned.[9]

Healing and Place: Sagrado Corazón

Sagrado Corazón is a small stucco niche in an urban row of continuous structures covered with faded light-blue paint; it is flanked by a barber shop and a restaurant. It is located in Boyle Heights, an older area than

Interior of Sagrado Corazón botanica. Used by permission of the author.

most others of East Los Angeles, and densely populated by mostly Mexican immigrants and Mexican American families.[10] The façade of the building is dominated by a display window and a glass door. In the window is a wide array of products for sale: images of Catholic saints, sprays, powders, herbs, potions, spices, special soaps for baths, candles, incense, and *aguas,* or various types of prepared waters. A large hand-painted sign directly outside the entrance reads "love, health, money." The sign further indicates that inside one can obtain card readings and spiritual consultations, as well as fast, effective weight loss without diet or exercise. This is a place where dreams can be made to come true.

Upon entering the space one is bombarded by a cacophony of images, creating dissonance and disorientation. Perhaps the dominant sight and sound is a small color television located atop a tall bookshelf to the left of the entrance. From there Spanish-language programming blares incessantly. In the left rear of the square floor plan there is a glass counter and display case behind which the clerk sits and watches. She does not typically greet visitors, in fact she studiously avoids meeting their eyes with hers. At times the clerk is Hortencia's teenage daughter. On the counter there are several upright images of La Virgen de Guadalupe with burning votive candles. On the wall behind the counter hang images of Guadalupe, the saints, and a Sacred Heart. To the right are five white plastic lawn chairs where people wait, often for several hours, to see Hortencia.

Hortencia arrives in the morning before ten and typically stays until six or seven in the evening. The shop is closed on Sundays. On Tuesdays and Fridays she accepts walk-in clients on a first-come first-served basis; these days, she explains, possess the most powerful energies. She asks her clients no questions except what they seek. Clients come to the front counter, and the clerk puts their name on a list and tells them the approximate waiting time. On these days Hortencia seldom comes into the shop space. A window in one of her two work rooms in the back affords her a view into the front room. Hortencia's private chambers are partitioned off from the main space by dry wall. There are two discrete rooms in the rear of the space that function as Hortencia's work rooms. In one she has a desk, chairs, and a large table serving as an altar on which stand a Virgin of Guadalupe, a Sacred Heart of Jesus, and candles and incense. Prepared waters line the walls. The second room holds a padded massage table covered with clean white sheets, where Hortencia performs her work as a *sabadora*, or massage therapist.

The high bookshelves lining the walls of the front room are packed with sundry merchandise, reflecting the diverse interests and faiths of patrons. In one corner are items that can be purchased in neighborhood markets: shampoo, soap, toothpaste, hair cream, deodorant, dishwashing and laundry detergent. On the other walls are racks of Mexican spices, fresh herbs, and teas of various kinds. Painted clay images of many official Catholic saints popular in Mexico and elsewhere in Latin America are represented and sold at the botanica. These include especially St. Francis, El Santo Niño de Atoche, San Martín de Porres, and Santa Barbara. In addition to saints there are replicas of the Buddha, Shango and Eluguia (two of the main spiritual entities in *Santería*), numerous Hindu deities, and various Latin American manifestations of the Virgin Mary, including Los Lagos, Cobra, Caridad, Zapopan, and especially Guadalupe. Perhaps the most striking and prominent saints are those not officially recognized by the Catholic church, including San Simón, El Niño Fidencio, Juan Soldado, and Don Pedrito Jaramillo. These saints share space and authority with the official Catholic saints without distinction.

Most of the shelves hold a variety of sprays and candles that are labeled according to their functions. Available only in aerosol cans is the *tres machos*. This spray is meant to invoke three strong male spirits and is used also in Santería. Mexican espiritualistas often spray tres machos before a ceremony. An espiritualista priestess once commented to me that she enjoys the light floral scent of the spray. But other candles and sprays sold at the center offer more specialized services. Available only in cans is the Uña de Gato, or the Cat's Nail. When I asked what purpose the Uña de Gato spray serves, I was told that it was for general good luck and well-being. Striking to me also was a large color poster advertising the Uña de Gato spray. On it a handsome Latino man sporting a mustache, dark suit, and tie holds the can in his right hand and smiles. Around him float three images: Guadalupe, an Aztec deity, and an image of Jesus Christ.

The candles are the dominant items on the shelves of the vestibule; there are candles for just about every conceivable type of problem. Candles are encased in colorful glass, and are painted with images and text. One candle reads (in Spanish): "Do as I say, now." This candle is adorned by two images, on one side a man submits to a woman, the other side depicts a woman submitting to a man. There are candles representing each sign of the zodiac, many of the saints and manifestations of the Virgin Mary, Jesus, popular saints, and various wishes, including "Instant money," "Shut your mouth," "Go away," "Protect me from evil," "Work," "Love," "Romance," "Seduction," "Instant luck," "Big money," "Lottery," "Health," and "Power." Here, a person can purchase hope, control, and power.

Hortencia prescribes these items to her clients, but she does not earn a commission on their sale. She receives a flat salary from the shop owners. Sagrado Corazón is owned by a group of investors who also own several of the other botanicas around Los Angeles and employ various curanderos and curanderas. Hortencia was reluctant to speak of the owners. There is no question, however, that Hortencia is the curator of Sagrado Corazón.

(Re)Making Myth, (Re)Making Body and Soul

The center appeals to the interests of many different visitors: some casual clients come only to purchase herbs and spices, while others come to purchase a new lease on life. On days other than Tuesday and Friday Hortencia sees clients by appointment and tends to the mundane business of the shop—ordering merchandise, balancing bank accounts, and other organizational activities. She prefers to see people during her walk-in hours.

On Tuesdays and Fridays the center is filled with a dozen or so people at a time waiting to see Hortencia. On a particularly busy day she sees upward of thirty clients. People are charged according to the service. A basic consultation is ten dollars, but Hortencia regularly adjusts the cost upward or downward according to the services rendered and the patient's means. Typically the customers remain silent while waiting. They survey the walls of merchandise, stare at the television, tend their children, or read newspapers, occasionally looking up cautiously to examine people as they enter and exit. Privacy is respected.

Casual visitors come in out of curiosity and browse; others rush in, quickly select some herbs, and go directly to the register to pay. One such customer explained that she was buying special Mexican-grown plants that aid in sleeping, upset stomachs, colds, and general aches and pains.[11] She does not visit the shop for the services offered, but to buy the things she regularly had in Mexico. Speaking for the casual customers, she told of how difficult it was to find these herbs, *medicinas* or medicines, in other stores. "We come here to buy the things that we have grown accustomed to in Mexico."

The patrons at Sagrado Corazón are mostly women, and most have children in tow. Some men come alone or with other male companions. Seldom do women and men come in couples. One twenty-six-year-old man said that he lived alone in the United Sates, working and sending money to his family in Aguas Calientes, Mexico. He was a practicing Catholic who attended Mass weekly and took communion. Seeking the aid of a curandera generally violated the laws of the Catholic Church as he saw it, but, as he put it, "The Catholic Church does not understand everything, and they are not always correct about everything." His words summed up the position of many of the people I spoke with there. He would not tell me what he sought from Hortencia, but it wasn't a card reading he was after: "I'm here for some other business that I can't tell you."

Many of the men I spoke to at Sagrado Corazón sought help from Hortencia to ease the stresses of separation from their families who remained in Mexico. Numerous men came to Hortencia for extra assistance in finding work. For some, the problem was that, in spite of their best efforts, they had run out of money. Hortencia offered the seekers discernment that uncovered the root of the problem, and solutions to it. To cure the problem she offered them rituals aimed at improving their "auras," which she claimed would eventually lead to finding a job, earning more money, or making their money last longer.

Gerardo Feliz, a handsome *guerito* man of twenty-six from Jalisco, Mexico, described a problem of a different nature. He seemed quite nervous while waiting for Hortencia one Friday afternoon. After a brief introductory chat, he told me that he had been visiting Hortencia regularly for about six months; he was there for the fourth time. He sadly recounted the problems with his immediate family back home, *con mi casa,* and especially with his wife. "In these times a man can no longer count on a woman's fidelity," he confided. He was reluctant to say much more. Hortencia was helping him discern the situation and the proper course of action. He told me he trusted Hortencia and related to her as a son relates to his mother. He had only very cursory and infrequent communication with his mother and had not told her of the family troubles. He believed the problem stemmed at least partially from his absence of almost two years. During his first trip he had been away less than a year, but now he had found a lucrative job as assistant manager of a restaurant; the restaurant owners would not let him go home and return to his job.

The women who frequent the center come with similar problems centering on family separation, employment, love, money, and health. Unlike the men, however, they come not only for spiritual aid but also for physical treatments, seeking Hortencia's services as a sabadora, or massage therapist. None of the men I spoke with during my time there called upon Hortencia for massage therapy, though many came for a limpia.

One of the problems I heard repeatedly while there was a tale of labor exploitation. Many of the undocumented women who patronize Sagrado Corazón work in the United States at menial service jobs, such as house cleaners and seamstresses at sweatshops in downtown Los Angeles. These women told of the long hours they spent toiling for their employers. After a week or two they would ask for the money they had been promised, only to be told that they would have to wait longer and keep on working. So on it went until, finally, the women realized that they had been deceived, and that no money would be paid to them. "What could I do?" they would ask me rhetorically in resignation and despair. I suggested Catholic social services or a legal agency in the area. Without fail their response was the same: "But I have no papers, I could be deported." What did they seek, then, from Hortencia? "A consultation and healing." Sagrado Corazón for them was the first step on a fresh course of action; a new path; catharsis and rejuvenation; a renewed sense of dignity, self-worth, and power; a kind of symbolic and spiritual justice, but not vengeance. With ancient Mesoamerican rituals filtered through centuries of Catholic colonialism, innovation, and border crossings, this Hortencia could provide, though, somewhat ironically, it can only be rendered for a small fee. Sagrado Corazón is not, by any means, a multinational corporation nor is Hortencia an owner of the "means of production." And yet, her work and her business are bound up with the capitalist social system and modes of work, compensation, and exchange.

On several occasions I noticed mothers at Sagrado Corazón with their teenage gangbanger sons. What did they seek from Hortencia? One mother answered that her son was full of bad energies and needed to be cleansed so that he would be put back on the right path. Her son told me that he needed help so that he could stop "messing up." Why not seek the aid of the church, I asked. "The priest can't do much for him," another mother answered, "just tell him to pray and to stay in school." Was visiting Hortencia against the Catholic religion, I asked. "I don't know," answered one mother. "Maybe it is, but it seems to be the only thing that works."[12]

Leticia, or Letty, a Chicana who is twenty-two years old, told me that she had first come to Hortencia about a year before for "female problems." Hortencia prescribed a cure that worked. She was back now because she had had increasingly bad luck at her job. "I just quit my job at a restaurant," she explained. "My boss was verbally abusing me. He was calling me dumb and stuff. I couldn't stand it. Now I don't have a job, and my parents have to support me." What could Hortencia do for her? "I feel all dirty, like I've been violated. I'm here because I need a limpia."[13] I asked if she was a Catholic and went to Mass. She responded that she was Catholic, but that she seldom went to church because she found it boring. "I pray to the Virgin at home, you know, Guadalupe, and I come here once in a while."

With Lara Medina I interviewed a group of four Chicanas, including "Dolores Multiplicadas," mentioned at the beginning of this chapter. We spoke in English. Dolores, the eldest, did most of the talking. I asked first how she had learned of Hortencia. She said she had heard of her through friends, who had heard of her through other friends, "just word of mouth." I asked what she had heard. "That she reads cards, and that she is pretty accurate," she replied. She had started coming in just the last couple of weeks. I asked what it was she sought there. "Well, it seems that everything goes wrong for me, and in fact she [Hortencia] told me that, that everything goes wrong for me, you know, she said everything in my life goes wrong for me—and it's true. You know, in terms of jobs, relationships, just everything. She told me the truth before I even talked to her." Her friends had come along to have their cards read but did not want to talk about it. All said that they were Catholics and went to church about every other week.

Dolores is involved in a Catholic retreat center, and she was wearing a T-shirt with the center's name on it when we spoke. Lara asked how she combined the work of Hortencia with her Catholic life. She responded that the retreat center was for people who were Catholic but not very active, "you know, people who never really felt it. But it is good, really, really good. I was raised Catholic but never really felt it; I wasn't really going much, and I looked around for a while. I was ready to become Christian [she meant evangelical Christian], but then I got invited to this [Catholic retreat center] and I went; so I was able to accept Catholic back again. Now I understand it, my communion, my confirmation, I know what it's about. I even felt the Holy Spirit too. For me it felt like, it was weird, like I was bouncing off the walls. It was like a high feeling, I mean I don't get high but I guess that's what high feels like. It was really neat, I liked it [laughs]."

Lara then asked her how she combined her experience with Hortencia with her experience with the Holy Spirit. Dolores replied: "To tell you the truth, I feel guilty [laughs]." I asked if she thought the Catholic Church was against visiting a curandera. She replied that she believed it was. "Well, because you're messing with other things and not him [points upward]." Her friends looked at her disapprovingly, and she answered their stares with a firm, "Well, it's true." I asked her younger companions if they believed that Sagrado Corazón was Catholic, and if it was okay to go there. "No, it isn't Catholic," one replied. They all agreed. Another companion disagreed and said, "Well, she [Hortencia] believes in Catholicism." To this the other replied, "Well, I know she does but, well, when we have problems we should pray to him [God]."

I asked the younger woman about Guadalupe and whether she prayed to her. Her answer was that she "didn't know much about that. I don't know much about saints. I really don't. What about you?" she asked Dolores. Dolores said she didn't know about saints either, except for Guadalupe. What did she know, I asked. "Well, if you pray to her and everything she'll be there for you." I asked her what she wanted from Hortencia. "I was just curious," she replied, "I wanted to know what was ahead for me. I'm stuck, and I don't know where to go next." "Do you think Hortencia can help to unblock your path?" Lara asked. "We'll see. I don't know, but I hope so."

A Curandera Speaks

Hortencia told me that both Catholics and evangelicals visit her at the center. The only difference between them, she said, "is that when they get here the evangelicals are more secretive; they visit me with a bad conscience." Hortencia said this with a touch of contempt, because for her conscience is the key to ethical religious practice. I asked her what she believed the Catholic Church taught about her work at Sagrado Corazón. Without hesitation she responded:

> They believe it's bad. Because they themselves believe that no one can do anything but God. And you yourself know that this is against the Catholic religion from whatever aspect you view it. This is against it. But if you yourself are content [*tranquila*] that you are not harming anyone,

then it's good, and for that reason I go to Mass. I am satisfied [*tranquila*] with myself. I'm not going to honor God if I know that I am sinning against him—it's one or the other thing—either you are with God or you are against him. But I am content because I am trying to do good. I try to do only good. I have to maintain my good *conscience*.

Any priest will tell you [that curanderismo is wrong]. My priest back in my village in Mexico would tell me all the time, "Hortencia, you [*tu*]"—excuse my use of the informal, but that is how he would address me—"you need to change your ways, because if you continue lying to people you are going to die." He himself saw that I could help people. But I *never* myself said that it was I who was helping people. No one can help people without God. I'm not going to go around saying that I am the greatest curandera in the world. I do what I can do to help the people [*la gente*]. And, well, perhaps that is why God, he helps me, because he sees my desire to do the good.

There are people who sometimes come here and say, "I would like this to happen to such and such person." I'm not here for that. If you need to resolve a problem with someone, you know what, just go and have it out with him and that's it; your anger will pass. Why would you want to do harm to the people? That will only work against you yourself.

What I do here is try and help people. People come to me with all sorts of problems. Mostly, people have money problems, they don't have enough money for their families [*casa*]. So, for example, if someone comes to me and says they don't have enough money, I tell them to take a special herb, a one-dollar bill, a [special] small rock, and a red perejer [a Mexican herb]. Take a glass of water, and in that water you will put that rock, and that red perejer, and then the dollar. Do you know what a dollar means? Do you have a one-dollar bill, and I'll show you. No? [She moves to the window that opens into the vestibule and calls for Daisy, the receptionist, to bring her a one-dollar bill.] Do you know what religion the dollar bill comes from? Now we are really talking about religion. It comes from the Masons. And why do you think it was the Masons? Because they wanted to make this the strongest country of all. [She takes the dollar bill, pointing.] This pyramid signifies positive energy. The eye is the eye of the Holy Spirit that you see there. Are you Catholic? I'm Catholic, as I told you, and when you go to Mass you will see the same Holy Spirit symbolized. These are things I'm telling you so that you will learn how things work. Take water, for example. Water is a material [*materia*]. Water is made by God. *Man didn't make water.*

Everything has a mystery. Just like the recitation I was telling you. El perejer, I was telling you, that is a plant that comes from the earth [*la tierra*] that is made by God, not by man. Just like the rocks. The rocks are a materia because they are not made by man but are made from nature [*la naturaleza*]. Okay? When you have four of those rocks it signifies harmony for all. People who know a lot about rocks will tell you that the four roses [*cuatro rosados*] are to create harmony, to bring happiness to your house, and to bring peace. So, you take a piece of foundation from your house, with your perejer, and put it in your water with the dollar bill. These are three things that symbolize the earth. It doesn't have to be there more than seventy-two hours. You then put it in the doorway of your house or in the doorway of your business. After three days you take the dollar from your water and let it dry in the sun. After it is dry you put it in your wallet; and that is one way to bring prosperity. Because it is made from things that are purely natural. People don't have to pay in order to be helped. That is one way to help people who come with need.

At one point I asked Hortencia if her practices were rituals. She said no, in the sense that rituals for her signified something much bigger, and she then went into a long discourse dissociating her work from the rituals of Afro-Cuban religions such as Santería—animal sacrifices and even, she added with mortification, human beings. She forcefully distinguished her work from those who are involved with graverobbing, which "is wrong." She described the practices she prescribes as works, *trabajos,* or as "offerings that you give for your prosperity." I asked her where she learned her work. She replied:

I can't tell you that I learned anything. I had premonitions. How do I explain to you? These are things that *Diosito* can give you. It's like a sixth sense. When I want to cleanse [*limpiar*] a person to bring prosperity, I do it with apple and honey, because that will create abundance, and honey will bring good luck. Cinnamon [too] will bring good luck. These are things that come from times long past, ancient times, you know. One doesn't know how one knows these things. I can't explain. I can tell you that my spiritual child [*niño espiritual*] guides me, he tells me what to say, he whispers in my ear.

I was seven years old when I first discovered my gift. It is something unexplainable. I can tell you that I wouldn't wish it on anyone. Let me tell you that in the first place where I come from is a very small village, and people would say that I had the devil inside of me. Why? Because of the reactions my body would bring. Things would fall when I got a little aggressive—I'm not very aggressive, but a little. My mom would say, "Don't ever tell your brothers [*hermanos*] anything," because it could happen. If I would say to my sister, "I hope you get hit in your mouth," well, in a little while, she would come with her mouth broken. These are things I cannot explain.

Hortencia related a long and, by her own description, tragic (*fea*) story about her grandfather and a premonition she had that, if heeded by her family, would have prevented the tragedy. She also said that she has revelatory dreams, and she had recently had one in which she was hugging and comforting her mother. The next day she learned that her mother needed surgery. She also claimed that she dreams about earthquakes two or three days before they happen.

I can't explain to anyone because this hurts me and causes great distress [*mortifica*] inside of me. I identify myself as a curandera, but I don't describe my work with people as curing them, but as helping them. Because there are many things that you can't cure. And you won't fool anyone. If someone comes to me and says, "I have a pain in my chest," the first thing I say to them is "go and see your doctor." It's like the plants, my son [*mi hijo*]. The plants can help you, but over a long period of time. If someone has high blood pressure I can say, "Drink this tea," but if that person has high blood pressure he can have a stroke—he needs to go to the doctor. There are many ways to help people, but a person shouldn't get involved with something in which they don't belong. This is to say that when you come to me to have your cards read I can do that for you because that is what I can do—look a bit at your future, look a bit at your problems to understand what you can do to help yourself, or what I can do to help you resolve your problems. But I won't get involved with things that I have no business in.

Look, that lady who is in the other room, her egg indicated that there was a person who was harming her. You see, your being is one whole [*conjunto*]: your body and your spirit. So, if someone hurts your body they also hurt your spirit, and vice versa. Like that lady who is in the other room, what I have to do for her is make sure her spirit is healthy, so that her body will heal. It's a lie, all those, what do they call them, spiritual operations. Or just because they touch you somewhere you've been healed. It has to be someone who has God [*que tenga Dios*]. Yes, sometimes they help. There are people who have that great gift, but there are people who are charlatans, and they take advantage of people. I can tell you about many people who come here complaining about how they went to such-and-such a place and how they got tricked into spending a lot of money. That is not helping someone. When you want to help someone, if you can't help, you tell him that you can't. "Go with your doctor, he will help you." In those cases based on bad luck [*mala suerte*] I can help, and I say, "Yes, I can help"; cleaning your aura or cleaning your spirit—those are things I can do. But to get involved in things I can't do, that would work against me, and the people who are trusting in me. I do my work to help people.

On another occasion Hortencia told me about a woman who had been through many conventional medical treatments that were ultimately unavailing. The woman could not eat or sleep. She was feeling generally anxious and depressed. Hortencia then took me out to the waiting room where the woman was sitting. Hortencia asked the woman to tell me how

Hortencia had helped her. The woman said, "I was ill [*asustado*], and the only thing that helped me was Hortencia."

Ya No Tengas Susto: The Poetics of Religious Healing

Sagrado Corazón is a paradox: it is at once an extraordinary and a common place. In other words, it is a public locus for the intersection of the sacred and the profane. In its extraordinary sense, it is a sacred space where hope abounds and miracles take place. Optimism, which for many is so difficult to achieve, is in no short supply at Sagrado Corazón. At this storefront botanica, hope and faith are created, nurtured, and packaged as the ability to control life itself, to affect destiny, to turn events in one's favor—all these things and more are available at Sagrado Corazón. The idea is relentlessly compelling, a universal in human history: that religious rituals and invisible powers can directly influence our fortunes and bring to us the people and things we desire if we offer them the correct prayer and performance.

The claims of divine intervention and power made at Sagrado Corazón are not unlike those made by a Mexican American home-based Catholicism, which delineates the sacred cosmos in terms of the specific functions of saints.[14] What differentiates curanderismo and Mexican American popular Catholicism is the cosmogony of saints, and the function of saints. The saints in Sagrado Corazón, and in curanderismo generally, include those who are officially sanctioned by the Catholic Church, but also those who are not counted among the ranks of the Vatican-sanctioned, but who symbolize, resonate with, and sacralize a condition of oppression, victimization and injustice—and the ambiguous moral choices the poor must often make in their struggles to survive—to confront and change the susto that poverty and racism bring.

Take for example the saint "Jesús Malverde," or (literally) "Jesus Bad-Green." At Sagrado Corazón one can find many products that bear his image and boast his intervention, including aerosol sprays, candles, and texts. Jesús Malverde, or Jesus "Bad-Green," is the appellation given to a community-sanctioned saint who is enshrined in Culican, Mexico. Malverde is the patron saint of drug traffickers. One *corrido* dedicated to him begins: "Jesús Malverde, angel of the poor, I've come to ask you a great big favor."[15] Not only drug dealers but law-abiding Mexicans and Chicanos make the pilgrimage to petition the saint who has been named *El Narcosantón*—the Big Drug Saint. El Narcosanton arises from a social condition that has pressed people to the limits of their conventional resources. For some who feel they must traffic in drugs or otherwise break the law as a matter of economic necessity, Malverde is the saint of choice. And yet if prayers to Malverde are answered favorably, his devotees will offer devotional recompense not only to Malverde but also to Guadalupe and to official Catholic saints.[16]

But the function of the saints in popular Catholicism and curanderismo is also inflected with cultural understandings and thus changed from the function accorded them by official doctrine. In official Catholicism, saints act only as moral exemplars who point to and act as intercessors to God, praying on behalf of the petitioners. In popular Catholicism and curanderismo the official saints, spirits of deceased loved ones, and unofficial saints possess power to effect change themselves.[17] Seen in this light, curanderismo is not so much a discrete religious system as a logical extension of popular Catholicism: the difference is not one of kind, but of degree. This in part explains how believers can participate in multiple religious practices with little or no cognitive dissonance. Believers who identify as Catholics may also claim multiple religious identities, for each is an extension of a singular religious soul constituted by a core set of beliefs that overlap with and extend into practices that may appear at variance with one another but are ultimately all, in effect, derivative.[18]

Additionally, many of the things promised by the mythology of Sagrado Corazón are those also offered by evangelical churches. In most Mexican American and other Latino evangelical circles, religious discourse is translated into native vernaculars, and the grammar of belief, salvation, and blessings is given to"local deployments."[19] For these overlapping religious premises, curanderismo can be considered not as isolated from Mexican American Catholicism and evangelicalism, but as part of a broad network of faith-based mechanisms that enable the poor and the oppressed to navigate the often difficult terrain of their lives. Thus, the question of Sagrado Corazón regards not so much the general beliefs, but the specific idioms and rituals through which these beliefs are expressed and reiterated. In effect, the sensation of the sacred is ubiquitous throughout Latina/o communities, and Sagrado Corazón is but one marker on a continuum where the sacred is routinely (re)imagined and encountered, conjured and manifested.

In another sense Sagrado Corazón is a common and ordinary place, for it is first and foremost a business. It is a store, a standard marker in the landscape of North American capitalism. Sagrado Corazón is not an altogether altruistic enterprise existing solely for the purpose of helping those in need. Sagrado Corazón is privately owned by entrepreneurs who also own and finance several other botanicas in East Los Angeles. Hortencia and other curanderas are hired by the owners to manage and operate the botanicas. Sagrado Corazón is in place to make a profit, and inasmuch as the profit motive dominates the relationships of gift and exchange operative there, Hortencia's work—even if unintentionally—is consistent with corporate United States, since it supports a distinctly capitalist *religious* sensibility: money buys happiness. A distinction must be drawn, however, between Hortencia's beliefs and practices and the motives of the owners of the shop, who enjoy the most financial gain. Still, with this ordinary business purpose in mind, the many "profane" or secular items (such as dishwashing soap and hair creams) sold alongside the articles that have a distinctively religious purpose are perfectly consistent with the mandate of profit—a divine commandment in the religion of North American capitalism. That both religious and secular items are bought from a wholesale distributor, marked up, sectioned off into discrete display areas, tagged with prices, and sold for profit along with Hortencia's services renders the whole venture less than mystical—unless, of course, one is enchanted by the mystical spectacle of the American marketplace more generally.

Curanderismo was once restricted to private homes and kinship networks. Today it has shifted from the familiar intimate space of home to the public space of commodity consumption. In fact, Mexican American urban religious landscapes are in general experiencing a radical transformation. Currently storefront religions—be they botanicas, spiritualist temples, or evangelical churches—compete for space and patrons with grocery stores, moviehouses, restaurants, barber shops, and the like. The space of the sacred and the space of the profane, which was for Durkheim so clearly distinguishable, is for Mexican-descent Angelenos increasingly dissolving into one another, and becoming one fluid mass of capitalist desire.

But there is an assumptive familiarity to storefront religious practice that is utterly logical to postmoderns in East Los Angeles: the ritual of capital exchange. That is, people pay for what they want; when applied to the sacred the appeal is nonetheless rational. People seek the services of a religious specialist as they would seek the services of a doctor, lawyer, electrician, beautician, and the like; and now these services are increasingly offered in the same consumer spaces. If the seeker wants a miracle, then he or she need only shop around for the curandera or curandero with the best reputation (cost, product/service), visit the practitioner's place of business—which is open and accessible to the public—pay the set fee, and expect results. But are not explicitly Christian services available through the same mechanism of exchange?

Curanderismo was once organized predominantly around an elaborate system of gifting.[20] Traditionally the cycle began with the healer recognizing his or her gift of healing powers, which came directly from God.

From gratitude and obligation, the healer would gift those who sought healing. In turn, the person or persons who received the gift of healing, or whatever divine services they sought, would be obliged to gift the curandera in return, and obliged also to gift to others as they had been gifted. *El don*, "the gift," was the principle that once guided social relations in curandera practice. The gift that seekers would offer to healers was never fixed or predetermined; it was at the discretion of the seeker and conformed to whatever means he or she possessed.[21] With the emergence of storefront healing centers, however, this pattern is changing. Market value and laws of supply and demand together with the costs of maintaining a healing "business" now delimit exchange in curanderismo. The charisma of blessings and gift so central to religious narratives is giving way to the rationale of capitalist ideology. As a result, religious expectations are conjoined with financial means, and religious spaces serve multiple purposes. Sagrado Corazón, for example, is at once a medical clinic of sorts, a religious article store, a sacred place of magic and devotion, an extension of devotional images and practices fostered by the Catholic Church, and a store that is in business for profit. As such it is the epitome of a postmodern religious place, whose success is found precisely in its ability consistently to transform religious irony and indeterminacy into efficacious social functionality.

Hence, patrons of Sagrado Corazón come with various needs, usually at moments of crisis. Seekers fall into categories based on frequency of visits and intensity of beliefs: casual and onetime visitors, occasional visitors, and regular clients. As Hortencia claimed, visitors are of all faiths, but they are all Latino, for Hortencia does not speak English. This one common element suggests a core set of beliefs originating and nurtured in aspects of Mexican American and other Latino cultures that get expressed in discrete yet ironically consistent practices. For example, the belief that divine healing is possible is held by Latina/o evangelicals, Catholics, and curanderas even while it is eschewed as medieval superstition by rational Catholic and Protestant institutions.

It is of no small significance that all the believers in this study who were asked about their faith replied with no uncertainty that they were indeed Catholic. And yet they also confessed that visiting the Sagrado Corazón botanica (which is how the question was phrased) was contrary to the teachings of Catholic doctrine. But the seekers nonetheless persisted in their visits to see Hortencia. When asked about this seeming contradiction, Hortencia's answer was clear and utterly pragmatic, articulating the perspective of the patrons of Sagrado Corazón: these are matters of personal conscience. And as long as one is convinced that he or she is doing good work in the world, there is no need to be burdened by sin in spite of perceived Catholic teachings.

This appeal to conscience is a triumph of Gloria Anzaldúa's mestiza consciousness. Anzaldúa argues that the definitive characteristic of mestiza consciousness is "a tolerance for contradictions, a tolerance for ambiguity."[22] This consciousness, or soul, is the impulse for (meta)physical, geopolitical, and symbolic boundary transgression: border crossings. As Hortencia and those interviewed confessed, they believed the practice of curanderismo to be contrary to the teachings of the Catholic Church. And yet, they professed also a Catholic identity while concomitantly defying the Catholic Church. Only a "tolerance for contradiction" would enable them to do thusly. For Anzaldúa, this consciousness emerges from a lifetime of struggle, from experiencing injustice and subsequently transforming pain into tactical maneuvers. In the borderlands, the tragic soul of a poet is nurtured. Thus, Hortencia boldly remytholigized her world, forcefully assuming poetic license with Catholic narrative. Assuming poetic control over religion when managing one's world—thought narrative and practice—is what I call religious poetics.

In conclusion, I want to suggest that participants in this study were practicing a type of what I call "religious poetics"—inasmuch as they renarrated religious discourse so that it became more conducive to their struggles. Even those, like Dolores, who professed a feeling of "guilt" for being at Sagrado Corazón were nevertheless assuming poetic creativity with Catholicism in practice, for Dolores (and others) believes that Catholicism was elastic enough to bend to her needs without breaking.

While most of the folks I watched and talked with at Sagrado Corazón lacked the vocabulary to describe powerfully what they were doing, in their various ways they, too, participated in producing a fresh religious mythology, or mythopoesis, insofar as they followed the teachings of Hortencia. Together they deftly delineated an ethics of healing and, even more, an ethics of borderland religions which brought together many disparate elements of religious life with Catholicism, memory, and culture in an attempt to survive. At the center of Hortencia's poetic religious ethics lies, in her own words, a commitment to "conscience." In her heart and soul she believes that what she is doing is helping people: she appeals to conviction, and that conscience enables her poetics of material salvation and power to forcefully unfold and take place.

The participants in this study saw the Catholic Church as key to who they were and to who they were becoming. Yet they simultaneously understood the church as a human institution mediating the sacred, and Hortencia as a human who, not so unlike the priests, manifested the divine: both received and disseminated God, and both could work in concert when deploying the sacred in their quotidian efforts to survive. Further research on curanderismo should take into account not only the lives of Catholics who visit curanderas, but Protestants and those professing other faiths who frequent healing centers. How, for example, does the emergent, largely Latina/o Los Angeles–based neo-Indigenous movement, indigenismo, interface with curanderismo? There need to be more in-depth case studies on botanicas that would include histories of the centers and closely charted individual stories. Such work should clearly distinguish gender patterns, as well as socioeconomic factors. More, understanding of religion generally but especially Mexican American religion in particular would be greatly enhanced by carefully documented accounts of healing practices written in English. Finally, meticulously recorded lives of individual healers and their religious poetics would serve an understanding of Mexican American religion well.[23] For it is in these stories that religious poetics take center stage.

Roberto S. Goizueta

The Symbolic World of
Mexican American Religion

NOT LONG AGO, my family and I participated in the Good
Friday celebration of the Mexican American community in the Pilsen
neighborhood of Chicago (eloquently described by Karen Mary Davalos
earlier in this volume). Together with thousands of others, we walked
with Jesus Christ as he carried his cross through the narrow streets of
Pilsen on his way to Calvary (that is, Harrison Park). After returning
home from the Via Crucis, my wife, children, and I were discussing what
we had just witnessed and experienced. At one point in the conversation,
my seven-year-old son asked me a question: "Dad, what is more important, life or love?" Like a good theologian, I instinctively gave him the
most logical answer: "Life, of course; unless you have life, you can't love."
His facial expression indicated that he was not quite convinced. "No," he
retorted, "I think it's the other way around: without love, you can't have
life." "Hmmm," I said, "I hadn't thought of that."

Over the next few days I spent a lot of time thinking about that exchange. I wondered why our experience of the Via Crucis in Pilsen might
have prompted both his question and, especially, the answer he himself
had given to the question. The following reflections are the result of my
own attempt to understand the Via Crucis and other Mexican American
popular religious traditions in the light of the question my son had asked:
"What is more important, life or love?"

In its symbols, narratives, and rituals, the Mexican American community (and indeed the entire U.S. Latino community) engages the universal human reality of death in powerful yet complex ways. To the outside observer, the reality of death may appear to play *the* central role in Mexican American popular Catholicism. From the ubiquitous crucifixes, such as that of Nuestro Señor de los Milagros (Our Lord of Miracles) in San Antonio, to the celebrations of El Día de los Muertos (the Day of the Dead), the Mexican American world seems to center on a preoccupation with human mortality, suffering, and the experience of death. The centrality of death in Mexican American culture is particularly striking when set against the backdrop of a dominant U.S. culture, in which the reality and experience of death seem largely absent from public consciousness; human pain, suffering, and death are viewed as enemies of life, barriers to the "good life," and obstacles to be overcome in the "pursuit of happiness." Indeed, as the social psychologist Ernest Becker noted three decades ago, one might argue that all modern Western cultures are constructed around and founded upon a "denial of death"; the raison d'être of individual personality structures as well as social structures is to mask or obscure the universal reality of suffering and death by creating the illusion that, by implementing the right psychological and technological instruments, human beings can actually achieve absolute control over their environment and, indeed, over themselves.[1]

In Mexican American popular Catholicism, one encounters an alternative, countercultural view. Mexican American popular Catholicism undermines the modern Western dichotomous worldview in which life and death are perceived as contradictory or mutually exclusive realities. Popular Catholicism also challenges the church to discover among the poor and marginalized the prophetic love of God.

It is my conviction that God is indeed revealed in the religious practices of the people, especially the poor and marginalized. Elsewhere in this volume Orlando Espín articulates clearly and forcefully the central significance of the *sensus fidelium* (the "faithful intuitions" of the people) for the church and its tradition; these faithful intuitions are a privileged locus of God's self-revelation. A central task of the theologian, then, is to "read" and interpret the sensus fidelium as this is made manifest in the popular religious practices of the community.[2]

Subverting Major Dichotomies

Mexican Americans and, indeed, all U.S. Latinos and Latinas live a mestizo reality; as Luis León asserts in his essay, our lives unfold on the border between cultures, between races, between nations, between conflicting worldviews; we live in a borderland that defines our existence.[3] On the border, we are forced by circumstances to live in a world of "both / and" rather than "either / or." Living in multiple worlds simultaneously, we know that it is an illusion to speak of "reality" as if it were an objective, universal datum immune to human construals and constructions; we are suspicious of attempts to circumscribe what counts for reality. If forced by historical circumstance to live on the border, in a world of both / and, we nevertheless struggle to embrace that world as a gift from God, a privileged place wherein we might struggle to affirm the value of *all* life and *all* persons.

Paradoxically perhaps, the popular religious practices of Mexican American culture reflect and express a view of life—*all* life—as a gift. Mexican American popular religious practices embody an organic worldview, wherein the human person sees himself or herself as part of a relational network and a temporal continuum embracing all of reality, material and spiritual. This organic, holistic worldview is at odds with post-Enlightenment notions of time and space, of the material and the spiritual, and of the person's place within time and space, within the material and the spiritual dimensions of reality. Finally, such an organic worldview reveals a very different understanding of the human experience of suffering and death.

Individual and Community

First, the worldview underlying these popular religious celebrations reflects a particular notion of the human person, a particular "theological anthropology" (that is, an understanding of the nature of the person and his or her relationship to the sacred). Indeed, this aspect is often what Euro-Americans find most striking about Mexican American popular Catholicism, namely, its decidedly communal character. Whether vis-à-vis one's family, one's barrio, one's ancestors, or God, the Mexican American always exists *in relationship.* This is evident in the familial character of the Día de los Muertos celebrations, in which so much care is taken to affirm and reinforce family ties with both the living and the dead. It is also evident in the public, communal processions of Good Friday, in which the people accompany Christ in his Passion, and accompany each other on the Way of the Cross, thereby identifying their own personal struggles with those of Jesus and their companions.

What is taking place in these celebrations is precisely an "identification," an affirmation of identity. In other words, the community here is not merely extrinsic to the individual participant, an optional—even if desirable—supplement to the individual's own identity; rather, the community forms and shapes the person's own identity. Here, personal identity is not so much achieved through an individual's choices and decisions as it is received from one's family, one's community, and, above all, from God.

For Mexican Americans, a community is not a collection of fundamentally autonomous individuals who have freely chosen to enter into an association with other individuals ("a voluntary association of like-minded individuals"). Rather, community is the very source of personal identity. Individuals are not the building blocks of community; community is, instead, the foundation of individual personhood. Community precedes personal existence, not the reverse. The human experience, or praxis, in which God is revealed, and upon which the theologian is called upon to reflect, is not simply the action of a historical agent but an *inter*action *in the course of which* we become empowered to act as individual historical agents; human agency is not the source of community but its by-product.[4]

Nevertheless, the historical experience of the "second mestizaje" (Virgilio Elizondo's term to describe the encounter between Mexican and Euro-American cultures) threatens this communal worldview.[5] As Luis León notes in his analysis of the impact of social fragmentation on curanderismo in the United States, the individualistic consumerism that characterizes this society can very quickly turn Mexican American popular religion into merely another commodity to be bought and sold for individual gain. Similar observations could be made about many other areas of life in which the dominant culture is breaking down communal bonds, especially among Mexican American youth.[6]

Though increasingly influenced by the second mestizaje, an inherently communal theological anthropology remains at the heart of the Mexican American understanding of identity as reflected in popular Catholicism. Like all drama, the ritual performance associated with popular religious celebrations forges an identification between the actors or participants and their roles, whether these be the roles of the crowds, Roman soldiers, Mary, or Christ himself in the Via Crucis, or the roles of spirits and skeletons in the Día de los Muertos celebrations. It is the very identity between community and self that makes these celebrations so powerful and, conversely, provokes such visceral reactions from Mexican Americans when the celebrations are not honored or, as too often still happens in the United States, when the celebrations are discouraged or prohibited. At stake in these rituals is the very identity, that is, the very existence of the Mexican American people as a people—an identity that depends upon the people's ability to maintain an intimate connection with one another, their ancestors, and the divine. Without that connection, the individual Mexican American literally does not exist; to "be" at all is to be-in-relation. Thus, to sever the relationship, and thus the means whereby that relationship is forged and affirmed, is to kill the person.

The function of home altars, food offerings to deceased relatives, visits to gravesites on Día de los Muertos, or the carrying of the cross, the physical reenactment of Jesus' crucifixion, the recital of the *Pésames* or condolences to Jesus' grieving mother on Good Friday is precisely that of cementing the bonds that link us to one another and that therefore define each of us as human persons. If a person is, at least in part, a physical, historical being, so too must the ties that bind us to one another be, at least in part, physical and historical. To remove those ties is thus to threaten our very existence, not only as a community but also as individual persons (since without community there is no individual person).

In the case of Mexican Americans and other U.S. Latinos, this intrinsically communal identity is, by definition, pan-American, transcending national borders. Thus, as Timothy Matovina points out, popular religious practices such as those surrounding Our Lady of Guadalupe function as bridges between the country of origin, Mexico, and the adopted country. The community that defines the person thus transcends not only generational boundaries, incorporating our ancestors as well as our progeny, but also geographic boundaries. The mestizo character of the Mexican American community defines both time and space.

Likewise, implied in this notion of a transgenerational, pan-American community is a profound sense of personal responsibility. In the case of the curandera Hortencia, this sense of responsibility precludes her from using the gift of healing, which she has received from God, as an instrument of merely individual gain; like all gifts, it is to be used for the benefit of the entire community.

The Material and the Spiritual

A second important way in which Mexican American popular Catholicism reflects a communal, organic worldview is through the Mexican American understanding of the interconnectedness of the material and spiritual dimensions of reality. One of the most widely recognized manifestations of this characteristic of Mexican American culture is the so-called spiritual realism of so much Mexican American and Latin American literature, in which the historical and spiritual worlds often intermingle almost willy-nilly. Events and characters that to an outsider may appear as "magical" or "fantastic" are to the Mexican American merely one more aspect of everyday existence, one more dimension of reality, a reality rich and diverse enough to encompass the magical as well as the mundane, the ethereal as well as the material.

The fluidity of the border between the spiritual and the material is evident during the Día de los Muertos celebrations, as described earlier by Lara Medina and Gilbert Cadena. Thus, for example, the ritual of placing a deceased relative's favorite foods or photographs on his or her grave or on a home altar in order to give pleasure to the deceased person presupposes a worldview in which there is no clear separation between the spiritual and material realms. The deceased person is *really* present and participating in every aspect of our everyday lives. Indeed, what is called into question by such rituals is precisely any definition of reality that clearly circumscribes it, excluding from the definition any nonempirical reality. The nonempirical world is as real as, if not more real than, the empirical world—without, however, denying the importance of the latter. This understanding of reality is particularly true of all interpersonal relationships, as these are mediated by love, which can be known as real only by experiencing it, not—like empirical reality—by simply "taking a good look." One must certainly evaluate empirically the fruits of love to determine whether it is genuine love, but the empirical results alone are not sufficient: the same empirical action (for example, giving money to the poor) may be undertaken as an act of genuine love or as an act of egotism, to display one's superiority. The empirical evidence is essential, but not sufficient, to determine that love is real.

This intermingling of the spiritual, or transcendent, and the material is also evident in the dramatic reenactment of the Via Crucis on Good Friday, in which the line between the real and the "merely" imagined also becomes blurred. Is Christ really crucified every year at the end of the community's procession? The many actors and participants in the annual Via Crucis would be hard pressed to deny the reality of the events. The pain, anguish, and tears on the faces of the participants at every Via Crucis celebration is evidence that, at least for them, what is transpiring in their midst is indeed real. Time and again, participants describe the experience as events that are indeed "really" happening: the Roman soldier cringes as he pounds the nails through Jesus' hands and feet, and members of "the crowd" find themselves crying real tears as they watch the soldiers whipping Jesus and nailing him to the cross.[7]

These popular religious practices thus suggest a profoundly sacramental worldview that rejects any clear separation between the symbolic and the real, or between the "sign" and the "signified"; what the symbol represents is in fact experienced as *truly* present in and through the symbol. The dramatic reenactment of the Via Crucis makes really present, here and now, the real Via Crucis, the real Jesus Christ. In and through the dramatic action, he enters into a real relationship with us, and we with him.

This dramatic interaction becomes a source of profound strength for the participants, precisely because through the interaction Jesus and Mary really identify with them. This process of empowerment is poignantly conveyed in Karen Mary Davalos's account of the women who participated in the Pilsen Via Crucis. One woman explains: "The Via Crucis is something we live in the barrio." (She does not say that the Via Crucis is *like* what we live in the barrio; rather, it *is* what we live in the barrio.)

This notion of reality distinguishes Mexican American popular Catholicism from post-Enlightenment views that establish a clear separation between a symbol, or sign, and what the symbol "points to," or signifies. For modern post-Enlightenment forms of religion, the real is *behind* (and thus separate from) the symbol; for popular Catholicism, the real is *in* (and thus practically—though not theoretically—indistinguishable from) the symbol. For the former, a symbol is always "merely" a symbol; for the latter, a symbol is the most complete representation of reality, precisely because the symbol unites the material and the spiritual, the empirical and the nonempirical. The participant certainly knows that the actor playing the part of Jesus Christ is not in fact Jesus Christ—and would acknowledge this if asked. However, while in the midst of the ritual action itself, this theoretical though "real" distinction gives way to an experience of organic unity: for the moment, the actor becomes what he represents.[8]

This is no more an example of idolatry than is the belief that, in the eucharistic liturgy, the consecrated bread and wine become the body and blood of Christ; indeed, anti-Catholic accusations of cannibalism and iconoclastic condemnations of religious images issue from mistaken notions of the relationship between sign and signified. These notions assume that there are only two possible ways of understanding that relationship: either the (material) sign and the (spiritual) signified remain completely separate, or else they become identified, resulting in idolatry. In Mexican American popular Catholicism, the sign is neither separate from nor identified with the spiritual reality that is signified. Rather, the sign *mediates* the signified; the former is both distinct from and one with the latter. (This relationship is similar to traditional, Catholic sacramental realism: thus the consecrated bread and wine on the altar are empirically bread and wine but really the body and blood of Christ—an essential theological distinction that nevertheless does not fully capture the single, unified experience of eucharistic communion.)

Unfortunately, the sacramental realism of popular Catholicism is often perceived as naïve or infantile by Christians under the sway of post-Enlightenment epistemologies. Peter Casarella has described the separation of sign and signified as a modern tendency to view the truth of the visible world with suspicion by conceiving of an idealized, self-contained, and logically precise theoretical screen. Or, in Husserl's words: "Immediately with Galileo . . . begins the surreptitious substitution of idealized nature for prescientifically intuited nature." In Galileo's wake, appearances of the non-idealized, "objective" world were well on their way to becoming mere appearances. . . . We moderns are still heirs to his distrust of appearances. Unless our bare perception of an event in the natural world is accompanied by a complex, *non-intuitive* explanation, we fear that we have not gotten to the bottom of things. Non-technical views are thought of as "superficial," which literally means "skimming the surface." Faith in the power of the scientific viewpoint compels us to take our distance from the appearance as appearance. If we really want to understand the world, we need an explanation that will unmask the illusion of what we perceive with our own eyes.[9]

Consequently, any form of religion that affirms the *reality* of the appearance as appearance, the intrinsic connection between a symbol and what it re-presents, will be derogated or dismissed as unsophisticated and naïve. Conversely, the only adequate "connection" between the (material) sign and the (spiritual) signified will be a rational, theoretical connection (hence, a connection understood only by the "educated," "rational" person).

For Mexican Americans, however, that connection is intrinsic to the reality itself. It is a connection known not primarily by stepping back from the sign in order to observe and analyze it, thereby uncovering what it "really" means, but by entering into, engaging, and participating in the sign—a reality known best not through analysis but through participation. In the act of participation, in the experience of the sign, sign and signified are one. In León's essay, Hortencia speaks of the mystery that resides at the very heart of matter itself; even material existence is experienced as at once empirical and nonempirical.

The very reality of the sign (material symbol or ritual) is what guarantees the reality of the concrete interrelationships that give birth to and nurture life itself. An abstract relationship is no relationship at all, any more than an abstract individual is a person. Insofar as relationships are real, they are mediated by the concrete, historical symbols in which we all participate jointly and through which we are thus united with one another; in these real symbols, the spiritual and the material become one. Jesus Christ is truly carrying his cross alongside us on Good Friday as surely as our deceased relatives are truly breaking bread with us during the elaborate fiestas of the Day of the Dead.

If our dead friends and relatives have a real presence in our everyday lives, thereby blurring the distinction between the spiritual and the material, so too then is the distinction between past and present blurred. Though deceased, our ancestors are as much a part of our community as are those persons physically alive today.[10] Traditions such as the Via Crucis and Día de los Muertos are, therefore, essential means for inviting the past into the present and affirming the continuing participation of our ancestors in our everyday lives. The individual person is given his or her identity by a community that extends across many generations. The community's traditions are its way of affirming those transgenerational bonds.

Conversely, where individual identity is perceived as the achievement of an autonomous, "self-made" individual, such traditions will be eschewed; indeed, tradition itself will be viewed as the unwarranted imposition of external constraints upon the (presumably) autonomous individual's exercise of his or her freedom or upon the individual's right to determine his or her identity for himself or herself. This is precisely the danger that Mexican Americans perceive as they struggle to carry on their popular religious traditions in the profoundly individualistic dominant culture of the United States. Because of its individualistic worldview, the dominant culture tends to be antagonistic not only to these particular traditions—for all the reasons outlined above—but to tradition per se as a threat to individual autonomy.

The Public and the Private

Mexican American popular traditions bring religion into the public square, thereby breaching the boundary between private life and public life and challenging another modern epistemological dichotomy. Much has been written about the post-Enlightenment "privatization" of religion; the life of faith becomes circumscribed within the sphere of the private conscience and domestic life, effectively immunizing the "public" realm from any real religious influence. In modern Western culture, religious faith tends to be seen as a matter of private choice or personal taste; the proper locus of faith is thus the individual conscience.

To breach this presumptive barrier between the realm of religion (private conscience) and the realm of "rational" activity (the public arena) is to risk being accused of "mixing religion and politics"; to introduce religious faith into public discussions is to risk being dismissed as a religious fanatic. Religion is thereby relegated to the realm of private opinion and personal taste, individual choices that, by their nature, have no warrants beyond the individual (such as, for instance, aesthetic or culinary taste). And the public sphere is immunized from religious critique.[11]

As analyzed by Timothy Matovina, Our Lady of Guadalupe symbol-

izes a very different understanding of the relationship between the public and the private. An explicitly religious (and therefore "private") symbol, Guadalupe is also nevertheless an equally powerful national,
political symbol that has played an important role in the history of Mexico and continues to be found at every level of the Mexican American experience. The image of Guadalupe can today be found not only in
churches and homes but also on storefront walls and on the tattooed arms
of Mexican American "gangbangers."

Both the Via Crucis and the Día de los Muertos celebrations exemplify
how Mexican American popular Catholicism breaks down this separation between the public and the private. Here, religious faith and practices are brought out from the private realm of the home and the church
into the public realm of the streets and cemeteries. Not only religious faith
but the reality of death itself enter the public—and hence political—arena
from which these fundamental realities have been excluded in modern
societies: Mexican Americans walk alongside Jesus Christ in public and
communicate with their deceased relatives in public. The distinction between a public demonstration (*manifestación*) and a religious procession
is thus blurred. (This is illustrated, for example, by recent events in the
heavily Mexican American town of Cicero, Illinois, whose mayor attempted to prevent Good Friday processions by applying town statutes
that limit public demonstrations.) As Karen Mary Davalos explains in her
essay, the processions often stop not only at expressly "religious" sites,
such a churches, but also at "secular" sites, such as prisons, bars, and
schools. Likewise, in the celebrations of the Day of the Dead described by
Medina and Cadena, the participants do not make clear distinctions between religious art, to serve the ends of private devotions, and secular art,
intended for the public square.

Through these practices, then, Mexican Americans stake out a place for
their religious faith in the public arena, thereby breaching another barrier established by the dominant culture. In the process, the religious values expressed subvert—at least for a time—the economic, productive,
utilitarian values associated with the public arena (for example, traffic
stops, businesses close). For a day, the public celebration of communal life
as an end in itself supplants "business as usual," where productivity, ef-
ficiency, and utility reign. The intrinsic value of human life as a gift is celebrated in an arena in which the value of life is determined by economic
criteria. During these celebrations, the sheer gratuity and, indeed, "use-
lessness" of life take priority over "useful" activity. Such processions thus
transform public space, claiming it as cultural space within the larger,
dominant culture. This public space gives expression to an alternative

way of living, one that construes life in a radically different way, as a gift to be celebrated rather than as an instrument of profit. The transformative power of popular religion as it enters the prohibited territory of public space is attested by a young man named Jorge, who has played various roles in the Pilsen Good Friday procession. Jorge notes that the number of bars that formerly dotted the 18th Street route of the Via Crucis has dwindled over the years as the people have brought their prayers into the street, praying for and to the alcoholics themselves. For Jorge, the social power of the sacred is clearly palpable; the signs of that power are visible on the street itself.

This public space is not abstract; it is itself embodied in a particular, concrete way. As Davalos notes in her analysis of the Via Crucis in Chicago, this public space is white, professional, and male. It is characterized, she argues, by an architecture of domination that "territorializes" space in such a way that the possibility of crossing borders, an experience that defines the Mexican American qua mestizo/a (someone who is both Mexican and American, both European and indigenous), is effectively denied. The architecture of domination is supposedly fixed and unchangeable; the Via Crucis changes people, even if only for a few minutes. Davalos cites some of the bodily changes that take place during the procession: gangbangers bow their heads out of respect as the procession passes by, and men doff their hats. Yet this process is not itself without internal conflicts and contestations.

Thus it is instructive to examine the distinctive, even ritualized roles played by men and women in the Via Crucis, as well as in other popular rituals. Often the "private" work entailed in preparing for the events is undertaken primarily by women, while the "public" rituals are led by men. Consequently, while the Via Crucis represents a breaching of the public/private barrier *ad extra,* that barrier may often remain stubbornly intact *ad intra,* especially in the identification of "women's work" with the private realm of behind-the-scenes preparations and "men's work" with the public ritual itself. Insofar as women begin to challenge this barrier, it will become an area of contestation within the Mexican American community itself. The Pilsen community acknowledges this fact, suggests Davalos, in the prayers offered during the event, some of which address the issue of violence against women in the Pilsen community.

Davalos also asserts that, in a special way, the Via Crucis is about women. The figures of Mary, Veronica, and the women of Jerusalem allow the Mexican American women in Pilsen to identify and explain their own roles in their communities and families. As Davalos points out, women's identification with Mary can be ambivalent—both empowering and, at times, restricting. Yet this identification with Mary in her suffering and, during the Via Crucis, with Veronica makes possible a "resistance from the position of the subaltern" within the dramatic action itself.

Likewise, Timothy Matovina observes, in his historical analysis of Guadalupan devotion in San Antonio, that popular religious images of the Virgin often function ambiguously, especially in the lives of women. Even as images like that of la morenita promote a sense of dignity, empowering women to move beyond the confines of the roles traditionally assigned them by men, the same images—when applied exclusively to women by men—may also function to relegate women to those very roles.

Life and Death

Finally, insofar as Mexican American popular Catholicism blurs the distinction between person and community, past and present, the real and the imagined, and the spiritual and material, the private and the public, it blurs the distinction between life and death. This is a key point to bear in mind when interpreting the Mexican American Via Crucis and Día de los Muertos celebrations, since both are ostensibly celebrations of death, suffering, and human mortality. Indeed, if these celebrations are viewed through cultural lenses that dichotomize life and death, the rituals will inevitably be interpreted as morbidly masochistic exhibitions that disempower and debilitate the participants. Where death is seen as the enemy of life, and life itself is viewed in individualistic terms (life = the life of an autonomous individual), the Way of the Cross and Day of the Dead celebrations will inevitably be rejected, or even condemned, as obstacles to a community's sense of self-worth and self-dignity (since the "self" here is the autonomous self).

To avoid such a misinterpretation, it is important to remind ourselves that, for Mexican Americans, personal life is always, by definition, *interpersonal* life. Since the person is always, by definition, a person-in-relationship, "life" is always life-in-community. To affirm life is to affirm communion. Conversely, "death" is, by definition, the abrogation of relationships, or the destruction of community. Thus, although an individual may die physically, he or she may really remain alive insofar as the relationships that define him or her remain in force. Indeed, in Mexican American culture, the life of the autonomous, "self-made" individual is no life at all, but a form of death; in Spanish, the word *individuo* usually has pejorative connotations.

Given this theological anthropology, it is possible to see the Via Crucis and Día de los Muertos celebrations as at once affirmations of life and ritual affirmations of the reality of suffering and death; far from mutually exclusive affirmations, they are seen as mutually implicit. If Jesus Christ's life is defined as much by his relationships as by the survival of an individual self, then his life survives death whenever those relationships survive all attempts to destroy them, and when they survive death itself. Consequently, when Jesus dies accompanied by his mother and the other women, and when he dies accompanied by us on Good Friday, life truly conquers death—the indestructibility of Jesus' life (and ours) is affirmed. And when, on the Day of the Dead, we accompany our deceased relatives and are accompanied by them, life conquers death—the indestructibility of our relationships and, therefore, our lives are affirmed. As one of Medina and Cadena's informants put it: "We can't forget our dead; because of them we are here. We have to keep fighting."

Conversely, if a loved one is left to die alone or is forgotten, he or she truly dies. If Christ is left to die alone, as a mere individual, his life is truly taken from him; without the living relationships that have made him who he is, he is dead. Indeed, this is precisely what the apostles do when they abandon him; they themselves become silent accomplices in Jesus' assassination. And this is why Mexican Americans *must* accompany Jesus on the way to Calvary; this act of accompaniment is the most fundamental affirmation of our belief in the reality and truth of Christ's life. And the same can be said of the Day of the Dead celebration. We *must* visit and accompany our deceased relatives and we *must* affirm their ongoing participation in our everyday lives. If not, death has conquered life.

The affirmation of life as intrinsically communal is also evident in the celebrations of Our Lady of Guadalupe. Matovina's study reveals how Guadalupe literally creates a community, a "people," bound to one another through their common love for la morenita and, more fundamentally, through her special love for them. These people, moreover, are the descendants of the indigenous victims of the Spanish conquest. The violence and death represented by the conquest become the seedbed of new life, that is, life as "a people."

Mexican American popular religious celebrations thus reflect an understanding of death not as the opposite of life but as an intrinsic part of life. The enemy of life is not death but *individual* life. The opposite of life is not death but life in isolation from loving relationships, for it is precisely those relationships that give birth to the individual self and continue to give life to the person. What, for the dominant U.S. culture, is the human ideal ("the rugged individual") is, for Mexican Americans, the most *in*human form of existence.

Hence, insofar as Mexican American popular Catholicism represents an affirmation of life-in-relationship over against a dominant culture that idolizes individualism (which, for Mexican Americans, amounts to death), it also functions in an implicitly, though profoundly, political way. Quite simply, the Via Crucis, Día de los Muertos, and Guadalupe celebrations are (tacitly) subversive affirmations of life in a society that undermines life by extolling autonomous individualism (that is, death) at the expense of those formative relationships that have shaped and defined us, thereby giving us life. What, to modern Western observers, appear to be ritualistic glorifications of suffering and death are revealed to be, in fact, celebrations of the power of life (that is, relationships, community, love) to conquer death (that is, isolation, autonomy, mere individual existence).

Moreover, this unity of life and death is characteristic of both the Iberian Catholic and the indigenous Mesoamerican traditions, which over centuries have fused and given rise to the elaborate Day of the Dead celebrations. If the Catholic tradition emphasizes the intrinsic connection between life and death, so too do Mesoamerican traditions refuse to draw clear and distinct boundaries between life and death. In their study, Medina and Cadena emphasize the indissolubility of this connection and the subversive character of this worldview vis-à-vis a dominant culture that denies the reality of death.

This understanding of the relationship between life and death has important ramifications for religious practice. Among Mexican Americans, Good Friday is arguably the single most popular day in the liturgical year, rivaled only by Ash Wednesday, (perhaps) Christmas, and the feast of Our Lady of Guadalupe. Participation in and attendance at Easter liturgies is, by comparison, strikingly less fervent and widespread. Likewise, the corpus on the crucifix usually appears bloodied, with wounds prominently displayed.

This emphasis on participation in Good Friday celebrations and the intense affection with which Mexican Americans venerate the crucified Christ must be viewed in the light of an intrinsically communal understanding of the person. Jesus' life is affirmed and vindicated if and when he remains accompanied to the bitter end—even if this Passion involves great individual suffering and death. Although his apostles abandon him, Mary, "the other women," and God do not—and, as we walk alongside him on Good Friday, we do not abandon him (nor, despite Jesus' concluding cry of abandonment, does God abandon him—a fact confirmed in Jesus' resurrection). On Calvary Jesus dies accompanied and loved; life has conquered death, even if the autonomous individual Jesus Christ has been killed. On the Via Crucis, Jesus' pain and humiliation do not destroy him because we, the people, walk alongside him, sharing his suffering. It is not suffering that humiliates and dehumanizes, but solitary suffering. It is not death that destroys life, but solitary death.

Hence, the resurrection is not the "end result" of Jesus' Passion; it is what Jesus already experiences as he walks along the Via Dolorosa accompanied by his mother and friends. What Mexican Americans celebrate on Good Friday is not the death of Jesus Christ the solitary individual but the life that issues from our common struggle, our common Via Dolorosa, a life that not even physical death can overcome. Likewise, the physical life that is resurrected is not the life of an autonomous individual, "Jesus Christ," but his life *in relationship*. This may be one reason why the gospels (especially John's) describe in such detail Jesus' postresurrection appearances. What takes place in and through those appearances is not just the empirical demonstration of Jesus' bodily resurrection but the reconciliation of Jesus with his best friends, the disciples who abandoned him out of fear for their own lives. Jesus invites them to "see and touch his wounds"; the apostles thereby acknowledge their own complicity in the violence that inflicted those wounds, and reaffirm their love for and faith in Jesus Christ. What is resurrected is not merely the individual Jesus but Jesus-in-relationship; the resurrection of an autonomous Jesus, in isolation from the loving relationships destroyed before his crucifixion, would not have been a real resurrection, a victory of life over death. The resurrected Jesus must appear to the apostles in order to be reconciled with them, in order to manifest the victory of life-in-relationship (the only true life) over death-as-autonomy.

That reconciliation/resurrection presupposes not a forgetting of past sufferings ("forgive and forget") but, on the contrary, a living memory of the history of suffering; if we are to forgive, we cannot forget. In the gospels, Jesus Christ forgives his friends not by forgetting the wounds they helped inflict but by showing them those very wounds, the bodily, material memory of the injustices he suffered—and by inviting (commanding?) them to "see and touch" the wounds. The wounds are thus the physical reminders of Jesus' communal identity, for, though borne by Jesus, they were inflicted by others, other persons whose interactions with him have left their indelible marks on his body.

Jesus' own life is defined by his relationships as much as our lives are defined by our own familial and communal bonds. Consequently, if the resurrection reflects the ultimate victory of life over death, it represents the victory of loving relationships (life) over solitary, isolated existence (death). Jesus' resurrection is, by definition, his resurrection together with his community. All life is defined by the bonds of love that give rise to and sustain life; love is the source of life.

It is in this light, moreover, that the special affection Mexican Americans demonstrate for Mary must be understood, whether that affection is expressed by accompanying her on the way to Calvary or by weeping beside La Dolorosa as she kneels over her son's lifeless body. If Christ is defined, above all, by his relationships, then we cannot truly know him unless we know his family, friends, and companions, especially that closest and most faithful of companions, his mother (just as, in order to know another person, we must also know his or her friends and family). The great love for Mary among Mexican Americans can be misinterpreted if Mary is perceived as an autonomous individual over against Jesus Christ. From a Mexican American perspective, love of Jesus and love of Mary do not compete for primacy; rather, they necessarily imply each other (since, as persons, Jesus and Mary imply each other).

A similar observation may be made with respect to the many practices associated with the veneration of saints, including deceased relatives, in the Mexican American community. If Jesus and Mary imply each other, so too do Jesus and the entire communion of saints imply each other. Jesus is not a solitary individual; he stands at the center of a family. Consequently, the reality of the church, particularly what Georges Bernanos called the "Church of the saints," is inherent in Mexican American popular Catholicism. It is this church of the saints, the transgenerational *communio sanctorum,* that is made manifest in the Día de los Muertos. In popular Catholicism the church is, above all, the communion of saints; the saints, both past and present, are the primary locus in which the church takes root.

The saints are not in competition with Jesus Christ for primacy in the religious pantheon; such an understanding of the relationship between Christ, the church, and the saints presupposes an individualistic theological anthropology, in which the atomic individual exists over against other individuals. Rather, for Mexican American Catholics, the opposite is the case: the primacy of Christ *implies and demands* a communion of saints. If Christ is alive, so too is that community through which he lives, his brothers and sisters.

Again one finds remarkable similarities between the Iberian Catholic and the indigenous worldviews, especially their views of the relationship between communal life and death: historically, the Catholic notion of the communio sanctorum and the indigenous practice of honoring the dead fused, giving rise to the Día de los Muertos celebrations. Indeed, as Medina and Cadena observe, that very similarity made it possible for the people of Mexico to appropriate and find meaningful the Spaniards' beliefs about life and death. The result was what the authors refer to as a "nepantla spirituality, a spirituality where diverse biological and cultural elements converge, at times in great tension and at other times in cohesion."

At a time when so much religion is dismissed as dry and perfunctory, the lives of the saints, the dead in our midst, become icons of God's abiding love for us, inspiring "texts" that proclaim and witness to that love. Thus, during celebrations like those that take place on Día de los Muertos, Mexican Americans approach their relatives and ancestors with the kind of reverence and love with which one would approach an icon. For like the icon, the loved one is a re-presentation of divine nearness, a nearness that is lived out every day of the year, but especially in celebrations such as the Day of the Dead and the Way of the Cross.

Church

This sense of God's everyday nearness and abiding presence in the community also has important implications for the Mexican American community's way of "being church," its way of practicing the faith as a community of faith. Both the Via Crucis and the Día de los Muertos celebrations exemplify a "way of being religious" that, though linked to parochial and clerical structures, is rooted in popular traditions. These traditions are preeminently lay in character, extending beyond the boundaries of the parish into the homes and barrios. Indeed, for reasons both historical and cultural, Mexican American popular Catholicism has its principal locus in the home, the family, and the neighborhood rather than in the geographic parish.

As a consequence, everyday religious authority and leadership are exercised by the persons who have historically carried out those functions in the domestic sphere, namely, women—especially the *abuelas*, or grandmothers, those women whose age and experience give them a special claim to authority. As Matovina details in his study, whether in pious societies, devotional services, parish fundraising drives, or local social events, Mexican American lay women and men have often exercised leadership roles that cross the boundaries between home and parish.[12]

This is not to say that the *padrecito*, or parish priest, is not respected or recognized as a religious leader; on an everyday basis, it is the women of the family who function as religious and spiritual leaders, whether as religious teachers or as liturgical leaders. Thus, Matovina cites the influential role played by the Hijas de María in the historical development of San Fernando Cathedral. The types of leadership (and survival) skills that women learned in the home—often of necessity—empowered them to exercise these skills in the parish community. Yet, as Matovina also makes clear, these lay leaders did not view their efforts as competing (at least openly or explicitly) with the role of the clergy but as complementing it, especially in instances when the priests at San Fernando encouraged and supported lay activities.

This extension of communal worship beyond the boundaries of explicitly clerical, parochial structures into the streets and homes calls into question any attempt to reduce liturgy—at least in the Mexican American Catholic community—to that which takes place within the physical walls of a church. Matovina describes attempts by the Claretians at San Fernando Cathedral to forge explicit links between the people's Guadalupan devotions and the parish's eucharistic celebrations.

For Mexican Americans, popular religious celebrations often constitute the very heart of their Catholic faith—again, for historical as well as cultural reasons. This difference can have pastoral consequences. In parishes in which the local pastor assumes that the number of "active Catholics" is limited to those who regularly attend Mass, scores of active Catholics—those who daily participate in a whole range of "paraliturgical" celebrations but who may not regularly participate in the formal church service—will become completely invisible to the official church and its clerical leaders.

This invisibility will also characterize, *a fortiori,* those forms of popular religious practice whose explicit relationship to the church is more tenuous or ambiguous, such as curanderismo. Nevertheless, the example of Hortencia demonstrates how lay religious leaders (especially women) play important roles as mediators between the sacred and the secular, the spiritual and the material, the public and the private. Deriving her healing role from God, the source of her gift, and from the community, the source of her popular legitimacy, Hortencia embodies a faith that, while not necessarily anticlerical, is not rooted primarily in parochial structures.

Liberating Theological Practice

The theological interpretation outlined above calls into question certain "ways of doing theology" that too often prescind from a systematic consideration of the ways in which the faith is actually lived.[13] That lacuna, in turn, leads not only to a misinterpretation of popular Catholicism but also to a depreciation of the foundational role of popular Catholicism in the church. More importantly, since there is no such thing as "popular Catholicism" except in its historical embodiment in the lives of particular persons and communities, that lacuna results in the marginalization and dehumanization of those persons and communities. Even among theologians who take as their starting point a preferential option for the poor, the lived faith of the people—especially through rituals such as those under consideration here—is too often dismissed as inherently apolitical or, worse, oppressive.

Latin American liberation theologians revolutionized Christian theology by articulating a "new way" of doing theology. That new way emphasized the historical struggles of the poor as the privileged context for theological reflection. Certainly, Christian theology has from the beginning looked to human experience as the locus of God's self-revelation. And from the beginning Christians have insisted on the central significance of social justice, or love of the poor as an ethical injunction implied in the faith itself. Liberation theologians brought together these two traditional theological insights to argue for a "preferential option for the poor."

Yet, at least in its first incarnations, liberation theology was often uncomfortable with popular religion. Precisely because so much of popular religion appears to condone and, indeed, promote a masochistic obsession with suffering and death, liberation theologians (like most of us, trained in modern Western educational centers) tended to view it with suspicion if not outright disparagement. If the struggle for justice is at the heart of the Christian faith, then popular religion may appear to focus attention on otherworldly concerns in such a way that the struggle for justice in this world is relativized; too often, ruling elites have in fact fostered this attention to otherworldly concerns as an instrument for maintaining their power over the lives of the poor.

The unfortunate consequence of this suspicion—which is not altogether without warrant—has been a failure to appreciate the profound ways in which, at its best, popular religion does indeed affirm life and expresses a hope-against-hope that, in the long run, constitutes the very foundation of the struggle for justice. Consequently, those theologians who, inspired by the methodological insights of liberation theology, take as their starting point the preferential option for the poor are becoming increasingly aware that the epistemological privilege of the marginalized persons in society embraces not only perspectives on expressly sociopolitical issues but, above all, the *lived faith* of the poor. The margins offer a privileged vantage point from which to view not only a society and its institutions but also, and most important, God and religious faith itself. To be in solidarity with the poor is thus not only to struggle politically alongside the poor but, especially, to worship the God whom they worship. When we are able to do that, we realize that that God is indeed a God of life—despite what our modern Western dichotomous epistemologies may tell us.[14]

Consequently, we come to a deeper understanding and appreciation of popular religion as the very foundation of the struggle for justice and liberation. The lived faith of the people, precisely because it is "of the people" themselves, confirms the dignity and value of their lives as persons and, above all, as a people in an environment in which that dignity and value are under constant attack. As we have suggested, traditions like those of Good Friday and the Day of the Dead reinforce those familial and communal bonds that make life and hope possible, even when those bonds are manifest in the context of solidarity in suffering and death. And above all, those bonds are the unimpeachable corroboration of God's own love and solidarity. A proper appreciation of popular religion will thus lead to a deeper understanding of "justice" and "liberation"; these will come to be seen not merely as the end result of historical struggle but as concomitants of that struggle, in and through which we come to know ourselves as loved by God and by others, thereby coming to an awareness of our own dignity as persons. The lived faith of the people is but the most basic and fundamental expression of that awareness.

This fundamentally if implicitly liberative function of popular religion is evidenced, for instance, in Matovina's beautiful description of Guadalupan devotion at San Fernando, especially as that devotion has empowered new Mexican immigrants and inspired Mexican Americans to resist racial prejudice and discrimination—not by explicitly calling for resistance so much as by reminding the people of their inherent dignity. A person's affirmation of his or her inherent dignity as a child of God is, after all, the starting point of any genuine liberation. This dignity is likewise affirmed in the curandera's service of healing. In a world that, as we have seen, refuses to separate the physical from the spiritual, and understands the personal as inherently communal, what is healed is not only the body of an individual but the person's whole world. In a society fraught with violence, conflict, and division, the curandera can be a witness to the possibility of living as a whole person, resisting the forces of fragmentation (both spiritual and physical), and thus living with dignity.

In the popular religious traditions of the Mexican American community, the loving relationships to God and others themselves become the seedbed of liberation, the seedbed of new life. Those loving relationships are the source of our identity, dignity, and power as individual human beings. In the end, then, the rich religious traditions of the Mexican American community enable us to discover that, yes, love is more important than life—because love is what defines life.

Orlando O. Espín

Mexican Religious Practices, Popular Catholicism, and the Development of Doctrine

THE MEXICAN RELIGIOUS practices and spiritual traditions discussed in this volume have their own integrity and value in the lives of practitioners. Indeed, they constitute an important element—arguably the central element—in the religion of Mexican and Mexican-heritage Catholics in the United States. How are we to think of such practices in the context of the Catholic Church? Are such practices and beliefs genuinely Catholic? And how does one decide?

These are fair questions, particularly relevant to pastoral leaders and others, clergy as well as laity, who are responsible for sustaining the life of the church. In the previous essay Roberto Goizueta provided one perspective by situating Mexican American religious practices within a sacramental religious imagination and moral universe that are identifiably Catholic. Here I approach the question from a somewhat different perspective, namely, the relationship between popular Catholicism and the development of Catholic doctrine and self-understanding over time. An understanding of this relationship is relevant to the faith of ordinary believers, but it bears even more directly upon the work of pastors, bishops, and lay leaders and ministers who must make daily decisions about church doctrines, identity, and practices.

I am a theologian. For over twenty years I have been intrigued by popular Catholicism, especially among U.S. Latinos/as and Latin Americans. Living and working in Brazil and the Dominican Republic, as well as in southern Florida, southern California, and west Texas, have provided me with numerous instances of a popular faith that has informed and sustained communities historically and culturally marginalized by society and church.

Viewing Catholicism in this way, from the ground up, poses intriguing questions. Why, for example, after centuries of evangelization, do the people of Socorro, Texas, hold fast to their devotion to St. Michael? Or why have Mexican Americans in San Diego battled city governments for permission to hold a procession to honor Our Lady of Guadalupe, and yet done so little to confront politicians on bread-and-butter issues? Why do Cuban Americans maintain their devotion to Our Lady of Charity yet seem to be uninterested in other, immensely more important elements of Catholicism?

It is said that Mexican Americans and all Latinos/as—Catholics and Protestants, as well as non-Christians and those with no particular religion—share the same historical and cultural roots, which were nurtured and shaped by Catholicism.[1] If this is true, then the issues raised by Latino/a popular Catholicism are not only historical or sociological but also eminently theological. If Catholicism has been embedded—or, in theological terms, inculturated—among so many different peoples and groups, each of which has given the Catholic Tradition new and vital expression, what has been the effect on the theological and doctrinal understanding of that Tradition? This question has been my challenge for at least two decades.

Five centuries of evangelization and pastoral work have profoundly affected and shaped the Mexican people's religious universe, and yet that universe still seems very different from "official" Catholic doctrinal expressions and liturgical practices. Perhaps the chief reason for this disjunction is that theologians and church leaders have not consistently taken popular faith into account. Indeed, they have regarded the faith of the people mostly as superstitious or aberrant. When we look beneath the externals, however, popular Catholicism is profoundly Christian, even if it sometimes appears mixed with elements that seem unacceptable to Christianity. More importantly, this popular religion is the operative faith of the majority of Mexicans and Mexican Americans in the United States, a situation that makes our question all the more pressing: What is the relationship between their faith and "official" Catholicism?

We should not exaggerate the tension between popular and official expressions of Catholicism. There is no divorce between the two, despite the clear differences between them. Historically it is virtually impossible to claim that either popular or official Catholicism, taken as a whole, is more "Catholic," more "authentic," or more "traditional" than the other.

Worldwide Catholicism is and has always been intensely and unavoidably diverse while somehow preserving a fundamental unity. Yet if the faith of U.S. Latino/a and Latin American Catholics is to be taken seriously by a "mainstream" Catholic theology that seems today largely reflective of its European past, some important tenets of mainstream Catholic theology have to be reconsidered and possibly challenged.

In the following pages I attempt to construct a theoretical framework within which Mexican American popular Catholicism can be understood theologically. A theological understanding of the development of doctrine provides the appropriate materials for constructing such a framework. I do not presume to construct a full theory of doctrinal development. I merely want to suggest that the ordinary development of doctrine occurs in and through popular Catholicism.

The four cases of Mexican American popular religion described in this volume demonstrate aspects of the dynamics of doctrinal development. Two of the cases—the devotion to Guadalupe at San Antonio's San Fernando Cathedral and the Via Crucis celebration in Chicago's Pilsen neighborhood—are clearly instances of popular Catholicism. The other two cases incorporate religious and nonreligious beliefs and practices that some of their practitioners perceive to be beyond the borders of the Catholic Tradition.

By "Tradition" I mean an interpretation of the past, made in and for the present and in anticipation of an imagined future. Neither the present, the past, nor the future is generic, abstract, universal, or homogeneous across time and space. Rather, ideas and imaginings about past, present, and future are culture-specific; they are shaped by people who live in societies defined by innumerable variables (class- and gender-based structures, conflict, power relations, and so on) that occur in various combinations and degrees of intensity from society to society. Any sufficient understanding of "Tradition," "memory," or "the development of doctrine" must take these historical, cultural, and epistemological contexts fully into account.[2]

Tradition and Continuity

There seems to be very little in religion that does not draw continuously on the memory of those who participate in it. A philosophical and theological argument could show that our understandings of the present and future are extraordinarily dependent on our memory, because memory provides identity as well as the various contexts in which to understand and function meaningfully in the present and to project a future.

Memory is much more than the simple, willful recall of past events; it is the present interpretation of the past, present, or future through a complex interplay of recall, assumptions, and associations of past events, specific interpretations, and meanings. At times memory in this sense is willfully engaged, but it can also be operative without our explicit consent. Put more directly, memory is always and inevitably a hermeneutic for the present.

Catholicism can be understood as the beliefs and practices reflecting or embodying a specific, collective, and always contemporary Christian interpretation of the past, present, and future. In turn, these interpretive beliefs and practices, which constitute Catholicism, shape the Catholic memory—that is, they drive the complex interplay of recall, assumptions, and associations of past events, specific interpretations, and meanings that are historically distinct to this religion. In its fullness, then, Catholic Tradition encompasses beliefs, practices, and memory—it encompasses, that is, both the collective interpretation of past, present, and future that is embodied in Catholic beliefs and practices, and the ongoing dynamism of Catholic memory.

Doctrines function within Tradition as reliable—that is, trustworthy—indicators of the perceived continuity between past, present, and future. Thus doctrines serve as frameworks for believers' corporate identity and criteria for correct belief.[3] Tradition, therefore, is not merely or mainly a recall of the past or a reference to it. Rather, it is the present's interpretation of the past in reference to the future.[4] Present interests and hopes for the future drive and legitimate the complex web of recall, assumptions, and associations that we call the past.

Thus continuity in Tradition exists if and when the people believe that continuity exists. Each generation of Catholics strives to legitimate its corporate identity by recalling from the past those associations, assumptions, and interpretations that seem to authorize and authenticate the present generation's claim to and interpretation of Catholic identity.

Historically Catholic theology has privileged the associations, assumptions, and interpretations contained in three basic sources: the text and message of Scripture, writings of early Christian authors and/or doctrines and practices of the early church, and past statements or doctrinal decisions made by recognized authorities of the church, as well as theories and proposals advanced by theologians of past generations. Claims to continuity with the Catholic tradition are as strong (or weak) as their grounding in these sources. A presentation of a community's Catholic identity, in other words, is considered legitimate—that is, "traditional"—to the extent that it is grounded in these sources.

There is a fourth source missing from this list, however: the religion of the people. Popular religious belief and practice is the gauge by which doctrines or practices are most frequently judged to be in continuity with Catholic identity and Tradition.

I am not suggesting that the people's Catholicism is the only or even the best criterion. But it is the ordinary, the most customary way of judging any claim to continuity with Catholic Tradition. The other three sources, in various ways and to varying degrees, do influence the judgment of legitimacy. But they are called upon only as needed, that is, as extraordinary gauges.

The everyday faith and faith-life of Catholics[5] is the ordinary means by which Catholic Tradition is interpreted and constructed, Catholic identity shaped, and continuity with the past claimed. This popular[6] Catholicism is the ordinary means for the complex mechanism of recall, assumptions, and associations of past events, specific interpretations, and meanings that are historically distinctive to Catholicism. This ordinary, collective interpretation is Catholic Tradition. Popular Catholicism acts both as a framework for the people's corporate Catholic identity and as a criterion for correct belief and behavior, as every generation of Catholics attempts to construct that identity for itself in continuity with preceding generations of Catholics. Doctrinal development, consequently, seems to occur ordinarily within the mesh and fabric of popular Catholicism. Five elements or dimensions seem to shape the ordinary development of doctrine as this development occurs in and through popular Catholicism.

Culture

Culture is first and foremost the historically and ecologically possible means through which a people construct and unveil themselves first to themselves, and secondarily to others, as meaningfully human. In the process of unveiling us to ourselves and to others as meaningfully human, culture constructs us as meaningfully human. And, because nothing human is acultural, doctrines and their development are cultural products too.[7]

Doctrinal development is cultural because it entails a crucial human and humanizing activity: the construction, discovery, clarification, and affirmation of life's meaning and, consequently for Christians, the meaning of revelation. In theological terms, God, the source of revelation, is not bound by culture. But given that revelation exists only where and when it is received as the Word of God, culture must play an essential role in the revelatory divine-human dialogue. When revelation is received and understood as the Word of God, when it is reflected upon, and when doctrine results from that reflection, culture acts as a necessary medium. Indeed, whenever doctrine is expressed or taught, received or lived by, culture acts as the unavoidable prism.

It thus seems evident that when Mexican Americans receive, understand, and express their understanding of Christian revelation, they necessarily do so *méxicoamericanamente*. For example, if Mexican Americans are to receive, understand, and express the Holy Spirit or Mary of Nazareth, the memory and significance of Christ's redemptive death, the communio sanctorum (communion of saints), the penultimate value of death, or the importance of healing and hope, all of which are recognizable elements of the Catholic Tradition, then these are to be believed and authentically embodied in the culture(s) of Mexican American Catholics. The symbols, beliefs, and rites associated with the Virgen de Guadalupe, the Via Crucis, the Día de los Muertos, and, more remotely, visits to a curandera can be legitimate for these Christians vis-à-vis Catholic Tradition.

On the other hand, theological analysis has shown the impact of sin on culture and on the unveiling of the meaningfully human. The sin of culture is clearly exemplified in patriarchy, gender discrimination and heterosexism, racism, class injustice, domestic violence, and fascination with social aggression. It would be totally unacceptable, however, to think that sin's evident and profound mark on all things human—and hence on culture—diminishes culture's importance or necessity for revelation, doctrinal development, and the theological task. Furthermore, it is unacceptable to contend that sin, though it does affect the fabric of popular Catholicism, is a justification for contending that the people's religion cannot be the ordinary context and means through which doctrine develops. Therefore, whatever corruptions or limitations sin has wrought within popular Catholicism—and, in the case before us, Mexican American Catholic beliefs and practices—it would be unacceptable to conclude that these flaws compromise their important role as legitimate bearers of and witnesses to (Christian) revelation within their cultural milieu.

Gradualism

Ordinary doctrinal development is unforeseen, peaceful, and slow. It can occur when more dramatic circumstances require adaptations and explanations of what is deemed "traditional" or necessary in Christianity. However, it happens more frequently through and within the daily life of Christians attempting to live what they understand Christianity to be. In addition, doctrinal development is only recognized long after the fact of its occurrence. Ordinarily it occurs through popular Catholicism, its symbols and practices, and in the contexts of daily life—that is, through ritual, symbol, and aphorism. The process often acquires technical, theological expression only later—after the church's sensus fidelium has already believed, acknowledged, and accepted the developed doctrine.[8]

In their daily lives Catholics experience God, believe as Christians and practice their faith-life, and, though often unconsciously, attempt to adapt and explain better to themselves and to others what they experience, believe, and practice. Usually they do so in the context of the other doctrines of the Tradition and in a way that allows their Catholicism to be effective in their daily lives. These adaptations and explanations are themselves grounded in earlier doctrinal developments and necessarily lead to further doctrinal developments.

Popular Catholicism is not laden with theologically explicit or sophisticated doctrinal statements because, in daily life, Catholics very seldom seem to need or expect them. Nevertheless, popular Catholicism is rich in ritual and practice, in ethical expectations and counsels, in deep religious experiences, in movements toward communal solidarity, and in aphoristic statements. All of this is the preeminent stuff of everyday religion. The four cases of Mexican American popular religion presented earlier exemplify these traits. They do not trade much in philosophically sophisticated creeds and theological texts; these are not part of everyday religion.[9]

Doctrinal development, after it has occurred in and through popular Catholicism, may be "officially" recognized, accepted, and defined. Or it may be rejected, or simply ignored. In still other cases, doctrinal development is accepted indirectly and gradually, almost by default or lack of resistance by the official teaching office, or magisterium, of the church. But none of this means that the development actually occurred only after its recognition, rejection, or acceptance by the church's magisterium.[10]

Significantly, much of what Christians (Catholic, Orthodox, and Protestant) believe has never been formally decided upon or defined by church councils or synods, and it is not explicitly enunciated in the Bible. Ordinary doctrinal developments are more frequently received and accepted by catechesis, Christian piety and devotions, common magisterial teaching, and liturgy, both official and popular, and by popular practices themselves. They may one day be defined dogmatically, or they may not be so defined.

Lo Cotidiano

The Spanish term *lo cotidiano* refers to "daily life" as it actually exists and is lived. It is everyday reality, with its routines and its surprises, its mysterious depths and its pedestrian quality. Thus, it is a constitutive dimension and element of the ordinary development of doctrine, because revelation, and the beliefs and practices that evolve from it, can be engaged by humans only in actual daily life. Indeed, revelation can happen only as revelation in lo cotidiano.

As experience, lo cotidiano is not reducible to the domestic, the private, or the individual, if by these is meant a sphere somehow secondary to the most significant events and trends within a supposedly more important national or international "public" sphere. Employment and unemployment, violence and war, educational systems, famine or plenty, mass media, global economics, information systems, international and national political decisions all have a direct impact on the daily realities of individuals, families, and communities, and do in fact occur within daily life and as part of it. Indeed, it might be argued that the so-called public sphere has any real effect on people's lives only if, when, and to the degree that it affects them existentially, in daily life.

If daily relationships constitute the foundation of the totality of social relationships,[11] then it is from within daily relationships that human beings engage in the process of doctrinal development. But doctrinal development is not a sinless process, because sin affects daily relationships and daily reality as much as it affects culture.

In Chicago's Via Crucis, the sinful and the graced dimensions of lo cotidiano are explicitly brought into the celebration, serving as catalysts and context for the Pilsen residents' understanding and development of christological beliefs. The same could be said about the Guadalupan celebrations in San Antonio and about the Día de los Muertos in Los Angeles, where daily life is the catalyst as well as the context for at least some ordinary doctrinal development among the participants.

The Sensus Fidelium

The ordinary development of doctrine is guided by the sensus fidelium. The sensus fidelium is composed of "faith-full" and meaningful intuitions that make Christian people sense that something is true (or untrue) vis-à-vis the gospel, that someone is (or is not) acting in accordance with the Christian gospel, or that something important for Christianity is not being heard. This intuition in turn allows for and encourages a belief and a style of life and prayer that express and give witness to the fundamental Christian message—God as revealed in Jesus Christ.

The Catholic Tradition holds that the whole church has received the revelation of God and accepted it in faith. And, as a consequence, the whole church is charged with proclaiming, living, and transmitting the fullness of revelation. Therefore, the necessary task of expressing the contents of Tradition (which includes Scripture) is not and cannot be limited to the ordained ministers or theologians of the church. The whole church has this mission, and the Holy Spirit was promised to the whole church for this task.[12] Christian laity, consequently, are indispensable witnesses and bearers of the gospel; indeed, they are as indispensable as the magisterium. Furthermore, because the foundational origin of the sensus fidelium is God, it can be said that this "sense of the faithful" is infallible, preserved by the Spirit from error in matters necessary to revelation.[13] In other words, the "faith-full" intuition of Christian laypeople transmits the contents of Tradition and thus intuitively recognizes or "senses" the proper interpretation and application of Scripture.

The main problem with studying the sensus fidelium as a necessary component of Tradition is, precisely, its being a sense, an intuition. This sense is never discovered in a pure state. The sensus fidelium is always expressed through the symbols, language, and culture of the faithful and, therefore, is in need of intense, constant interpretive processes and methods similar to those required for the written texts of Tradition, including Scripture. Without this careful examination and interpretation of its means of expression, the true "faith-full" intuition of the Christian people could be inadequately understood or even falsified. Because of this possibility of ambiguity or error, theology and the magisterium play essential hermeneutic roles.

In order to discern and interpret the sensus fidelium it is necessary to ascertain the authenticity of the intuitions, that is, their coherence and fundamental coincidence with the other witnesses of revelation.[14] It is also important to assess the appropriateness of the expressions, that is, their validity as vehicles for the communication of revelation, while realizing that no human expression is ever totally transparent to God and the gospel. This process calls for confrontations with the criteria employed by Catholics when judging the legitimacy of claims to continuity within the Catholic Tradition.

The first of these confrontations must be with Scripture, because that which claims to be a necessary component of Catholic Tradition must prove itself to be in fundamental coherence with the Bible. Although not everything that Christians hold to be revealed is expressly stated in Scripture,[15] nothing held to be revealed can ever contradict the Bible or be incapable of showing its authentic development from a legitimate interpretation of Scripture.

The second confrontation must be with the written texts of the Tradition, which include conciliar definitions of doctrine; the teachings of early bishops, theologians, and other church writers during the first seven or eight centuries C.E.; the documents of the magisterium of the church; and the various theological traditions and authors. Down through the ages the church, contemplating divine revelation, has arrived at normative decisions on the proper understanding of some dimensions or elements of that revelation. As a consequence, all intuitions that claim to be "faith-full" must be in basic agreement, but as sensus, with those normative decisions of the church, and must also show some degree of coherence with the general doctrinal and spiritual trajectory of the history of the church.

The third confrontation must be with the historical and sociological contexts in which the "faith-full" intuitions and their means of expression appear. If a "sense" of the faith expressed variously through popular Catholicism is to be discerned as a true bearer of Tradition, it must be capable of promoting the results that Christians expect from their living of the gospel within their concrete historical and sociological contexts. In the same way, the vehicles through which the intuition of faith expresses itself must somehow be coherent with Catholicism's necessary proclamation and practice of justice, peace, liberation, and reconciliation, which are indispensable dimensions of a daily life lived according to God's will. The expressions of the sensus fidelium must facilitate and not hinder the people's participation in the building of the reign of God. This third confrontation demands an awareness of culture and of economic and political reality, as well as an awareness of the hidden class, gender, and ethnocultural biases and interests that may blind us to dimensions of revelation present precisely in the "faith-full" intuitions of the people. This third confrontation also calls us to become aware of the cultural and ideological limits and biases of the very theological tools we are employing to study the sensus fidelium.

If the infallible, "faith-full" intuitions of the Christian people can be expressed only through culturally given means, then it is possible and very likely that different Christian communities can communicate the same intuition through different cultural means. It is in this context, and as a consequence of what we have been discussing, that popular Catholicism is an authentic expression of fundamental, infallible intuitions of Christianity. Popular Catholicism is indeed a bearer of the sensus fidelium.

Limitations in the Expressions of the Sensus Fidelium

Nevertheless, the discernment of the authenticity of expressions of the sensus fidelium cannot afford to be naïve with regard to the limitations of all expressions of the sensus fidelium as transmitted in popular Catholicism.

There are those limitations, in the first place, that come from the cultural, sociopolitical, linguistic, and economic contexts in which the Christian gospel is proclaimed, understood, and lived. The "faith-full" intuitions, when expressed, will evidently employ the means made available through the people's cultural and linguistic codes. But the Christians who communicate their sense of faith will also exhibit in these expressions their experiences and social location of privilege or oppression in society. Their faith will be their response to the gospel; thus their history, their struggles, failures and victories, their social class, gender roles, and other specific markers of identity will shape their affirmations of Christian truth. The whole of their social, human reality acts as a filter of the gospel. But if the Christian people's reality is mainly a wounded and invaded context, the truth that the Spirit stirs within them will express itself in a wounded and invaded manner. It is certainly the function of the entire church to discern the truth amidst its wounded expressions. However, it is crucial that this discernment not be guided by or based on the presupposition that expressions of faith offered by the poor and marginalized are inferior to those of the intellectual, ecclesiastical, or political elites. Otherwise, the discernment would itself be vitiated.[16]

In the universe of popular Catholicism, sociohistorical and cultural reality has offered opportunities and also created limitations. The experience of poverty and injustice, for example, seems to have inclined Latino/a religious imagery to symbols and devotions that are explicitly associated with compassion and suffering, as in our four cases of Mexican American popular religion. The same can be said of the emphasis Mexican Americans (and other Latinos/as) place on the extended family and on other social networks. These have moved the people to conceive symbols and devotions that stress solidarity, community, and familylike networks with the living and the dead. Indeed, many Latinos project features of family life onto the religious realm.

The active presence of these socio-historical and cultural dimensions has created adequate vehicles for the sensus fidelium, but, when not properly understood and received, or when distorted by an unjust reality, they can also produce doctrinal exaggerations and deviations. Discernment can help avoid doctrinal deviation through the threefold confrontation with Scripture, the texts of the Tradition, and the sociohistorical context itself. And this discernment must also confront the racist, gender, or class ideologies that inevitably insinuate themselves into the theological, ecclesiastical, or pastoral judgment of those who either by training or by ecclesial function might be engaged in the discernment.

A second group of limitations confronting popular religious expressions of the sensus fidelium are those inherent in the idea and reality of the sensus itself. The sensus fidelium, strictly speaking, is not the practices or beliefs through which it makes itself known—the sensus fidelium, in other words, is not equivalent to or coextensive with popular Catholicism. It is, rather, the "faith-full" intuition of the Christian people, moved by the Spirit, that "senses," adheres to, and interprets the Word of

God. It is also clear, of course, that every intuition must be mediated and that every mediation will necessarily involve the reality of the ones experiencing the intuition. This is just as true of Latino/a popular Catholicism as it is of the expressions of all the other cultural bearers of the sensus fidelium in the church. Even if difficult to discern in actual practice, it is theoretically possible and even necessary to affirm that the "faith-full" intuitions of Christians are not coextensive with or equivalent to the expressions they employ as vehicles for the former. But what is left of the intuition after it has been distinguished from its expressions? What is an intuition without some mediation to make it understandable or, indeed, even perceivable?[17]

The act of discerning the truth that lies behind the expression can never proceed without the use of some kind of symbolic means in order to understand the truth. But can the symbol mediating the truth still be considered an intuition in the strict sense of the sensus fidelium? The seriousness of these questions should be obvious, since so many culturally given, ideologically tainted, and socially repressive mediations are considered in today's church to be vehicles of the intuitions of sensus fidelium and of many officially sanctioned doctrines and practices as well.

These limitations notwithstanding, we must recall that all bearers of the Tradition are called to participate in mutual discernment; they are all part of the church, of the communio sanctorum. If discernment is multidirectional and shared, coherence with revelation and Tradition may be established by and for each generation. In other words, although the sensus fidelium needs to be discerned by confrontations with the ecclesial magisterium, the texts of Tradition, sociocultural reality, and Scripture, all these other bearers of Tradition must themselves be discerned by the sensus fidelium. Thus, any consequent doctrinal developments are the result of these mutual discernments and not the unilateral product of the magisterium's judgment over the rest. It is the whole church that is infallible, and it is within this overall ecclesial infallibility that we must understand the infallibility of the magisterium and of the sensus fidelium. The communio sanctorum must be the context and justification of all doctrinal discernment.

Mexican Religious Traditions and the Development of Doctrine

Each of the four case studies of Mexican American religious practices suggests both the richness and the limitations of popular expressions of the sensus fidelium. Are the "faith-full" intuitions communicated through and embedded in these four particular cultural expressions of popular Catholicism coherent with Catholic Tradition?

The Guadalupe devotions at San Fernando Cathedral in San Antonio discussed by Timothy Matovina illuminate ritual as a bearer of doctrine, and thus as vehicle of the sensus fidelium. Matovina emphasizes that these rituals, which together shaped and expressed the participants' devotion, served as affirmations of human dignity against racism, bigotry, and poverty. One group, the émigrés, empowered the sense of worth of another group, the Mexican Americans, and encouraged the latter's continuing struggle for justice, even as the émigrés themselves were empowered. This case also shows how practical discernment occurred in the nexus of the laity's and the clergy's beliefs and practices, in mutual critique and affirmation. The feast of Guadalupe further empowered action in the political arena, thereby rejecting attempts to privatize religion and its existential consequences. In this instance, women exercised social leadership even within the confines of a patriarchal context.

The Via Crucis described by Karen Mary Davalos also highlights ritual as a means of affirmation and empowerment in a context of injustice. Ritual provides the setting and impetus for the people's concrete and focused critique and analysis of that injustice. Community-building and community identity are grounded in the participants' struggle to identify, publicly name, and confront, albeit symbolically, the occasions and sources of injustice. The reconfiguration of public space in the Via Crucis is a rejection of the privatization of religion which negates the potential role of religion to denounce social sin and advocate a more just social order. In Pilsen, it seems, God is not only publicly "on the side" of Pilsen's poor; God suffers "as the poor," because God is publicly poor in the Pilsen neighbors' retelling and reinterpreting of the Tradition. Therefore, something crucial about God's commitments and God's being needs to be said through and in the Via Crucis.

The celebration of the Día de los Muertos in East Los Angeles, as described by Lara Medina and Gilbert Cadena, also demonstrates the people's identification and critique of injustice. More specifically, solidarity is affirmed against the clergy's disregard or forgetfulness of this necessary Christian ecclesiological and ethical dimension. The dangerous memory of the martyrs, and of the community's "saints," further recovers the importance of the communio sanctorum. The church and Christian identity are built not on official ecclesiastical statements or good intentions, but on the people's faith, mutual empowerment, and solidarity, especially in the struggle for justice and in the unmasking of injustice, and through the preservation of the people's identity. Thus the universal church is confronted with its own sins and called to conversion.

Luis León's report on a curandera's work in East Los Angeles uncovers the community's urgent need for healing, support, and hope in the face of poverty, displacement, and exploitation. Although the curandera construes the boundaries of Catholicism loosely, it could be theologically fruitful to view her concerns and those of many of her clients from the perspective of nepantla. Here, then, cries for justice, healing, and hope can cross possible religious boundaries to be shared and become explicit within the "nepantlic" dimension of Catholic Tradition.

In these cases we are dealing with the expression of doctrines that are indispensable in and to Christianity. Often these doctrines were developed and expressed without assistance from, or even in opposition to, the opinions and convictions of the ministers and theologians of the church. The lived religion of the people demands recognition from the other bearers of the Tradition even as a mutual critique necessarily continues. Although much more would need to be said and clarified, it seems clear that, despite their acknowledged limitations, the practices and beliefs described in the case studies can serve as bearers of the sensus fidelium, and thus can be said to participate in the overall process of the ordinary development of doctrines.

Conclusion

How does doctrine ordinarily develop among Christian people? There are no historically proven or sanctioned recipes, no absolute rules in ordinary or extraordinary doctrinal development, regardless of the tendency, among some historians and theologians, to focus on the magisterium's reception or rejection of doctrines as the only important event in the process of doctrinal development.

The preceding pages have demonstrated the need for a much broader, more accurate, and more realistic approach to the study of doctrinal development. Theological study of popular Catholicism is indispensable to the study of doctrines and their development within the Catholic Tradition, and this Tradition has been profoundly affected and shaped by the people's faith and daily experience. The four cases of Mexican American religion that form the heart of this volume indicate the much broader and deeper epistemological issues we must deal with in developing a theology of doctrinal development. We can no longer—and actually never could—theologize without engaging the faith of the people, in all its complex diversity. To refuse such engagement would be to betray not only proper methodology but also, ultimately, fidelity to the gospel and to the Catholic Tradition.

Notes

Introduction

1. Alejandro García-Rivera, "Let's Capture the Hispanic Imagination," *U.S. Catholic* 57 (July 1994): 34–35.

2. The term *Mexican American* is not the only self-designation used by people of Mexican heritage born and/or living in the United States. Since the 1960s some U.S. residents of Mexican descent have rejected the term as assimilationist and instead called themselves Chicanas and Chicanos, usually as a means of expressing a strong ethnic consciousness and orientation toward social struggle and justice. Many recent Mexican arrivals call themselves *mexicanos* or simply Mexicans, while some native-born Texans of Mexican heritage call themselves Tejanos. Still others identify themselves as *mestizos* to accentuate their mixed descent from Native American and Spanish ancestors. The essays in this volume attempt to reflect the langauge and meanings the authors encountered in interviews and in primary documentary sources, respecting both the diverse terminology of individual informants and general usage in specific locales, communities, and historical eras.

3. Charles R. Morris, *American Catholic: The Saints and Sinners Who Built America's Most Powerful Church* (New York: Times Books, 1997), 431; Jay P. Dolan, *The American Catholic Experience: A History from Colonial Times to the Present* (1985; reprint, Notre Dame, Ind.: University of Notre Dame Press, 1992), 125, 417; James Hennesey, *American Catholics: A History of the Roman Catholic Community in the United States* (New York: Oxford University Press, 1981).

4. See, e.g., Michael J. Baxter, "Writing History in a World without Ends: An Evangelical Catholic Critique of United States Catholic History," *Pro Ecclesia* 5 (fall 1996): 440–69; William L. Portier, "Americanism and Inculturation, 1899–1999," *Communio* 27 (spring 2000): 139–60; Michael J. Baxter, "The Unsettling of Americanism: A Response to William Portier," *Communio* 27 (spring 2000): 161–70; Peter R. D'Agostino, "The Scalabrini Fathers, the Italian Emigrant Church, and Ethnic Nationalism in America," *Religion and American Culture* 7 (winter 1997): 121–59; idem, "Italian Ethnicity and Religious Priests in the American Church: The

Servites, 1870–1940," *Catholic Historical Review* 80 (October 1994): 714–40; idem, "The Triad of Roman Authority: Fascism, the Vatican, and Italian Religious Clergy in the Italian Emigrant Church," *Journal of American Ethnic History* 17 (spring 1998): 3–37.

5. Silvano M. Tomasi, *Piety and Power: The Role of Italian Parishes in the New York Metropolitan Area, 1880–1930* (Staten Island, N.Y.: Center for Migration Studies, 1975), 140; Dolores Liptak, *Immigrants and Their Church* (New York: Macmillan, 1989); Stephen J. Shaw, *The Catholic Parish as a Way-Station of Ethnicity and Americanization: Chicago's Germans and Italians, 1903–1939* (Brooklyn, N.Y.: Carlson, 1991); Joseph Fitzpatrick, *One Church, Many Cultures: The Challenge of Diversity* (Kansas City, Mo.: Sheed and Ward, 1987), 103–18.

6. Gilberto M. Hinojosa, "The Enduring Hispanic Faith Communities: Spanish and Texas Church Historiography," *Journal of Texas Catholic History and Culture* 1 (March 1990): 20–41; Robert E. Wright, "Local Church Emergence and Mission Decline: The Historiography of the Catholic Church in the Southwest during the Spanish and Mexican Periods," *U.S. Catholic Historian* 9 (winter / spring 1990): 27–48; Michael E. Engh, *Frontier Faiths: Church, Temple, and Synagogue in Los Angeles, 1846–1888* (Albuquerque: University of New Mexico Press, 1992); Timothy Matovina, *Tejano Religion and Ethnicity: San Antonio, 1821–1860* (Austin: University of Texas Press, 1995); Susan M. Yohn, *A Contest of Faiths: Missionary Women and Pluralism in the American Southwest* (Ithaca: Cornell University Press, 1995); Michael Charles Neri, *Hispanic Catholicism in Transitional California: The Life of José González Rubio, O.F.M. (1804–1875)* (Berkeley, Calif.: Academy of American Franciscan History, 1997).

7. Henry Granjon, *Along the Rio Grande: A Pastoral Visit to Southwest New Mexico in 1902,* ed. Michael Romero Taylor, trans. Mary W. de López (Albuquerque: University of New Mexico Press, 1986), 39; Timothy Matovina and Gerald E. Poyo, eds., *¡Presente! U.S. Latino Catholics from Colonial Origins to the Present* (Maryknoll, N.Y.: Orbis, 2000), 44–89.

8. Roberto R. Treviño, "*La fe:* Catholicism and Mexican Americans in Houston, 1911–1972" (Ph.D. diss., Stanford University, 1993), 104–7. See also Matovina, *Tejano Religion and Ethnicity,* 57–58.

9. For the argument that Mexican American customs and religious traditions (as well as those of other Latinos) will endure longer than those of European Catholic immigrants, see Matovina, *Tejano Religion and Ethnicity,* 83–93; idem, "No Melting Pot in Sight," in *Perspectivas: Hispanic Ministry,* ed. Allan Figueroa Deck, Yolanda Tarango, and Timothy Matovina (Kansas City, Mo.: Sheed and Ward, 1995), 35–39.

10. Joseph P. Chinnici and Angelyn Dries, eds., *Prayer and Practice in the American Catholic Community* (Maryknoll, N.Y.: Orbis, 2000); Joseph P. Chinnici, *Living Stones: The History and Structure of Catholic Spiritual Life in the United States* (New York: Macmillan, 1989); Timothy Kelly and Joseph Kelly, "Our Lady of Perpetual Help, Gender Roles, and the Decline of Devotional Catholicism," *Journal of Social History* 32 (fall 1998): 5–26; "Participation in Catholic Parish Life: Religious Rites and Parish Activities in the 1980s," Report no. 3 of the Notre Dame Study of Catholic Parish Life, 1989. See also the forthcoming study on Euro-American Catholic devotionalism edited by James O'Toole, which, like this volume, resulted from a project on the history of twentieth-century U.S. Catholicism sponsored by the Cushwa Center for the Study of American Catholicism at the University of Notre Dame.

11. For good summations of contemporary Mexican American ritual and devotional traditions, see Virgilio Elizondo, *Christianity and Culture: An Introduction to Pastoral Theology and Ministry for the Bicultural Community* (Huntington, Ind.: Our Sunday Visitor, 1975), 182–94; Rosa María Icaza, "Prayer, Worship, and Liturgy in a United States Hispanic Key," in *Frontiers of Hispanic Theology in the United States,* ed. Allan Figueroa Deck (Maryknoll, N.Y.: Orbis, 1992), 134–53; *Faith Expressions of Hispanics in the Southwest,* rev. ed. (San Antonio: Mexican American Cultural Center Press, 1990).

12. Vatican II, "Constitution on the Sacred Liturgy," nos. 13, 14; Juan Sosa, "Liturgical Piety or Popular Piety?" *Liturgy* 24 (November–December 1979): 8; Vatican II, "Decree on the Missionary Activity of the Church," no. 22; Rosa María Icaza, "The Cross in Mexican

Popular Piety," *Liturgy* 1, no. 1 (1981): 27–34; Arturo Pérez, *Popular Catholicism: A Hispanic Perspective* (Washington, D.C.: Pastoral Press, 1988). The sixteen documents of Vatican II are available in various English translations, including the one used here, *The Documents of Vatican II*, ed. Walter M. Abbott (New York: America Press, 1966). *Liturgy* is the journal of the Liturgical Conference in Washington, D.C.; the discrepancy in volume numbers for the two *Liturgy* articles cited in this note reflects a new format and numbering for that journal beginning in 1981.

13. For a helpful presentation of three models for Hispanic ministry prevalent among Catholic leaders in the United States, along with an insightful analysis on the strengths and weaknesses of each model, see Allan Figueroa Deck, "Models," in Deck, Tarango, and Matovina, *Perspectivas*, 1–6.

14. Terrence W. Tilley, *Inventing Catholic Tradition* (Maryknoll, N.Y.: Orbis, 2000); John E. Thiel, *Senses of Tradition: Continuity and Development in Catholic Faith* (New York: Oxford University Press, 2000). Another treatment of this topic can be found in Orlando O. Espín's forthcoming book, tentatively titled *Grounding Our Future: A Theology of Tradition and Doctrinal Change*.

15. Virgilio Elizondo's classic work on this topic is *Mestizaje: The Dialectic of Cultural Birth and the Gospel*, 3 vols. (San Antonio: Mexican American Cultural Center Press, 1978). See also idem, *Galilean Journey: The Mexican-American Promise*, rev. ed. (Maryknoll, N.Y.: Orbis, 2000); idem, *The Future Is Mestizo: Life Where Cultures Meet*, rev. ed. (Boulder: University Press of Colorado, 2000); Timothy Matovina, ed., *Beyond Borders: Writings of Virgilio Elizondo and Friends* (Maryknoll, N.Y.: Orbis, 2000). See also Allan Figueroa Deck, *The Second Wave: Hispanic Ministry and the Evangelization of Cultures* (New York: Paulist, 1989), esp. 26–53.

16. For an investigation of this topic, see Orlando O. Espín, *The Faith of the People: Theological Reflections on Popular Catholicism* (Maryknoll, N.Y.: Orbis, 1997), 133–42.

17. Elizondo, *Galilean Journey*, 23; Ricardo Ramírez, "Liturgy from the Mexican American Perspective," *Worship* 51 (July 1977): 296. Significant works on the first mestizaje, as well as the concept of mestizaje, include James Lockhart, *The Nahuas after the Conquest: A Social and Cultural History of the Indians of Central Mexico, Sixteenth through Eighteenth Centuries* (Stanford: Stanford University Press, 1992); Jorge J. E. Gracia, *Hispanic/Latino Identity: A Philosophical Perspective* (Malden, Mass.: Blackwell, 2000). See also note 15 above.

18. Rafael Pérez-Torres, *Movements in Chicano Poetry: Against Myths, against Margins* (Cambridge: Cambridge University Press, 1995), 48.

19. Gracia, *Hispanic/Latino Identity*, 111.

20. Frances E. Karttunen, *An Analytical Dictionary of Nahuatl* (Austin: University of Texas Press, 1983), s.v. See also Rudy Busto, "The Predicament of *Nepantla*: Chicano/a Religions in the 21st Century," *Perspectivas: Occasional Papers* (Hispanic Theological Initiative) 1 (fall 1998): 7–20.

21. Gloria Anzaldúa is probably the most articulate of Chicano/a writers attempting to spell out this internal psychic experience of "borderlands" as foundational to an understanding of what it means to be *mestizo/a*, or the result of worlds in collision with each other. See Gloria Anzaldúa, *Borderlands/La Frontera: The New Mestiza* (San Francisco: Spinsters / aunt lute, 1987), esp. 78–80.

22. For parallel studies among non-Latino Catholics and other religious groups in the United States, see Robert A. Orsi, *The Madonna of 115th Street: Faith and Community in Italian Harlem, 1880–1950* (New Haven: Yale University Press, 1986); idem, *Thank You, St. Jude: Women's Devotion to the Patron Saint of Hopeless Causes* (New Haven: Yale University Press, 1996); Ann Taves, *The Household of Faith: Roman Catholic Devotions in Mid-Nineteenth-Century America* (Notre Dame, Ind.: University of Notre Dame Press, 1986); Colleen McDannell, *Material Christianity: Religion and Popular Culture in America* (New Haven: Yale University Press, 1995); David D. Hall, ed., *Lived Religion in America: Toward a History of Practice* (Princeton: Princeton University Press, 1997); David Morgan, *Visual Piety: A History and Theory of Popular Religious Images* (Berkeley: University of California Press, 1998).

23. National Conference of Catholic Bishops, *The Hispanic Presence: Challenge and Commitment* (Washington, D.C.: United States Catholic Conference, 1984), no. 3. A fascinating analysis of the interrelationship between the evangelization of Hispanics and the dominant U.S. culture itself is in Deck, *Second Wave,* 92–119.

24. Although most studies of Mexican American religious traditions have tended merely to describe the traditions, several have also offered significant insights into the symbolic worldview underlying them. See, e.g., Elizondo's works, mentioned in note 15 above, and the works cited in the notes below.

25. In recent decades several books addressing these topics have had a wide readership, such as Ernest Becker, *The Denial of Death* (New York: Free Press, 1973); Robert N. Bellah, *Habits of the Heart: Individualism and Commitment in American Life* (Berkeley: University of California Press, 1985); Stephen L. Carter, *The Culture of Disbelief: How American Law and Politics Trivialize Religious Devotion* (New York: Basic Books, 1993).

26. For example, while the Via Crucis in Pilsen encompasses the promotion of social justice and social change, in parishes like St. Bridget's on Manhattan's Lower East Side some Latino parishioners have protested against their pastor's explicit connection of this religious tradition with the plight of contemporary urban Latinos. See Wayne Ashley, "The Stations of the Cross: Christ, Politics, and Processions on New York City's Lower East Side," in *Gods of the City: Religion and the American Urban Landscape,* ed. Robert A. Orsi (Bloomington: Indiana University Press, 1999), 341–66. Similarly, although in Los Angeles Chicano artists and activists revived the Día de los Muertos tradition, in places like San Antonio the tradition is carried on in a somewhat different way in Catholic parishes. See Virgilio Elizondo and Timothy Matovina, *San Fernando Cathedral: Soul of the City* (Maryknoll, N.Y.: Orbis, 1998), 107.

27. Anzaldúa, *Borderlands/La Frontera,* 79.

28. For a parallel analysis of the interrelationship between Guadalupe celebrations and social relations in a contemporary Mexican village, see Mary O'Connor, "The Virgin of Guadalupe and the Economics of Symbolic Behavior," *Journal for the Scientific Study of Religion* 28, no. 2 (1989): 105–19.

29. Ana María Díaz-Stevens, "The Saving Grace: The Matriarchal Core of Latino Catholicism," *Latino Studies Journal* 4 (September 1993): 60–78; Jeanette Rodriguez, *Our Lady of Guadalupe: Faith and Empowerment among Mexican American Women* (Austin: University of Texas Press, 1994). See also Timothy Matovina, "Our Lady of Guadalupe Celebrations in San Antonio, Texas, 1840–41," *Journal of Hispanic/Latino Theology* 1 (November 1993): 88–93; idem, "Lay Initiatives in Worship on the Texas *Frontera,* 1830–1860," *U.S. Catholic Historian* 12 (fall 1994): 107–20.

30. A parallel analysis of how Cubans and other exiles engage in religious traditions that are "translocative" and "transtemporal" is in Thomas A. Tweed, *Our Lady of the Exile: Diasporic Religion at a Cuban Catholic Shrine in Miami* (Oxford: Oxford University Press, 1997), esp. 94–95, 117, 132, 138–39.

31. See, e.g., Espín, *Faith of the People,* 100–101.

32. Our analysis here is consistent with the work of scholars such as Kay F. Turner, "Mexican American Women's Home Altars: The Art of Relationship" (Ph.D. diss., University of Texas, 1990); C. Gilbert Romero, *Hispanic Devotional Piety: Tracing the Biblical Roots* (Maryknoll, N.Y.: Orbis, 1991), 83–97; Treviño, "*La fe,*" 143–49.

Companion in Exile

1. Josefina Rodríguez, interview by author, 1 August 1995.

2. *Hoja parroquial de San Fernando* (hereafter *Hoja parroquial*), 29 November 1931, Catholic Archives at San Antonio, Chancery Office, Archdiocese of San Antonio (hereafter CASA); *Express,* 6 December 1931; "San Fernando Cathedral Chronicles, 1930–1954," 18, Archives of

Claretian Missionaries, Western Province, U.S.A., Claretian Center, Los Angeles (hereafter ACM); "Actos de la Sociedad de Vasallos de Cristo Rey de la Catedral de San Fernando," 1925–1934, 108, CASA; *Hoja parroquial,* 13 December 1931; Arthur J. Drossaerts, American Board of Catholic Missions report, 1928, CASA. See also *Hoja parroquial,* 15 and 22 November 1931, 6 December 1931; *Southern Messenger,* 3 and 10 December 1931; *Express,* 10 December 1931; *Light,* 10 December 1931; *La Prensa,* 12–14 December 1931. All translations of Spanish-language sources are my own. I gratefully acknowledge Dr. Jaime R. Vidal for checking several translations. All newspapers cited in this essay were published in San Antonio.

3. *"Cabildo* [town council] of the Villa de San Fernando and others, Statements on feast days, 12 February–6 May 1772," typescript, 5:46b, Nacogdoches Archives, Center for American History, University of Texas; Timothy Matovina, "Guadalupan Devotion in a Borderlands Community," *Journal of Hispanic/Latino Theology* 4 (August 1996): 6–26; idem, "New Frontiers of Guadalupanismo," *Journal of Hispanic/Latino Theology* 5 (August 1997): 20–36.

4. Terry G. Jordan, "A Century and a Half of Ethnic Change in Texas, 1836–1986," *Southwestern Historical Quarterly* 89 (April 1986): 392–97; Jean A. Meyer, *The Cristero Rebellion: The Mexican People between Church and State, 1926–1929,* trans. Richard Southern (Cambridge: Cambridge University Press, 1976); Francisco E. Balderrama and Raymond Rodríguez, *Decade of Betrayal: Mexican Repatriation in the 1930s* (Albuquerque: University of New Mexico Press, 1995); San Antonio Public Service Company, *Economic and Industrial Survey* (San Antonio, 1940), 167, cited in Richard A. García, *Rise of the Mexican American Middle Class: San Antonio, 1929–1941* (College Station: Texas A&M University Press, 1991), 29.

5. "Growth of the San Antonio Archdiocese: In Town Parishes by Chronology," typescript, CASA; García, *Rise of Mexican American Middle Class,* 157–58.

6. Mary of Providence Stecker, "The History of San Fernando Cathedral" (M.A. thesis, Catholic University of America, 1940), 46; "San Fernando Cathedral Census Book thru ca. 1901," CASA; "San Fernando Cathedral Annual Parish Reports," 1911–1940, CASA; *Express,* 10 December 1930, p. 6.

7. Robert E. Lucey, "Are We Good Neighbors?" opening address for the Conference on the Spanish-Speaking People of the Southwest, July 1943, Incarnate Word College, San Antonio, cited in Alonso S. Perales, *Are We Good Neighbors?* (1948; reprint, New York: Arno, 1974), 11; Gilberto M. Hinojosa, "Mexican-American Faith Communities in Texas and the Southwest," in *Mexican Americans and the Catholic Church, 1900–1965,* ed. Jay P. Dolan and Gilberto M. Hinojosa (Notre Dame, Ind.: University of Notre Dame Press, 1994), 36; John L. Davis, *San Antonio: A Historical Portrait* (Austin: Encino, 1978), 41; Charles A. Arnold, *Folklore, Manners, and Customs of the Mexicans in San Antonio, Texas* (1928; reprint, San Francisco: R and E Research Associates, 1971), 43; *La Prensa,* 4 June 1923; David A. Badillo, "Between Alienation and Ethnicity: The Evolution of Mexican-American Catholicism in San Antonio, 1910–1940," *Journal of American Ethnic History* 16 (summer 1997): 62–83; Selden C. Menefee and Orin C. Cassmore, *The Pecan Shellers of San Antonio: The Problem of Underpaid and Unemployed Mexican Labor* (Washington, D.C.: U.S. Government Printing Office, 1940), 16–19, reprinted in *Mexican Labor in the United States* (New York: Arno, 1974); Julia Kirk Blackwelder, *Women of the Depression: Caste and Culture in San Antonio, 1929–1939* (College Station: Texas A&M University Press, 1984), 139–45. The San Fernando parishioners interviewed for this study are too many to enumerate, but I would especially like to thank Mary Esther and Joe Bernal, Carmen Cedillo, Janie Dillard, Janie García, Felipa Peña, Esther Rodríguez, Gene and Sylvia Rodríguez, and Josefina Rodríguez for their generous gifts of time and insightful commentaries.

8. García, *Rise of Mexican American Middle Class,* 74–75; Davis, *San Antonio,* 36–41; William J. Knox, *The Economic Status of the Mexican American Immigrant in San Antonio, Texas* (1927; San Francisco: R and E Research Associates, 1971); "Officers of the City Government," typescript, San Antonio Public Library.

9. *La Prensa,* 28 February 1930, 6.

10. Victor S. Clark, *Mexican Labor in the United States,* Bureau of Labor Bulletin no. 78 (Washington, D.C.: Department of Commerce, 1908), reprinted in Manuel P. Servín, *An Awakened Minority: The Mexican Americans* (New York: Macmillan, 1974), 58; J. Luz Saenz, *Los Mexico-Americanos en la gran guerra y su contingente en pró de la democracia, la humanidad y la justicia* (San Antonio: Artes Gráficas, 1933), 289; Cynthia E. Orozco, "The Origins of the League of United Latin American Citizens (LULAC) and the Mexican American Civil Rights Movement in Texas with an Analysis of Women's Political Participation in a Gendered Context, 1910–1929" (Ph.D. diss., University of California at Los Angeles, 1992); Julie Leininger Pycior, "*La Raza* Organizes: Mexican American Life in San Antonio, 1915–1930, as Reflected in *Mutualista* Activities" (Ph.D. diss., University of Notre Dame, 1979), 172–86; García, *Rise of Mexican American Middle Class,* 253–99.

11. *La Prenza,* 26 November 1916 and 16 February 1930; *El Imparcial de Texas,* 23 December 1920; Hermino Ríos and Guadalupe Castillo, "Toward a True Chicano Bibliography: Mexican-American Newspapers, 1848–1942," *El Grito: A Journal of Contemporary Mexican-American Thought* 3 (summer 1970): 23–24; Hermino Ríos, "Toward a True Chicano Bibliography: Part II," ibid., 5 (summer 1972): 47; Nora Ríos-McMillan, "A Biography of a Man and His Newspaper," *Americas Review* 17 (fall/winter 1989): 139; Leininger Pycior, "*La Raza* Organizes," 96–104; Arnold, *Folklore, Manners, and Customs,* 7–10; Kathleen May Gonzalas, *The Mexican Family in San Antonio, Texas* (1928; San Francisco: R and E Research Associates, 1971), 1–2.

12. Manuel Gamio, *Mexican Immigration to the United States: A Study of Human Migration and Adjustment* (1930; reprint, New York: Arno, 1969), 128–30; idem, *The Mexican Immigrant: His Life-Story* (1931; reprint, New York: Arno, 1969); David G. Gutiérrez, *Walls and Mirrors: Mexican Americans, Mexican Immigrants, and the Politics of Ethnicity* (Berkeley: University of California Press, 1995), esp. 56–68.

13. *La Prensa,* 13 February 1933; Gamio, *Mexican Immigration,* 128; Leininger Pycior, "*La Raza* Organizes," esp. 85–89, 223; Arnold, *Folklore, Manners, and Customs,* 19–21.

14. Ríos-McMillan, "Biography of a Man and His Newspaper"; Federico Allen Hinojosa, *El México de Afuera y su reintegración a la patria* (San Antonio: Artes Gráficas, 1940); Roberto R. Treviño, "*Prensa y Patria:* The Spanish-Language Press and the Biculturation of the Tejano Middle Class, 1920–1940," *Western Historical Quarterly* 22 (November 1991): 451–72. I am grateful to Juanita Luna Lawhn, whose extensive research and insightful analysis helped me understand the function and significance of *La Prensa.* The Ríos-McMillan article was one of several on *La Prensa* published in *Americas Review* 17 (fall/winter 1989). A copy of the Hinojosa book is available at the Nettie Lee Benson Latin American Collection, University of Texas, Austin.

15. Arthur J. Drossaerts, pastoral letter, 31 January 1936, CASA; Juanita Luna Lawhn, "Victorian Attitudes Affecting the Mexican Woman Writing in *La Prensa* during the Early 1900s and the Chicana of the 1980s," in *Missions in Conflict: Essays on U.S.-Mexican Relations and Chicano Culture,* ed. Renate von Bardeleben, Dietrich Briesemeister, and Juan Bruce-Novoa (Tübingen: Narr, 1986), 65–71; idem, "*El Regidor* and *La Prensa:* Impediments to Women's Self-Definition," in *Third Woman: The Sexuality of Latinas,* ed. Norma Alarcón, Ana Castillo, and Cherríe Moraga (Berkeley, Calif: Third Woman Press, 1989), 134–42; Gamio, *Mexican Immigrant,* 235; Gonzalas, *Mexican Family,* 37–39; Vicki L. Ruiz, "'Star Struck': Acculturation, Adolescence, and Mexican American Women, 1920–1950," in *Small Worlds: Children and Adolescents in America, 1850–1950,* ed. Elliott West and Paula Petrik (Lawrence: University Press of Kansas, 1992), 61–80; idem, *From Out of the Shadows: Mexican Women in Twentieth-Century America* (Oxford: Oxford University Press, 1998).

16. "San Fernando Cathedral Chronicles, 1914–1930," 12; Hinojosa, "Mexican-American Faith Communities," 58; *Anales de la Congregación de Misioneros Hijos del Inmaculado Corazón de Maria* (hereafter *Anales*), 1917–1918, 185, ACM. Exiled women religious also served in San

Antonio during these decades, but they were not prominent in the San Fernando congregation.

17. Cristóbal Fernández, *Compendio histórico de la Congregación de los Hijos del Inmaculado Corazón de María,* vol. 2 (Madrid: Editorial Coculsa, 1967), 587–615; "Historia de la Catedral de San Fernando," manuscript, c. 1945, ACM. This unsigned manuscript was written by a Claretian.

18. *Anales,* 1909–1910, 249; R[afael] Serrano, "Missionary Work among the Mexicans," *Southern Messenger,* 30 June 1910; *Anales,* 1905–06, 601–2; Stecker, "History of San Fernando Cathedral," 57–58; *Southern Messenger,* 7 and 14 December 1911; "San Fernando Cathedral Chronicles, 1914–1930," 54, 113, 291; ibid., "1930–1954," 7–41, 81; *Hoja parroquial,* 8 June 1930, 25 January, 22 February, 8, 15, and 22 March, 5 and 12 April, 8 and 29 November, and 6 December 1931; "Historia de la Catedral," 52–53. Numerous reports of Claretian preaching and leadership in devotional services can be found in the *Anales* and in the "San Fernando Cathedral Chronicles." For interviews of today's older San Fernando parishioners, see note 7.

19. *Hoja parroquial,* 8 June 1930, 4, 11, and 18 October and 8 November 1931; "Actos de la Sociedad de Vasallos," 1925–1934, 103–9; "San Fernando Cathedral Chronicles, 1914–1930," 291; ibid., "1930–1954," 17, 20.

20. *Hoja parroquial,* 19 April 1931; "San Fernando Cathedral Chronicles, 1930–1954," 18, 41; *Hoja parroquial,* 12 April–24 May and 15 November–13 December 1931; *Southern Messenger,* 3 December 1931; *Express,* 6 December 1931.

21. Edmundo Rodríguez, "The Hispanic Community and Church Movements: Schools of Leadership," in *Hispanic Catholic Culture in the U.S.: Issues and Concerns,* ed. Jay P. Dolan and Allan Figueroa Deck (Notre Dame, Ind.: University of Notre Dame Press, 1994), 209, 210; *La Fe Católica,* 27 March 1897–4 August 1900, Center for American History, University of Texas, Austin; *Hoja parroquial,* 5 January–28 December 1930.

22. *Anales,* 1913–14, 562; "Actos de la Sociedad de Vasallos," 1925–1934, 24; "Actos de la Sociedad de Vasallas de Cristo Rey de la Catedral de San Fernando," 1926–1933, 9. Numerous entries in the "San Fernando Cathedral Chronicles" for 1914–1954, *Hoja parroquial,* and the minutes of Vasallos and Vasallas reflect Claretian efforts to support parish associations. I am grateful to Josefina Rodríguez, a member of the Vasallas for over five decades, for lending me the 1926–1933 minutes of the women's section and various annual reports. At her request, these documents will be housed in the special collections at Our Lady of the Lake University, San Antonio.

23. "Actos de la Sociedad de Vasallos," 1925–1934, 1, 33, 2–3, 6, 20, 51; ibid., 1940–1945, 1–21; "Actos de la Sociedad de Vasallas," 1926–1933; "San Fernando Cathedral Chronicles, 1914–1930," 165–300; ibid., "1930–1954," 1–118; *Hoja parroquial,* 1930–1931. See also *Reglamento de la Asociación Nacional de los Vasallos de Cristo Rey,* 7, CASA, whose cover has a photograph of the Vasallos member medallion.

24. *Hoja parroquial,* 11 May and 23 November 1930, 15 November 1931; *La Prensa,* 11 December 1923; "San Fernando Cathedral Annual Parish Reports," 1911–1940. For the religious and social activities of the Hijas, see "San Fernando Cathedral Chronicles, 1914–1930"; ibid., "1930–1954," 1–118; *Hoja parroquial,* 1930–1931; and various newspaper reports, e.g., *Southern Messenger,* 6 December 1917, 15 December 1921, 5 December 1929, 4 December 1930, 5 December 1940; *La Prensa,* 9 December 1923.

25. Yolanda Tarango, "The Hispanic Woman and Her Role in the Church," *New Theology Review* 3 (November 1990): 58; Hinojosa, "Mexican-American Faith Communities," 62.

26. "Actos de la Sociedad de Vasallos," 1925–1934, 47, 49, 53–55.

27. *Hoja parroquial,* January–December 1930; "San Fernando Cathedral Chronicles, 1914–1930," 282–300; ibid., "1930–1954," 3–6; "Actos de la Sociedad de Vasallos," 1925–1934, 80–95; "Actos de la Sociedad de Vasallas," 1926–1933, 81–104 (from loose pages preserved in an envelope). For outdoor processions to celebrate el Santo Entierro, first communion rites,

and Christ the King, see, e.g., "San Fernando Cathedral Chronicles, 1930–1954," 52; *Hoja Parroquial,* 18 May and 19 and 26 October 1930. Reports of public Guadalupe processions are in note 28.

28. *Light,* 11 December 1905, 12 December 1910, 12 December 1914, 9 and 13 December 1916, 10 December 1931, 12 December 1933; *Southern Messenger,* 19 December 1907, 15 December 1910, 7 December 1911, 17 December 1914, 14 December 1916, 6 December 1917, 15 December 1921, 5 December 1929, 11 December 1930, 3 and 10 December 1931, 8 December 1932, 7 and 21 December 1933; *La Prensa,* 13 December 1914, 12 December 1915, 13 December 1916, 12 December 1923, 12 and 13 December 1926, 11 December 1927, 12 December 1928–1930, 12–15 December 1931, 11 December 1932, 10, 11, and 13 December 1933, 12 and 13 December 1934, 12 December 1935, 12 December 1936; *Express,* 13 December 1914, 11 December 1915, 13 December 1921, 11 December 1928, 10 December 1930, 6 and 10 December 1931, 10 December 1932, 10 December 1933, 11 December 1940; *El Regidor,* 15 December 1915; *Anales,* 1917–1918, 182–183, 185, 190; *Hoja parroquial,* 7 December 1930, 15, 22, and 29 November and 6 and 13 December 1931; poster announcing "Solemne Triduo a Nuestra Madre Santísima de Guadalupe en la Catedral de San Fernando," 1933, Catholic Archives of Texas, Austin. See also annual December listings in "San Fernando Cathedral Chronicles, 1914–1930"; ibid., "1930–1954"; "Actos de la Sociedad de Vasallos," 1925–1934; ibid., 1940–1945; "Actos de la Sociedad de Vasallas," 1926–1933.

29. *La Prensa,* 10 October 1920, 12 December 1924, 1925, 1929, 1931, 1933; *Magazín de la Prensa,* 13 December 1931.

30. *La Prensa,* 12 December 1916; *Light,* 12 December 1914; *La Prensa,* 12 December 1934; *Hoja Parroquial,* 13 December 1931; *La Prensa,* 14 December 1919, 11 December 1921, 12 December 1925, 13 December 1926, 12 December 1928, 13 December 1930, 11 December 1932, 13 December 1934, 12 December 1937; *Express,* 10 December 1930.

31. *La Prensa,* 17 October 1920, 13 December 1934, 13 December 1916.

32. Juan Bruce-Novoa, "*La Prensa* and the Chicano Community," *Americas Review* 17 (fall/winter 1989): 154; Hinojosa, *El México de Afuera,* 9–10; *La Prensa,* 13 December 1914.

33. Matovina, "Guadalupan Devotion in a Borderlands Community," 13–16.

34. *La Prensa,* 12 December 1934, 12 December 1929, 17 October 1920, 12 December 1930, and 13 December 1933.

35. *La Prensa,* 12 December 1924 and 1925.

36. "San Fernando Cathedral Chronicles, 1914–1930," 186–87.

37. Luna Lawhn, "Victorian Attitudes Affecting Mexican Woman Writing," 66–67; Elizabeth A. Johnson, "The Marian Tradition and the Reality of Women," *Horizons* 12 (spring 1985): 117 (quotation), 116–35; Elizabeth A. Johnson, "Mary and the Female Face of God," *Theological Studies* 50 (September 1989): 500–526; *La Prensa,* 11 December 1932. Jovita González also published a Guadalupe article in *La Prensa* (12 December 1933, p. 4), but it is a short summary of the traditional Guadalupe apparition narrative and does not relate any of her own reflections.

38. *Light,* 13 December 1916; Gonzalas, *Mexican Family,* 16–17; *La Prensa,* 12 December 1925 and 1935.

39. Arnold, *Folklore, Manners, and Customs,* 21, 22–24; *El Imparcial de Texas,* 19 December 1918; devotional books and pamphlets, Rare Book Collection, item nos. 129–36 (all in one envelope), CASA.

40. *Hoja parroquial,* 29 November and 13 December 1931.

41. Patti Elizondo, "The Serenata Guadalupana Experience," typescript, December 1994.

"The Real Way of Praying"

I am thankful to the following people for help in this research: Chuck Dahm for his encouragement; Julie A. Satzik, at the Archdiocese of Chicago's Joseph Cardinal Bernardin

Archives and Records Center, who helped me locate some obscure items; Karen Brodkin, Monica Russel y Rodriguez, and Marie Pitti, who read earlier versions of this essay; Dolores Delgado Bernal, Rusty Barceló, and the other participants in the Mujeres Activas en Letras y Cambio Social (MALCS) 1999 Summer Institute; the audience of anthropologists at the American Ethnological Society annual meeting of 2000 and at University of California, Irvine, who provided valuable feedback; Heather O. Leider and Luz Vera for transcription; Jorge L. Fajardo for inspiring the opening of this essay; and John Cinnamon and the participants in the Pacific Lutheran University Anthropology Lecture Series. I also acknowledge the material support of David and Alice and the Mexican Fine Arts Center Museum for giving my family and me a place to stay while I conducted research in 1998, and Loyola Marymount University for summer grants that year. I am especially grateful to Felix Just for his insight and basic tutorials in theology. Finally, I acknowledge David Gaylord for his artistic metaphors, which make the narrative sing.

1. Lately I have been very concerned about my unintentional reproductions of master narratives of Mexicanos and Chicanos. My overarching aim is to contribute to a decolonial social science based on human dignity. In this opening I experiment with another style that hopefully does not echo the aura of exoticism and foreignness found in some ethnographic texts. The passage is from a conversation with a former student who had participated in a Via Crucis in Los Angeles. It echoed much of what I heard in Chicago, and I have edited the story to convey more easily the fluidity with which his memory moved from past to present, from spiritual procession to performance, and from representation to incarnation.

2. See also Renato Rosaldo, *Culture and Truth: The Remaking of Social Analysis* (Boston: Beacon Press, 1989); José E. Limón, *American Encounters: Greater Mexico, the United States, and the Erotics of Culture* (Boston: Beacon Press, 1998).

3. This essay draws on ethnographic research conducted in Chicago from 1989 through 1998. During the most intensive period of fieldwork (May 1990–November 1992), more than forty Mexicanas invited me into their lives, sharing their stories of immigration, employment, family, and faith. I also followed them to a variety of devotional practices inside and outside of the Catholic Church, including the Via Crucis. Follow-up trips in 1994, 1996, and 1998 allowed me to maintain relationships in Chicago, observe the Good Friday commemoration, and meet new people through family and parish networks. In the summer of 1998 I interviewed the core coordinators of the Via Crucis, the priests and nuns who assisted them, and an additional handful of people who participate annually in the event. This methodology encouraged me to use their experience and memories as my guide when I consulted historical material to develop an understanding of Chicago's past, the origins of the event, immigration to the Midwest, and urban planning. Robert H. Stark's dissertation, documenting the first Via Crucis, was particularly useful. See Robert H. Stark, "Religious Ritual and Class Formation: The Story of Pilsen, St. Vitus Parish, and the 1977 *Via Crucis*" (Ph.D. diss., University of Chicago, 1981). The Archdiocese of Chicago's Joseph Cardinal Bernardin Archives and Records Center (hereafter AAC) provided additional information about the first Way of the Cross.

4. See Akhil Gupta and James Ferguson, "Beyond 'Culture': Space, Identity, and the Politics of Difference," *Cultural Anthropology* 7, no. 1 (February 1992): 6–23.

5. Paul S. Taylor, *Mexican Labor in the United States: Chicago and the Calumet Region* (Berkeley: University of California Press, 1932).

6. Juan R. García, *Mexicans in the Midwest, 1900–1932* (Tucson: University of Arizona Press, 1996), 234.

7. Ibid., 223–24, 238–39; Mark Reisler, *By the Sweat of Their Brow: Mexican Immigrant Labor in the United States, 1900–1940* (Westport, Conn.: Greenwood Press, 1976), 228.

8. Louise Año Nuevo Kerr, "The Chicano Experience in Chicago: 1920–1970" (Ph.D. diss., University of Illinois at Chicago, 1976), 8; Gary Orfield and Ricardo M. Tostado, eds., *Latinos in Metropolitan Chicago: A Study of Housing and Employment* (Chicago: Latino Institute, 1983), 51.

9. Felix Padilla, *Latino Ethnic Consciousness* (Notre Dame, Ind.: University of Notre Dame Press, 1985).

10. Chicago Fact Book Consortium, *Local Community Fact Book: Chicago Metropolitan Area Based on the 1970 and 1980 Censuses* (Chicago: Chicago Review Press, 1984), 75–79.

11. Louise Año Nuevo Kerr, "Chicano Settlements in Chicago: A Brief History," *Journal of Ethnic Studies* 2, no. 1 (1975): 29.

12. Ruth Horowitz, *Honor and the American Dream: Culture and Identity in a Chicano Community* (New Brunswick, N.J.: Rutgers University Press, 1983), 49.

13. Historical information in this section is from St. Vitus Administrative Files, 1977–1991, box BB 10044.07, AAC; Parish Bulletins Files, box HH 10715.04, AAC.

14. See Dorothy Collin, "Christmas, Coffins, Tears in Pilsen after Fire Tragedy," *Chicago Tribune*, 27 December 1976.

15. Stark, "Religious Ritual," 196.

16. Elaine Markoutsas, "Two Neighborhoods Mourn Fire Victims," *Chicago Tribune*, 4 January 1977.

17. Dominic A. Pacyga and Ellen Skerrett, *Chicago, City of Neighborhoods: Histories and Tours* (Chicago: Loyola University Press, 1986), 6; Gregory D. Squires, Larry Bennett, Kathleen McCourt, and Philip Nyden, *Chicago: Race, Class, and the Response to Urban Decline* (Philadelphia: Temple University Press, 1987), 99.

18. All names used are pseudonyms. This practice brings complications with it. Although it protects the identity of the people who participated in the research, as professional ethics require, it also limits the efforts of historians. More important, it unwittingly contributes to a colonial social science, in which the subjects of anthropology remain anonymous objects, while the author does not.

19. Claudia Aguirre, interview by author, 31 July 1998. The responses of all those interviewed have been modified for the sake of clarity.

20. The event is no longer the primary responsibility of one parish. The following parishes have been involved: St. Vitus (closed in 1990), Providence of God, St. Pius V, St. Procopius, St. Ann, St. Adalbert, Holy Trinity, St. Paul, St. Michael, and, sporadically, St. Francis of Assisi. Sharing administrative, budgetary, and planning decisions, generally eight parishes send two representatives apiece to sit on the core committee, which in turn manages the media; obtains a parade license; coordinates with the police, sanitation, and parks departments; selects the participants; invites volunteers for crowd control; sews the costumes; determines the theme for the event; writes reflections for each station; and determines the guidelines by which participants are chosen. The core group divides the responsibilities and decision-making power among the parishes, so that each controls a part of the Passion story (usually two stations), the reflections and markers (altars and crosses) for their stations, and the selection of participants and guards. However, the parishes do not appear to have equal authority over the event, since a few have permanent control of the more significant roles. For example, Holy Trinity selects two apostles, Veronica, the drummer, three Roman soldiers, and ten guards; St. Procopius selects Mary, Simon of Cirene, the Roman centurion, two soldiers, and ten guards; and St. Michael selects the two thieves, two soldiers, and ten guards. For the role of Jesus, the parishes use a rotating lottery system.

21. Stark, "Religious Ritual," 308.

22. Pacyga and Skerrett, *Chicago, City of Neighborhoods*, 258.

23. Although conflict is certainly one of the dynamics of the core committee, so is cohesion. Laughing in seriousness and in jest, several coordinators told me that it takes a "miracle" each year to bring together eight parishes to organize the event. Through consensus decision-making, the coordinators resolve their different interpretations of Scripture, the use of commentary or teachings based on the Bible, and incorporation of the non-Spanish-speaking observers. Time, as one coordinator told me, also served to improve solidarity, and the shared commitment to the event is enough for them to put aside their differences.

This belief in the Via Crucis itself as a force that creates unity has historical precedent. In 1977 St. Vitus parishioners believed that the Via Crucis would help reconcile the bitter disagreement between Pilsen Neighbors Community Council and Casa Aztlán. The competing views on a bilingual/bicultural principal for the new Benito Juarez High School led to a physical fight and continuing tensions between the leaders of the two organizations. During the procession the narrator made several references to solidarity and unity, and one observer noted that leaders from Pilsen Neighbors and Casa Aztlán were seen walking side by side (Stark, "Religious Ritual," 283). The call to unity continues to be a part of the reflections, and observers consistently claim that the Via Crucis is a symbol of unity and solidarity within Pilsen and in the Mexicano population in general. Many participants and observers claim that the Via Crucis helps the community to sustain that solidarity throughout the year.

24. "Yo tengo un mural. . . ¿sabe lo que es mural? Es un *picture* donde va identificando como va a caminar. Primera estación, segunda estación, tercera estación. . . . Cada estación tiene un mural. Y de allí el mural y luego la escritura, un mural y lo escritura, otra vez. . . . Cinco años para atrás, le han ido modernizando y han dejado escrituras de lo sagrado. Han metido otras cosas. Muchos estamos de acuerdo; muchos no estamos de acuerdo." Antonio Covarrubias, interview by author, 17 July 1998.

25. Information in this section is based on an open-ended interview on 22 July 1998 with three women, each of whom had represented the women of Jerusalem on several occasions. The eldest woman, approximately seventy years old, had participated in the Via Crucis three times and had observed the event since its inception. Another woman, approximately forty years old, had participated six times. The third woman, also in her forties, was a member of the coordinating committee and had walked 18th Street as a woman of Jerusalem a few times. Additional information comes from ongoing conversations with a few people I have known since 1989, interviews with members of the core committee who had represented Mary, and interviews available in the public record.

26. Quoted in Constanza Montaña, "Passion Play Unites Pilsen: Way of Cross Is a Community Tradition," *Chicago Tribune,* 26 March 1991.

27. Karen Mary Davalos, "*La Quinceañera:* Making Gender and Ethnic Identities," *Frontiers: A Journal of Women Studies* 16, no. 2/3 (1996): 101–27.

28. A police escort and a parade permit stop all automotive traffic. Observers of the first Via Crucis recall the inversion that occurred in 1977, when people took control of the procession away from the police and forced all traffic on Racine Avenue (or Ashland Avenue, depending on the version) to stop, including a Chicago Transit Authority (CTA) bus. Intentionally or otherwise, this action itself recalled another in 1972, when the St. Vitus congregation had stopped two CTA buses at the corner of 18th Street and Ashland as part of a campaign demanding more CTA jobs for Latinos. The protest erupted into a riot that resulted in thirty-three arrests and fourteen injuries. See Stark, "Religious Ritual," 177, 252, 302.

29. This interpretation is also found in Stark, "Religious Ritual," 1: "The fifth and final goal [of the St. Vitus Pastoral Team] was to prepare a *Via Crucis* that would be a representation of an historical yet transcendent event, but also an event that is happening daily in our community; Christ abandoned, Christ undocumented, Christ sick, Christ unemployed, Christ imprisoned. We wish to say through the Way of the Cross that Jesus Christ is alive and suffering in our city." The connection between Christ's presence and the daily conditions of Pilsen was also articulated in 1998 by the core coordinators and participants whom I interviewed.

30. Gary Rivlin, "Who Killed Rudy Lozano?" *Chicago Reader* 14, no. 30 (26 April 1985).

31. Quoted in Teresa Puente, "Pilsen Will Take a Walk in Jesus' Footsteps: Road to Crucifixion to be Re-enacted in Living Way of Cross," *Chicago Tribune,* 14 April 1995.

32. Kay F. Turner, "Home Altars and the Art of Devotion," in *Chicano Expressions: A New View in American Art,* exhibition catalog, project director Inverna Lockpez (New York: INTAR Latin American Gallery, 1986), 41.

33. Kay F. Turner, "Mexican American Home Altars: Towards Their Interpretation," *Aztlán* 13 (spring/fall 1982): 309–26.

34. Jorge Durand and D. S. Massey, *Miracles on the Border: Retablos of Mexican Migrants to the United States* (Tucson: University of Arizona Press, 1995).

35. Turner, "Home Altars," 41.

36. "History of the Archdiocese," Parishes Collection, New World Publications Archives, AAC. See also David A. Badillo, "The Catholic Church and the Making of Mexican-American Parish Communities in the Midwest," in *Mexican Americans and the Catholic Church, 1900–1965*, ed. Jay P. Dolan and Gilberto M. Hinojosa (Notre Dame, Ind.: University of Notre Dame Press, 1994), 237–308.

37. Formerly a butcher shop, Our Lady of Guadalupe Chapel opened in March 1941 as a mission and social center to serve the growing Mexican population of the West Side. Information in this section is based on interviews conducted from 1990 through 1992 with long-time residents and parishioners of the Immaculate Heart of Mary parish. See also Our Lady of Guadalupe Parish Folder, New World Publications Archives, AAC.

38. Antonio Covarrubias, interview by author, 17 July 1998.

39. Patricia Luz, interview by author, 27 July 1998. Like the young man at the beginning of this essay, Patricia spoke with a temporal continuum—"It happened and it's happening now"—that equates Mary in her sorrow with contemporary women who weep for their children.

40. Jorge Leyba, interview by author, 24 July 1998.

41. Aguirre, interview.

42. Dolores Yáñez, interview by author, 20 July 1998.

43. Dolores Yáñez, interview by author, 10 July 1998.

44. Yáñez, interview, 10 July 1998.

45. Chicago Fact Book Consortium, *Local Community Fact Book*, 86; Charles Bowden and Lew Kreinberg, *Street Signs Chicago: Neighborhood and Other Illusions of Big-City Life* (Chicago: Chicago Review Press, 1981).

46. Chicago Fact Book Consortium, *Local Community Fact Book*, 86.

47. Luz, interviews by author, 21 and 27 July 1998.

48. Barbara Hooper, "Split at the Roots: A Critique of the Philosophical and Political Sources of Modern Planning Doctrine," *Frontiers: A Journal of Women's Studies* 13, no. 1 (1992): 45–80.

49. Helán Page and R. Brooke Thomas, "White Public Space and the Construction of White Privilege in U.S. Health Care: Fresh Concepts and a New Model of Analysis," *Medical Anthropology Quarterly* 8, no. 1 (March 1994): 111; George Lipsitz, *The Possessive Investment in Whiteness: How White People Profit from Identity Politics* (Philadelphia: Temple University Press, 1998), vii, 3.

50. Some scholars view discussions of Mexicans and race as a useless fabrication, as if this concept applied only to African Americans. Following the work of critical race theorists, I take the view that Mexicans have been racialized as a matter of social inequality and subordination. See Martha Menchaca, "Chicano Indianism: A Historical Account of Racial Repression in the United States," *American Ethnologist* 20, no. 3 (1993): 583–603.

51. On "Mock Spanish" see Jane H. Hill, "Language, Race, and White Public Space," *American Anthropologist* 100, no. 3 (1998): 680. Advertisements for beer and tequila consistently promote Mock Spanish by anglicizing common phrases and expressions, such as *la vida loca*.

52. See, for example, Gloria Anzaldúa, *Borderlands/La Frontera: The New Mestiza* (San Francisco: Spinsters/aunt lute, 1987); José E. Limón, *Dancing with the Devil: Society and Cultural Poetics in Mexican-American South Texas* (Madison: University of Wisconsin Press, 1994); Ralph Cintrón, *Angels' Town: Chero Ways, Gang Life, and the Rhetorics of the Everyday* (Boston: Beacon Press, 1997).

53. The hill has been a problem for the city for some time. According to Stark, "the small knoll is actually the remains of a controversial landfill that covered up a large hole in the ground left from the days when a rock quarry was located there. The landfill failed to sink completely as the city has promised"; "Religious Ritual," 299.

Días de los Muertos

Epigraph: Participant in Días de los Muertos, 1 November 1998, Self Help Graphics, Los Angeles (SHG).

1. "Celebrate Día de los Muertos All Month Long," *BOCA* 1, no. 3 (October–November 1998): 6.

2. Amalia Mesa-Baines, "Curatorial Statement," in *Ceremony of Spirit: Nature and Memory in Contemporary Latino Art* (San Francisco: The Mexican Museum, 1993), 9.

3. Tomás Benitez, interview by authors, 12 January 1999.

4. Fray Bernardino de Sahagún, *Historia general de las cosas de la Nueva España,* vol. 2 (Mexico City: Porrúa, 1969); Diego Durán, *Historia de las Indias de Nueva España e Islas de la Tierra Firme,* vol. 1 (Mexico City: Porrúa, 1969). See also Juanita Garcíagodoy, *Digging the Days of the Dead: A Reading of Mexico's Días de Muertos* (Niwot: University Press of Colorado, 1998), 110–18; Susan Shumate Morrison, "Mexico's Day of the Dead in San Francisco, California: A Study of Continuity and Change in a Popular Religious Festival" (Ph.D. diss., Graduate Theological Union, Berkeley, 1992), 130–41.

5. Hugo G. Nutini, "Pre-Hispanic Component of the Syncretic Cult of the Dead," *Ethnology* 27 (January 1988): 57–78.

6. Garcíagodoy, *Digging the Days of the Dead,* 130.

7. Morrison, "Mexico's Day of the Dead," 156–63.

8. Judith Strupp Green, "The Days of the Dead in Oaxaca, Mexico: A Historical Inquiry," in *Death and Dying: Views from Many Cultures,* ed. Richard A. Kalish (Farmingdale, N.Y.: Baywood, 1980), 65–66.

9. For a further discussion of this process see J. Jorge Klor de Alva, "Aztec Spirituality and Nahuatized Christianity," in *South and Meso-American Native Spirituality,* ed. Gary H. Gossen and Miguel León-Portillo (New York: Crossroad, 1993), 173–97.

10. Elizabeth Carmichael Nutini and Chloe Sayer, *The Skeleton at the Feast: The Day of the Dead in Mexico* (Austin: University of Texas Press, 1992).

11. Sybil Venegas, "Day of the Dead in Aztlán: Chicano Variations on the Theme of Life, Death and Self Preservation" (M.A. thesis, University of California at Los Angeles, 1995), 18.

12. Linda Vallejo, interview by Lara Medina, December 1998.

13. Sybil Venegas, "The Day of the Dead in Los Angeles," flyer from the Los Angeles Photography Center, 1990.

14. Information supplied by Father Gary Riebe-Estrella, October 1999.

15. Sister Karen died in 1997 from heart failure. Her photograph occupied the central place on the altar painted on the portable canvas mural for the ritual celebration at Self Help Graphics in 1998.

16. We believe that Amalia Mesa-Baines, artist and scholar, first used this term for Días de los Muertos. See her *Ceremony of Memory* (Santa Fe: Center for Contemporary Arts of Santa Fe, 1988).

17. Amalia Mesa-Baines, "ALTARMAKERS: The Historic Mediators," in *Offerings: The Altar Show* (Venice, Calif.: Social and Public Arts Resource Center, 1984), 5.

18. Ofelia Esparza, interview by authors, 13 September 1999.

19. "Self Help Graphics Presents Day of the Dead / Dia de los Muertos," program, 1 November 1998, p. 2, SHG.

20. Venegas, "Day of the Dead in Aztlán," 4.

21. We are thankful to Davíd Carrasco for talking with us about the continuity between these ancient and contemporary practices, as well as the political implications of celebrating Días de los Muertos in the United States. For further exploration of these Indigenous Mesoamerican practices see Alfredo López Austin, *Tamoanchan, Tlalocan: Places of Mist* (Niwot: University Press of Colorado, 1997).

22. Mesa-Baines, "Curatorial Statement," 9.

23. Father Greg Baumann, interview by authors, Dolores Mission parish, 12 November 1998.

24. Laura Pérez, "Spirit Glyphs: Reimagining Art and Artist in the Work of Chicana *Tlamatinime*," *Modern Fiction Studies* 44, no. 1 (spring 1998): 43.

25. For further discussion on the limitations of syncretism, see Anthony Stevens-Arroyo and Andrés Pérez y Mena, eds., *Enigmatic Powers: Syncretism with African and Indigenous Peoples' Religions among Latinos,* Program for the Analysis of Religion Among Latinas/os, vol. 3 (New York: Bildner Center, 1995).

26. Miguel León-Portillo, *Endangered Cultures* (Dallas: Southern Methodist University Press, 1990), 10.

27. See Gloria Anzaldúa, *Borderlands/La Frontera: The New Mestiza* (San Francisco: Spinsters / aunt lute, 1987), for a seminal contemporary examination of *nepantla*. See also works by Chicana writers and artists, including Norma Alarcón, Santa Barraza, Ana Castillo, Yreina Cervantez, Sandra Cisneros, Ester Hernandez, Amalia Mesa-Baines, and Cherríe Moraga, among many others who have reimagined the possibilities of nepantla. See also Rudy Busto, "The Predicament of *Nepantla*: Chicano/a Religions into the 21st Century," *Perspectives: Occasional Papers* (Hispanic Theological Initiative) 1 (fall 1998): 7–20.

28. See Pérez, "Spirit Glyphs," for an insightful discussion of nepantla in Chicana art and writing.

29. Venegas, "Day of the Dead in Aztlán," 1, 13.

30. Mesa-Baines, "Curatorial Statement," 12.

31. Kay F. Turner, "Home Altars and the Art of Devotion," in *Chicano Expressions: A New View in American Art* (New York: INTAR Latin American Gallery, 1986), 41.

32. Mesa-Baines, "ALTARMAKERS," 5.

33. Garcíagodoy, *Digging the Days of the Dead,* 199.

34. See ibid., 197–231, for an insightful discussion of the calavera in Mexico.

35. Yvette Cabrera, "Day of the Dead: Cemeteries See Culture Clash," *Woodland Hills* (Calif.) *Daily News,* 31 October 1998, 1, 16.

36. Father Mike Kennedy, interview by authors, Dolores Mission parish, January 1999.

37. Olga Garcia, poem read at SHG, 1 November 1998.

"Soy una Curandera y Soy una Católica"

Epigraph: Jose E. Limón, *Dancing with the Devil: Society and Cultural Poetics in Mexican-American South Texas* (Madison: University of Wisconsin Press, 1994), 202.

1. Dolores Multiplicadas, interview by author, East Los Angeles, 17 September 1999. All names of interviewees in the text are pseudonyms. Unless otherwise noted, all interviews were conducted in Spanish by the author at Sagrado Corazón from June 1998 through September 1999. I thank Lara Medina for her help throughout this time.

2. *Tonantzin,* in Nahuatl, literally, "our mother," was the symbol of a fertility goddess. Malinche was the Maya concubine and lover of Cortez. She is known perjoratively as the great traitor of Mexico. La Llorona is the archetypical "weeping woman" in Mexico; she foretells tragedy, transformation, and change. See Octavio Paz, "Sons of La Malinche," in *The Labyrinth of Solitude: Life and Thought in Mexico,* trans. Lysander Kemp (New York: Grove, 1961).

3. Although there is a significant amount of Mexican ethnographic literature in Spanish from case studies conducted over a long period, there is little information in English on curanderismo, and none of the English-language literature adopts a religious studies perspective. For a review of some of this literature, see Robert Trotter and Juan Antonio Chavira, *Curanderismo: Mexican American Folk Healing*, 2d ed. (Athens: University of Georgia Press, 1997).

4. In what I call "religious poetics," believers renarrate religious discourse through practice, imbuing existing religious doctrines with poetic, contextual meanings. See Luis D. León, *La Llorona's Children: Religion, Life, and Death in the Borderlands* (Berkeley: University of California Press, 2002).

5. On the influence of pre-Tridentine Catholicism in the colonization of Mexico, see Orlando O. Espín, in *The Faith of the People: Theological Reflections on Popular Catholicism* (Maryknoll, N.Y.: Orbis, 1997), 32–62.

6. See the recent report by John Orr and Sherry May, "Religion and Health Services in Los Angeles: Reconfiguring the Terrain," Center for the Study of Religion and American Civic Culture, December 1999, available at http://www.usc.edu/dept/LAS/religion_online/publications/civic_profile/CivicProfile_99.html.

7. Davíd Carrasco, *Religions of Mesoamerica: Cosmovision and Ceremonial Centers* (San Francisco: Harper and Row, 1990), 170.

8. Bernard Ortiz de Motellano, *Aztec Health and Medicine* (New Brunswick, N.J.: Rutgers University Press, 1990), 220.

9. See Trotter and Chavira, *Curanderismo*.

10. Boyle Heights occupies an area of 3.27 square miles. Its population of 55,157 consists of 2 percent African Americans, 4 percent Asian Pacific Islanders, 93 percent Latinas/os, and one percent others. Thirty-nine percent of these households earn less than $15,000 per year, and 39 percent earn between $15,000 and $35,000 per year.

11. For an extensive list of Mexican healing herbs, see Annette Sandoval, *Homegrown Healing: Traditional Remedies from Mexico* (New York: Berkeley Books, 1998).

12. This account synthesizes discussion on three occasions; some of the conversation took place in English.

13. This interview was conducted in English.

14. See Jeffrey S. Thies, *Mexican Catholicism in Southern California* (New York: Peter Lang, 1993).

15. Anita Snow, "Drug Dealers Honor Patron Saint," *Santa Barbara New Press*, 4 September 1995.

16. For an extended discussion of this phenomenon, see James Griffith, *Saints and Holy Places: A Spiritual Geography of the Pimería Alta* (Tucson: University of Arizona Press, 1992).

17. See Thies, *Mexican Catholicism*.

18. For an extended discussion of this core set of beliefs, see León, *La Llorona's Children*.

19. Manuel Vasquez, "Pentecostalism, Collective Identity, and Transnationalism among Salvadorans and Peruvians in the U.S.," *Journal of the American Academy of Religion* 67, no. 3 (September 1999): 617–36.

20. Here, of course, I draw upon Marcel Mauss's seminal study on rites of gift and exchange, *The Gift: The Form and Reason for Exchange in Archaic Societies* (New York: W. W. Norton, 1990).

21. Trotter and Chavira, *Curanderismo*. See also Eliseo Torres, *The Folk Healer: The Mexican-American Tradition of Curanderismo* (Kingsville, Texas: Nieves Press, 1983).

22. Gloria Anzaldúa, *Borderlands/La Frontera: The New Mestiza*, 2d ed. (San Francisco: Spinsters/aunt lute, 1999), 79.

23. One model for this kind of work is Karen McCarthy Brown's *Mama Lola: A Vodou Priestess in Brooklyn* (Berkeley: University of California Press, 1991).

The Symbolic World of Mexican American Religion

1. Ernest Becker, *The Denial of Death* (New York: Free Press, 1973).

2. See also Orlando O. Espín, *The Faith of the People: Theological Reflections on Popular Catholicism* (Maryknoll, N.Y.: Orbis, 1997), 63–90.

3. On the relationship between identities and borders from two very different methodological perspectives, see also Gloria Anzaldúa, *Borderlands/La Frontera: The New Mestiza* (San Francisco: Spinsters/aunt lute, 1987); Homi Bhabha, *The Location of Culture* (London: Routledge, 1994).

4. On the communal self and the notion of accompaniment discussed below, see Roberto S. Goizueta, *Caminemos con Jesús: Toward a Hispanic/Latino Theology of Accompaniment* (Maryknoll, N.Y.: Orbis, 1995), 47–76. Gary Riebe-Estrella speaks of the "sociocentric organic" character of U.S. Latino/a culture; see his "*Pueblo* and Church," in *From the Heart of Our People: Latino/a Explorations in Catholic Systematic Theology*, ed. Orlando O. Espín and Miguel H. Díaz (Maryknoll, N.Y.: Orbis, 1999), 172–88.

5. See Virgilio Elizondo, *The Future is Mestizo: Life Where Cultures Meet* (Bloomington, Ind.: Meyer-Stone, 1988). See also idem, *Mestizaje: The Dialectic of Cultural Birth and the Gospel*, 3 vols. (San Antonio: Mexican American Cultural Center Press, 1978); idem, *Galilean Journey: The Mexican-American Promise*, rev. ed. (Maryknoll, N.Y.: Orbis, 2000); Timothy Matovina, ed., *Beyond Borders: Writings of Virgilio Elizondo and Friends* (Maryknoll, N.Y.: Orbis, 2000).

6. For analyses of the commodification of religious experience in late capitalist, consumerist culture, see Orlando O. Espín, "La experiencia religiosa en el contexto de la globalización," *Journal of Hispanic/Latino Theology* 7, no. 2 (November 1999): 13–31, esp. 20–23; Wade Clark Roof, *Spiritual Marketplace: Baby Boomers and the Remaking of American Religion* (Princeton: Princeton University Press, 1999); Thomas Frank and Matt Weiland, eds., *Commodify Your Dissent* (New York: W. W. Norton, 1997).

7. One might speak of this identification as empathy; see Alejandro García-Rivera, "The Whole and the Love of Difference: Latino Metaphysics as Cosmology," in Espín and Díaz, *From the Heart of Our People*, 67–74.

8. The historical and philosophical roots of the differences between these notions of symbol are examined in Louis Dupré, *Passage to Modernity: An Essay in the Hermeneutics of Nature and Culture* (New Haven: Yale University Press, 1993). For a classic essay on symbol as "making present" what it signifies, see Karl Rahner, "The Theology of the Symbol," in *Theological Investigations*, vol. 4 (Baltimore: Helicon Press, 1966), 221–52.

9. Peter Casarella, "Questioning the Primacy of Method: On Sokolowski's *Eucharistic Presence*," *Communio* 22 (winter 1995): 670–71.

10. In the words of William Faulkner, "The past is not dead; it is not even past"; quoted in David Tracy, *Plurality and Ambiguity: Hermeneutics, Religion, Hope* (Chicago: University of Chicago Press, 1987), 36.

11. On the privatization of faith, see Johann Baptist Metz, *Faith in History and Society: Toward a Practical Fundamental Theology* (New York: Seabury/Crossroad, 1980). See also Stephen L. Carter, *The Culture of Disbelief: How American Law and Politics Trivialize Religious Devotion* (New York: Basic Books, 1993).

12. The centrality of everyday life for Latinos/as is reflected in the increasing attention being given to the category of lo cotidiano (the everyday) in U.S. Latino/a theology. See, for example, María Pilar Aquino, "Theological Method in U.S. Latino/a Theology: Toward an Intercultural Theology for the Third Millennium," in *From the Heart of Our People: Latino/a Explorations in Catholic Systematic Theology*, ed. Orlando O. Espín and Miguel H. Díaz (Maryknoll, N.Y.: Orbis, 1999), 38–39; Orlando O. Espín, "An Exploration into the Theology of Grace and Sin," ibid., 121–52.

13. María Pilar Aquino presents a thoroughgoing critique of such abstract methods and the alternative method of U.S. Latino/a theology. See Aquino, "Theological Method," 6–48.

14. For a dramatic and powerful account of an Anglo-American priest who became "converted" to the faith of the poor, see Brian J. Pierce, "The Cross and the Crib: Hope from the Underside," *America*, 2 April 1994, 13–14.

Mexican Religious Practices, Popular Catholicism, and the Development of Doctrine

1. Church historian Justo L. González, a United Methodist, has repeatedly emphasized this shared ancestry. See his *Mañana: Christian Theology from a Hispanic Perspective* (Nashville: Abingdon Press, 1990), esp. 55, 63.

2. Serious philosophical issues are unquestionably at stake. However, given my specific focus here as well as the limitations of space, it is impossible to offer the analyses essential to a thorough understanding of Tradition and doctrinal development. For a more detailed treatment of this topic, see Terrence W. Tilley, *Inventing Catholic Tradition* (Maryknoll, N.Y.: Orbis, 2000); John E. Thiel, *Senses of Tradition: Continuity and Development in Catholic Faith* (New York: Oxford University Press, 2000); and my forthcoming book, tentatively titled *Grounding Our Future: A Theology of Tradition and Doctrinal Change*.

3. On the Catholic Tradition as "traditioning" and on the role doctrine plays therein, see Tilley, *Inventing Catholic Tradition*; Rolf J. Pöhler, *Continuity and Change in Christian Doctrine: A Study of the Problem of Doctrinal Development* (New York: Peter Lang, 1999); D. N. Bell, *A Cloud of Witnesses: An Introductory History of the Development of Christian Doctrine* (Kalamazoo: Cistercian Publications, 1989).

4. This seems extremely evident in Timothy Matovina's essay on San Fernando Cathedral's Guadalupan devotion from 1900 to 1940, when the parishioners reinterpreted the account of the Guadalupe apparitions and its meaning in and for Mexican history both from the perspective of their own experience and from the experience of their contemporary Mexico. They read back as history and tradition what in fact was their present understanding chiefly as a result of their desire and hope for a *new* Mexico. The parishioners were probably not aware of their hermeneutic creativity.

5. Popular Catholicism cannot be said to be strictly coextensive with the laity. However, it is clearly no exaggeration to affirm that popular Catholicism is and has been mostly created, practiced, and led by the laity, with or without hierarchical support. Particularly but certainly not exclusively in the Latino/a and Latin American contexts, women are and have been indispensable in creating and transmitting the formulations and expressions of popular Catholicism.

6. By "popular" I do not mean "widespread," although popular Catholicism certainly is. "Popular" is the adjective to the noun "people," and thus in our expression the term refers to Catholicism as practiced, believed, etc., by the common people who identify themselves with cause as part of the Catholic Tradition.

7. See Orlando O. Espín, "The God of the Vanquished: Foundations for a Latino Spirituality," in *The Faith of the People: Theological Reflections on Popular Catholicism* (Maryknoll, N.Y.: Orbis, 1997), 11–31; idem, "Popular Religion as an Epistemology (of Suffering): An Introduction on the Urgency of Epistemological Reflection," ibid., 156–79.

8. For a further explanation of sensus fidelium, see Orlando O. Espín, "Tradition and Popular Religion: An Understanding of the *Sensus Fidelium*," in *The Faith of the People*, 63–90.

9. I am in no way implying that popular Catholicism is lacking in philosophical or theological sophistication. The latter, however, is usually expressed through the common symbols, beliefs, and practices of the people, which, unfortunately and groundlessly, are rarely deemed "sophisticated" by the social elites. Antonio Gramsci's theory on the social construction of knowledge explains the causes and processes of this social situation. For good introductions to Gramsci's thought, see Hugues Portelli, *Gramsci y la cuestión religiosa*

(Barcelona: Editorial Laia, 1977); idem, *Gramsci y el bloque histórico* (Mexico City: Siglo XXI Editores, 1980); L. Gruppi, *O conceito de hegemonia em Gramsci* (Rio de Janeiro: Editora Graal, 1978); R. Ortiz, *A consciência fragmentada. Ensaios de cultura popular e religião* (Rio de Janeiro: Editora Paz e Terra, 1980).

10. The term *magisterium,* Latin for "group of teachers," is used in Catholicism to designate bishops who, by their ministry, are charged with officially teaching within and in the name of the church. Nevertheless, as a result of baptism, all Catholics share equally in the duty to announce the gospel, and as a result of the sensus fidelium, all have the responsibilities inherent in this "faith-full sense" of the people.

11. María Pilar Aquino, *Nuestro clamor por la vida* (San José, Costa Rica: DEI, 1992), 75.

12. See Vatican II, "Lumen Gentium," nos. 3, 4, 12. The sixteen documents of Vatican II are available in various English translations, including *The Documents of Vatican II*, ed. Walter M. Abbott (New York: America Press, 1966).

13. See Vatican II,"Lumen Gentium," no. 12.

14. In the Catholic Tradition those other witnesses are Scripture, ecclesial magisterium, liturgy, and theology. I argue that these cannot supplant the most ordinary witness to revelation, the sensus fidelium.

15. See Jaroslav Pelikan, *Development of Christian Doctrine: Some Historical Prolegomena* (New Haven: Yale University Press, 1969); George A. Lindbeck, *The Nature of Doctrine: Religion and Theology in a Postliberal Age* (Philadelphia: Westminster Press, 1984). See also Vatican II, "Dei Verbum," no. 9.

16. An in-depth analysis of power relations is a prerequisite to any such presupposition. Theologians and the magisterium must also look at their own stereotypes, their own biases and prejudices, even their own racism. Without a clear awareness of their own limitations, bishops and theologians run the risk of blocking within and among themselves the voice of the Spirit speaking through the laity (especially the poor, who in fact are the majority of all Catholics).

17. See Peter L. Berger and Thomas Luckmann, *The Social Construction of Reality: A Treatise in the Sociology of Knowledge* (New York: Anchor, 1999); Susan J. Hekman, *Hermeneutics and the Sociology of Knowledge* (Notre Dame, Ind.: University of Notre Dame Press, 1986). The sociology of knowledge is a pertinent contributor to this discussion.

Selected Bibliography

Abbott, Walter M., ed. *The Documents of Vatican II*. New York: America Press, 1966.
Alarcón, Norma, Ana Castillo, and Cherríe Moraga, eds. *Third Woman: The Sexuality of Latinas*. Berkeley, Calif.: Third Woman Press, 1989.
Anzaldúa, Gloria. *Borderlands/La Frontera: The New Mestiza*. 2d ed. San Francisco: Spinsters/aunt lute, 1999.
Aquino, María Pilar. *Nuestro clamor por la vida*. San José, Costa Rica: DEI, 1992. Translated by Dinah Livingstone as *Our Cry for Life*. Maryknoll, N.Y.: Orbis, 1993.
——. "Theological Method in U.S. Latino/a Theology: Toward an Intercultural Theology for the Third Millennium." In *From the Heart of Our People: Latino/a Explorations in Catholic Systematic Theology*, ed. Orlando O. Espín and Miguel H. Díaz, 6–48. Maryknoll, N.Y.: Orbis, 1999.
Arnold, Charles A. *Folklore, Manners, and Customs of the Mexicans in San Antonio, Texas, 1928*. Reprint, San Francisco: R and E Research Associates, 1971.
Ashley, Wayne. "The Stations of the Cross: Christ, Politics, and Processions on New York City's Lower East Side." In *Gods of the City: Religion and the American Urban Landscape*, ed. Robert A. Orsi, 341–66. Bloomington: Indiana University Press, 1999.
Badillo, David A. "Between Alienation and Ethnicity: The Evolution of Mexican-American Catholicism in San Antonio, 1910–1940." *Journal of American Ethnic History* 16 (summer 1997): 62–83.
——. "The Catholic Church and the Making of Mexican-American Parish Communities in the Midwest." In *Mexican Americans and the Catholic Church, 1900–1965*, ed. Jay P. Dolan and Gilberto M. Hinojosa, 237–308. Notre Dame, Ind.: University of Notre Dame Press, 1994.
Balderrama, Francisco E., and Raymond Rodríguez. *Decade of Betrayal: Mexican Repatriation in the 1930s*. Albuquerque: University of New Mexico Press, 1995.

Baxter, Michael J. "The Unsettling of Americanism: A Response to William Portier." *Communio* 27 (spring 2000): 161–70.

———. "Writing History in a World without Ends: An Evangelical Catholic Critique of United States Catholic History." *Pro Ecclesia* 5 (fall 1996): 440–69.

Becker, Ernest. *The Denial of Death*. New York: Free Press, 1973.

Bell, D. N. *A Cloud of Witnesses: An Introductory History of the Development of Christian Doctrine*. Kalamazoo: Cistercian Publications, 1989.

Bellah, Robert N. *Habits of the Heart: Individualism and Commitment in American Life*. Berkeley: University of California Press, 1985.

Berger, Peter L., and Thomas Luckmann. *The Social Construction of Reality: A Treatise in the Sociology of Knowledge*. New York: Anchor, 1990.

Bernardino de Sahagún, Fray. *Historia general de las cosas de la Nueva España*. Vol. 2. Mexico City: Porrúa, 1969.

Bhabha, Homi. *The Location of Culture*. London: Routledge, 1994.

Blackwelder, Julia Kirk. *Women of the Depression: Caste and Culture in San Antonio, 1929–1939*. College Station: Texas A&M University Press, 1984.

Brown, Karen McCarthy. *Mama Lola: A Vodou Priestess in Brooklyn*. Berkeley: University of California Press, 1991.

Bruce-Novoa, Juan. "*La Prensa* and the Chicano Community." *Americas Review* 17 (fall / winter 1989): 150–56.

Busto, Rudy. "The Predicament of *Nepantla:* Chicano/a Religions in the 21st Century." *Perspectivas: Occasional Papers* (Hispanic Theological Initiative) 1 (fall 1998): 7–20.

Carmichael, Elizabeth, and Chloe Sayer. *The Skeleton at the Feast: The Day of the Dead in Mexico*. Austin: University of Texas Press, 1992.

Carrasco, Davíd. *Religions of Mesoamerica: Cosmovision and Ceremonial Centers*. San Francisco: Harper and Row, 1990.

Carter, Stephen L. *The Culture of Disbelief: How American Law and Politics Trivialize Religious Devotion*. New York: Basic Books, 1993.

Casarella, Peter. "Questioning the Primacy of Method: On Sokolowski's *Eucharistic Presence*." *Communio* 22 (winter 1995): 668–701.

"Celebrate Día de los Muertos All Month Long." *BOCA* 1, no. 3 (October–November 1998): 6.

Chicago Fact Book Consortium. *Local Community Fact Book: Chicago Metropolitan Area Based on the 1970 and 1980 Censuses*. Chicago: Chicago Review Press, 1984.

Chinnici, Joseph P. *Living Stones: The History and Structure of Catholic Spiritual Life in the United States*. New York: Macmillan, 1989.

Chinnici, Joseph P., and Angelyn Dries, eds. *Prayer and Practice in the American Catholic Community*. Maryknoll, N.Y.: Orbis, 2000.

Cintrón, Ralph. *Angels' Town: Chero Ways, Gang Life, and Rhetorics of the Everyday*. Boston: Beacon Press, 1997.

D'Agostino, Peter R. "Italian Ethnicity and Religious Priests in the American Church: The Servites, 1870–1940." *Catholic Historical Review* 80 (October 1994): 714–40.

———. "The Scalabrini Fathers, the Italian Emigrant Church, and Ethnic Nationalism in America." *Religion and American Culture* 7 (winter 1997): 121–59.

———. "The Triad of Roman Authority: Fascism, the Vatican, and Italian Religious Clergy in the Italian Emigrant Church." *Journal of American Ethnic History* 17 (spring 1998): 3–37.

Davalos, Karen Mary. "*La Quinceañera:* Making Gender and Ethnic Identities." *Frontiers: A Journal of Women Studies* 16, no. 2 / 3 (1996): 101–27.

Davis, John L. *San Antonio: A Historical Portrait.* Austin: Encino, 1978.

Deck, Allan Figueroa. "Models." In *Perspectivas: Hispanic Ministry,* ed. Allan Figueroa Deck, Yolanda Tarango, and Timothy Matovina, 1–6. Kansas City, Mo.: Sheed and Ward, 1995.

———. *The Second Wave: Hispanic Ministry and the Evangelization of Cultures.* New York: Paulist, 1989.

Deck, Allan Figueroa, Yolanda Tarango, and Timothy Matovina, eds. *Perspectivas: Hispanic Ministry.* Kansas City, Mo.: Sheed and Ward, 1995.

Díaz-Stevens, Ana María. "The Saving Grace: The Matriarchal Core of Latino Catholicism." *Latino Studies Journal* 4 (September 1993): 60–78.

Dolan, Jay P. *The American Catholic Experience: A History from Colonial Times to the Present.* 1985. Reprint, Notre Dame, Ind.: University of Notre Dame Press, 1992.

Dolan, Jay P., and Allan Figueroa Deck, eds. *Hispanic Catholic Culture in the U.S.: Issues and Concerns.* Notre Dame, Ind.: University of Notre Dame Press, 1994.

Dolan, Jay P., and Gilberto M. Hinojosa, eds. *Mexican Americans and the Catholic Church, 1900–1965.* Notre Dame, Ind.: University of Notre Dame Press, 1994.

Dupré, Louis. *Passage to Modernity: An Essay in the Hermeneutics of Nature and Culture.* New Haven: Yale University Press, 1993.

Durán, Diego. *Historia de las Indias de Nueva España e Islas de la Tierra Firme.* Vol. 1. México City: Porrúa, 1969.

Durand, Jorge, and D. S. Massey. *Miracles on the Border: Retablos of Mexican Migrants to the United States.* Tucson: University of Arizona Press, 1995.

Elizondo, Virgilio. *Christianity and Culture: An Introduction to Pastoral Theology and Ministry for the Bicultural Community.* Huntington, Ind.: Our Sunday Visitor, 1975.

———. *The Future Is Mestizo: Life Where Cultures Meet.* 2d ed. Boulder: University Press of Colorado, 2000.

———. *Galilean Journey: The Mexican-American Promise.* Rev. ed. Maryknoll, N.Y.: Orbis, 2000.

———. *Mestizaje: The Dialectic of Cultural Birth and the Gospel.* 3 vols. San Antonio: Mexican American Cultural Center Press, 1978.

Elizondo, Virgilio, and Timothy Matovina. *San Fernando Cathedral: Soul of the City.* Maryknoll, N.Y.: Orbis, 1998.

Engh, Michael E. *Frontier Faiths: Church, Temple, and Synagogue in Los Angeles, 1846–1888.* Albuquerque: University of New Mexico Press, 1992.

Espín, Orlando O. "La experiencia religiosa en el contexto de la globalización." *Journal of Hispanic/Latino Theology* 7, no. 2 (November 1999): 13–31.

———. "An Exploration into the Theology of Grace and Sin." In *From the Heart of Our People: Latino/a Explorations in Catholic Systematic Theology,* ed. Orlando O. Espín and Miguel H. Díaz, 121–52. Maryknoll, N.Y.: Orbis, 1999.

———. *The Faith of the People: Theological Reflections on Popular Catholicism.* Maryknoll, N.Y.: Orbis, 1997.

Espín, Orlando O., and Miguel H. Díaz, eds. *From the Heart of Our People: Latino/a Explorations in Catholic Systematic Theology.* Maryknoll, N.Y.: Orbis, 1999.

Faith Expressions of Hispanics in the Southwest. Rev. ed. San Antonio: Mexican American Cultural Center Press, 1990.

Fernández, Cristóbal. *Compendio histórico de la Congregación de los Hijos del Inmaculado Corazón de María.* Vol. 2. Madrid: Editorial Coculsa, 1967.

Fitzpatrick, Joseph. *One Church, Many Cultures: The Challenge of Diversity.* Kansas City, Mo.: Sheed and Ward, 1987.

Frank, Thomas, and Matt Weiland, eds. *Commodify Your Dissent.* New York: W. W. Norton, 1997.

Gamio, Manuel. *The Mexican Immigrant: His Life-Story.* 1931. Reprint, New York: Arno, 1969.

——. *Mexican Immigration to the United States: A Study of Human Migration and Adjustment.* 1930. Reprint, New York: Arno, 1969.

García, Juan R. *Mexicans in the Midwest, 1900–1932.* Tucson: University of Arizona Press, 1996.

García, Richard A. *Rise of the Mexican American Middle Class: San Antonio, 1929–1941.* College Station: Texas A&M University Press, 1991.

Garcíagodoy, Juanita. *Digging the Days of the Dead: A Reading of Mexico's Días de Muertos.* Niwot: University Press of Colorado, 1998.

García-Rivera, Alejandro. "Let's Capture the Hispanic Imagination." *U.S. Catholic* 57 (July 1994): 34–35.

——. "The Whole and the Love of Difference: Latino Metaphysics as Cosmology." In *From the Heart of Our People: Latino/a Explorations in Catholic Systematic Theology,* ed. Orlando O. Espín and Miguel H. Díaz, 57–83. Maryknoll, N.Y.: Orbis, 1999.

Goizueta, Roberto S. *Caminemos con Jesús: Toward a Hispanic/Latino Theology of Accompaniment.* Maryknoll, N.Y.: Orbis, 1995.

Gonzalas, Kathleen May. *The Mexican Family in San Antonio, Texas.* M.A. thesis, University of Texas at Austin, 1928. San Francisco: R and E Research Associates, 1971.

González, Justo. *Mañana: Christian Theology from a Hispanic Perspective.* Nashville: Abingdon Press, 1990.

Gracia, Jorge J. E. *Hispanic/Latino Identity: A Philosophical Perspective.* Malden, Mass.: Blackwell, 2000.

Granjon, Henry. *Along the Rio Grande: A Pastoral Visit to Southwest New Mexico in 1902.* Edited by Michael Romero Taylor. Translated by Mary W. de López. Albuquerque: University of New Mexico Press, 1986.

Green, Judith Strupp. "The Days of the Dead in Oaxaca, Mexico: A Historical Inquiry." In *Death and Dying: Views from Many Cultures,* ed. Richard A. Kalish, 56–71. Farmingdale, N.Y.: Baywood, 1980.

Griffith, James. *Saints and Holy Places: A Spiritual Geography of the Pimería Alta.* Tucson: University of Arizona Press, 1992.

Gruppi, L. *O conceito de hegemonia em Gramsci.* Rio de Janeiro: Editora Graal, 1978.

Gupta, Akhil, and James Ferguson. "Beyond 'Culture': Space, Identity, and Politics of Difference." *Cultural Anthropology* 7, no. 1 (February 1992): 6–23.

Gutiérrez, David G. *Walls and Mirrors: Mexican Americans, Mexican Immigrants, and the Politics of Ethnicity.* Berkeley: University of California Press, 1995.

Hall, David D., ed. *Lived Religion in America: Toward a History of Practice.* Princeton: Princeton University Press, 1997.

Hekman, Susan J. *Hermeneutics and the Sociology of Knowledge.* Notre Dame, Ind.: University of Notre Dame Press, 1986.

Hennesey, James. *American Catholics: A History of the Roman Catholic Community in the United States.* New York: Oxford University Press, 1981.

Hill, Jane H. "Language, Race, and White Public Space." *American Anthropologist* 100, no. 3 (1998): 680–89.

Hinojosa, Federico Allen. *El México de Afuera y su reintegración a la patria.* San Antonio: Artes Gráficas, 1940.

Hinojosa, Gilberto M. "The Enduring Hispanic Faith Communities: Spanish and

Texas Church Historiography." *Journal of Texas Catholic History and Culture* 1 (March 1990): 20–41.

——. "Mexican-American Faith Communities in Texas and the Southwest." In *Mexican Americans and the Catholic Church, 1900–1965,* ed. Jay P. Dolan and Gilberto M. Hinojosa, 9–125. Notre Dame, Ind.: University of Notre Dame Press, 1994.

Hooper, Barbara. "Split at the Roots: A Critique of the Philosophical and Political Sources of Modern Planning Doctrine." *Frontiers: A Journal of Women's Studies* 13, no. 1 (1992): 45–80.

Horowitz, Ruth. *Honor and the American Dream: Culture and Identity in a Chicano Community.* New Brunswick, N.J.: Rutgers University Press, 1983.

Icaza, Rosa María. "The Cross in Mexican Popular Piety." *Liturgy* 1, no. 1 (1981): 27–34.

——. "Prayer, Worship, and Liturgy in a United States Hispanic Key." In *Frontiers of Hispanic Theology in the United States,* ed. Allan Figueroa Deck, 134–53. Maryknoll, N.Y.: Orbis, 1992.

Johnson, Elizabeth A. "The Marian Tradition and the Reality of Women." *Horizons* 12 (spring 1985): 116–35.

——. "Mary and the Female Face of God." *Theological Studies* 50 (September 1989): 500–526.

Jordan, Terry G. "A Century and a Half of Ethnic Change in Texas 1836–1986." *Southwestern Historical Quarterly* 89 (April 1986): 385–422.

Karttunen, Frances E. *An Analytical Dictionary of Nahuatl.* Austin: University of Texas Press, 1983.

Kelly, Timothy, and Joseph Kelly. "Our Lady of Perpetual Help, Gender Roles, and the Decline of Devotional Catholicism." *Journal of Social History* 32 (fall 1998): 5–26.

Kerr, Louise Año Nuevo. "The Chicano Experience in Chicago, 1920–1970." Ph.D. diss., University of Illinois at Chicago, 1976.

——. "Chicano Settlements in Chicago: A Brief History." *Journal of Ethnic Studies* 2, no. 4 (1975): 22–32.

Klor de Alva, J. Jorge. "Aztec Spirituality and Nahuatized Christianity." In *South and Meso-American Native Spirituality,* ed. Gary H. Gossen and Miguel León-Portillo, 173–97. New York: Crossroad, 1993.

Knox, William J. *The Economic Status of the Mexican American Immigrant in San Antonio, Texas.* M.A. thesis, University of Texas at Austin, 1927. San Francisco: R and E Research Associates, 1971.

León, Luis D. *La Llorona's Children: Religion, Life and Death in the Borderlands.* Berkeley: University of California Press, 2002.

León-Portillo, Miguel. *Endangered Cultures.* Dallas: Southern Methodist University Press, 1990.

Limón, José E. *American Encounters: Greater Mexico, the United States, and the Erotics of Culture.* Boston: Beacon Press, 1998.

——. *Dancing with the Devil: Society and Cultural Poetics in Mexican-American South Texas.* Madison: University of Wisconsin Press, 1994.

Lindbeck, George A. *The Nature of Doctrine: Religion and Theology in a Postliberal Age.* Philadelphia: Westminster Press, 1984.

Lipsitz, George. *The Possessive Investment in Whiteness: How White People Profit from Identity Politics.* Philadelphia: Temple University Press, 1998.

Liptak, Dolores. *Immigrants and Their Church.* New York: Macmillan, 1989.

Lockhart, James. *The Nahuas after the Conquest: A Social and Cultural History of the Indians of Central Mexico, Sixteenth through Eighteenth Centuries.* Stanford: Stanford University Press, 1992.

López Austin, Alfredo. *Tamoanchan, Tlalocan: Places of Mist.* Niwot: University Press of Colorado, 1997.

Luna Lawhn, Juanita. "*El Regidor* and *La Prensa:* Impediments to Women's Self-Definition." In *Third Woman: The Sexuality of Latinas,* ed. Norma Alarcón, Ana Castillo, and Cherríe Moraga, 134–42. Berkeley, Calif.: Third Woman Press, 1989.

———. "Victorian Attitudes Affecting the Mexican Woman Writing in *La Prensa* during the Early 1900s and the Chicana of the 1980s." In *Missions in Conflict: Essays on U.S.-Mexican Relations and Chicano Culture,* ed. Renate von Bardeleben, Dietrich Briesemeister, and Juan Bruce-Novoa, 65–71. Tübingen: Narr, 1986.

Matovina, Timothy. "Guadalupan Devotion in a Borderlands Community." *Journal of Hispanic/Latino Theology* 4 (August 1996): 6–26.

———. "Lay Initiatives in Worship on the Texas *Frontera,* 1830–1860." *U.S. Catholic Historian* 12 (fall 1994): 107–20.

———. "New Frontiers of Guadalupanismo." *Journal of Hispanic/Latino Theology* 5 (August 1997): 20–36.

———. "No Melting Pot in Sight." In *Perspectivas: Hispanic Ministry,* ed. Allan Figueroa Deck, Yolanda Tarango, and Timothy Matovina, 35–39. Kansas City, Mo.: Sheed and Ward, 1995.

———. "Our Lady of Guadalupe Celebrations in San Antonio, Texas, 1840–41." *Journal of Hispanic/Latino Theology* 1 (November 1993): 77–96.

———. *Tejano Religion and Ethnicity: San Antonio, 1821–1860.* Austin: University of Texas Press, 1995.

Matovina, Timothy, ed. *Beyond Borders: Writings of Virgilio Elizondo and Friends.* Maryknoll, N.Y.: Orbis, 2000.

Matovina, Timothy, and Gerald E. Poyo, eds. *¡Presente! U.S. Latino Catholics from Colonial Origins to the Present.* Maryknoll, N.Y.: Orbis, 2000.

Mauss, Marcel. *The Gift: The Form and Reason for Exchange in Archaic Societies.* New York: W. W. Norton, 1990.

McDannell, Colleen. *Material Christianity: Religion and Popular Culture in America.* New Haven: Yale University Press, 1995.

Menchaca, Martha. "Chicano Indianism: A Historical Account of Racial Repression in the United States." *American Ethnologist* 20, no. 3 (1993): 583–603.

Menefee, Selden C., and Orin C. Cassmore. *The Pecan Shellers of San Antonio: The Problem of Underpaid and Unemployed Mexican Labor.* 1940. Reprinted in *Mexican Labor in the United States.* New York: Arno, 1974.

Mesa-Baines, Amalia. "ALTARMAKERS: The Historic Mediators." In *Offerings: The Altar Show,* 5–7. Venice, Calif.: Social and Public Arts Resource Center, 1984.

———. *Ceremony of Memory.* Santa Fe: Center for Contemporary Arts of Santa Fe, 1988.

———. "Curatorial Statement." In *Ceremony of Spirit: Nature and Memory in Contemporary Latino Art,* 9. San Francisco: The Mexican Museum, 1993.

Metz, Johann Baptist. *Faith in History and Society: Toward a Practical Fundamental Theology.* New York: Seabury/Crossroad, 1980.

Meyer, Jean A. *The Cristero Rebellion: The Mexican People between Church and State, 1926–1929.* Translated by Richard Southern. Cambridge: Cambridge University Press, 1976.

Morgan, David. *Visual Piety: A History and Theory of Popular Religious Images.* Berkeley: University of California Press, 1998.

Morris, Charles R. *American Catholic: The Saints and Sinners Who Built America's Most Powerful Church.* New York: Times Books, 1997.

Morrison, Susan Shumate. "Mexico's Day of the Dead in San Francisco, California: A Study of Continuity and Change in a Popular Religious Festival." Ph.D. diss., Graduate Theological Union, Berkeley, 1992.

National Conference of Catholic Bishops. *The Hispanic Presence: Challenge and Commitment.* Washington, D.C.: United States Catholic Conference, 1984.

Neri, Michael Charles. *Hispanic Catholicism in Transitional California: The Life of José González Rubio, O.F.M. (1804–1875).* Berkeley, Calif.: Academy of American Franciscan History, 1997.

Nutini, Hugo G. "Pre-Hispanic Component of the Syncretic Cult of the Dead." *Ethnology* 27 (January 1998): 57–78.

O'Connor, Mary. "The Virgin of Guadalupe and the Economics of Symbolic Behavior." *Journal for the Scientific Study of Religion* 28, no. 2 (1989): 105–19.

Orfield, Gary, and Ricardo M. Tostado, eds. *Latinos in Metropolitan Chicago: A Study of Housing and Employment.* Chicago: Latino Institute, 1983.

Orozco, Cynthia E. "The Origins of the League of United Latin American Citizens (LULAC) and the Mexican American Civil Rights Movement in Texas with an Analysis of Women's Political Participation in a Gendered Context, 1910–1929." Ph.D. diss., University of California at Los Angeles, 1992.

Orsi, Robert A. *The Madonna of 115th Street: Faith and Community in Italian Harlem, 1880–1950.* New Haven: Yale University Press, 1986.

———. *Thank You, St. Jude: Women's Devotion to the Patron Saint of Hopeless Causes.* New Haven: Yale University Press, 1996.

Ortiz, R. *A consciência fragmentada. Ensaios de cultura popular e religião.* Rio de Janeiro: Editora Paz e Terra, 1980.

Ortiz de Motellano, Bernard. *Aztec Health and Medicine.* New Brunswick, N.J.: Rutgers University Press, 1990.

Pacyga, Dominic A., and Ellen Skerrett. *Chicago, City of Neighborhoods: Histories and Tours.* Chicago: Loyola University Press, 1986.

Padilla, Felix. *Latino Ethnic Consciousness.* Notre Dame, Ind.: University of Notre Dame Press, 1985.

Page, Helán, and R. Brooke Thomas. "White Public Space and the Construction of White Privilege in U.S. Health Care: Fresh Concepts and a New Model of Analysis." *Medical Anthropology Quarterly* 8, no. 1 (March 1994): 109–16.

Pelikan, Jaroslav. *Development of Christian Doctrine: Some Historical Prolegomena.* New Haven: Yale University Press, 1969.

Perales, Alonso S. *Are We Good Neighbors?* 1948. Reprint, New York: Arno, 1974.

Pérez, Arturo. *Popular Catholicism: A Hispanic Perspective.* Washington, D.C.: Pastoral Press, 1988.

Pérez, Laura. "Spirit Glyphs: Reimagining Art and Artist in the Work of Chicana *Tlamatinime.*" *Modern Fiction Studies* 44, no. 1 (spring 1998): 36–76.

Pérez-Torres, Rafael. *Movements in Chicano Poetry: Against Myths, against Margins.* Cambridge: Cambridge University Press, 1995.

Pierce, Brian J. "The Cross and the Crib: Hope from the Underside." *America,* 2 April 1994, 13–14.

Pöhler, Rolf J. *Continuity and Change in Christian Doctrine: A Study of the Problem of Doctorinal Development.* New York: Peter Lang, 1999.

Portelli, Hugues. *Gramsci y el bloque histórico.* Mexico City: Siglo XXI Editores, 1980.

———. *Gramsci y la cuestión religiosa.* Barcelona: Editorial Laia, 1977.

Portier, William L. "Americanism and Inculturation, 1899–1999." *Communio* 27 (spring 2000): 139–60.

Pycior, Julie Leininger. *"La Raza* Organizes: Mexican American Life in San Antonio, 1915–1930, as Reflected in *Mutualista* Activities." Ph.D. diss., University of Notre Dame, 1979.

Rahner, Karl. "The Theology of the Symbol." In *Theological Investigations,* 221–52. Vol. 4. Baltimore: Helicon, 1966.

Ramírez, Ricardo. "Liturgy from the Mexican American Perspective." *Worship* 51 (July 1977): 293–98.

Reisler, Mark. *By the Sweat of Their Brow: Mexican Immigrant Labor in the United States, 1900–1940.* Westport, Conn.: Greenwood Press, 1976.

Riebe-Estrella, Gary. *"Pueblo* and Church." In *From the Heart of Our People: Latino/a Explorations in Catholic Systematic Theology,* ed. Orlando O. Espín and Miguel H. Díaz, 172–88. Maryknoll, N.Y.: Orbis, 1999.

Ríos, Hermino. "Toward a True Chicano Bibliography: Part II." *El Grito: A Journal of Contemporary Mexican-American Thought* 5 (summer 1972): 40–47.

Ríos, Hermino, and Guadalupe Castillo. "Toward a True Chicano Bibliography: Mexican-American Newspapers, 1848–1942." *El Grito: A Journal of Contemporary Mexican-American Thought* 3 (summer 1970): 17–24.

Ríos-McMillan, Nora. "A Biography of a Man and His Newspaper." *Americas Review* 17 (fall/winter 1989): 136–49.

Rivlin, Gary. "Who Killed Rudy Lozano?" *Chicago Reader* 14, no. 30 (26 April 1985).

Rodríguez, Edmundo. "The Hispanic Community and Church Movements: Schools of Leadership." In *Hispanic Catholic Culture in the U.S.: Issues and Concerns,* ed. Jay P. Dolan and Allan Figueroa Deck, 206–239. Notre Dame, Ind.: University of Notre Dame Press, 1994.

Rodriguez, Jeanette. *Our Lady of Guadalupe: Faith and Empowerment among Mexican American Women.* Austin: University of Texas Press, 1994.

Romero, C. Gilbert. *Hispanic Devotional Piety: Tracing the Biblical Roots.* Maryknoll, N.Y.: Orbis, 1991.

Roof, Wade Clark. *Spiritual Marketplace: Baby Boomers and the Remaking of American Religion.* Princeton: Princeton University Press, 1999.

Rosaldo, Renato. *Culture and Truth: The Remaking of Social Analysis.* Boston: Beacon Press, 1989.

Rosales, F. Arturo. *Chicano! The History of the Mexican American Civil Rights Movement.* Houston: Arte Público Press, 1996.

Ruiz, Vicki L. *From Out of the Shadows: Mexican Women in Twentieth-Century America.* Oxford: Oxford University Press, 1998.

———. "'Star Struck': Acculturation, Adolescence, and Mexican American Women, 1920–1950." In *Small Worlds: Children and Adolescents in America, 1850–1950,* ed. Elliott West and Paula Petrik, 61–80. Lawrence: University Press of Kansas, 1992.

Saenz, J. Luz. *Los Mexico-Americanos en la gran guerra y su contingente en pró de la democracia, la humanidad y la justicia.* San Antonio: Artes Gráficas, 1933.

Sandoval, Annette. *Homegrown Healing: Traditional Remedies from Mexico.* New York: Berkley Books, 1998.

Serrano, Rafael. "Missionary Work among the Mexicans." *Southern Messenger,* 30 June 1910.

Servín, Manuel P. *An Awakened Minority: The Mexican Americans.* New York: Macmillan, 1974.

Shaw, Stephen J. *The Catholic Parish as a Way-Station of Ethnicity and Americanization: Chicago's Germans and Italians, 1903–1939.* Brooklyn, N.Y.: Carlson, 1991.

Sosa, Juan. "Liturgical Piety or Popular Piety?" *Liturgy* 24 (November–December 1979): 7–9.

Stark, Robert H. "Religious Ritual and Class Formation: The Story of Pilsen, St. Vitus Parish, and the 1977 *Via Crucis.*" Ph.D. diss., University of Chicago, 1981.

Stecker, Mary of Providence. "The History of San Fernando Cathedral." M.A. thesis, Catholic University of America, Washington, D.C., 1940.

Stevens-Arroyo, Anthony, and Andrés Pérez y Mena, eds. *Enigmatic Powers: Syncretism with African and Indigenous Peoples' Religions among Latinos.* New York: Bildner Center, 1995.

Squires, Gregory D., Larry Bennett, Kathleen McCourt, and Philip Nyden. *Chicago: Race, Class, and the Response to Urban Decline.* Philadelphia: Temple University Press, 1987.

Tarango, Yolanda. "The Hispanic Woman and Her Role in the Church." *New Theology Review* 3 (November 1990): 56–61.

Taves, Ann. *The Household of Faith: Roman Catholic Devotions in Mid-Nineteenth-Century America.* Notre Dame, Ind.: University of Notre Dame Press, 1986.

Taylor, Paul S. *Mexican Labor in the United States: Chicago and the Calumet Region.* Berkeley: University of California Press, 1932.

Thiel, John E. *Senses of Tradition: Continuity and Development in Catholic Faith.* New York: Oxford University Press, 2000.

Thies, Jeffrey S. *Mexican Catholicism in Southern California.* New York: Peter Lang, 1993.

Tilley, Terrence W. *Inventing Catholic Tradition.* Maryknoll, N.Y.: Orbis, 2000.

Tomasi, Silvano M. *Piety and Power: The Role of Italian Parishes in the New York Metropolitan Area, 1880–1930.* Staten Island, N.Y.: Center for Migration Studies, 1975.

Torres, Eliseo. *The Folk Healer: The Mexican-American Tradition of Curanderismo.* Kingsville, Tex.: Nieves Press, 1983.

Tracy, David. *Plurality and Ambiguity: Hermeneutics, Religion, Hope.* Chicago: University of Chicago Press, 1987.

Treviño, Roberto R. "*La fe:* Catholicism and Mexican Americans in Houston, 1911–1972." Ph.D. diss., Stanford University, 1993.

——. "*Prensa y Patria:* The Spanish-Language Press and the Biculturation of the Tejano Middle Class, 1920–1940." *Western Historical Quarterly* 22 (November 1991): 451–72.

Trotter, Robert, and Juan Antonio Chavira. *Curanderismo: Mexican American Folk Healing.* 2d ed. Athens: University of Georgia Press, 1997.

Turner, Kay F. "Mexican American Home Altars: Towards Their Interpretation." *Aztlán* 13 (spring/fall 1982): 309–26.

——. "Mexican American Women's Home Altars: The Art of Relationship." Ph.D. diss., University of Texas, 1990.

Tweed, Thomas A. *Our Lady of the Exile: Diasporic Religion at a Cuban Catholic Shrine in Miami.* Oxford: Oxford University Press, 1997.

Vasquez, Manuel. "Pentecostalism, Collective Identity, and Transnationalism among Salvadorans and Peruvians in the U.S." *Journal of the American Academy of Religion* 67, no. 3 (September 1999): 617–36.

Venegas, Sybil. "Day of the Dead in Aztlán: Chicano Variations on the Theme of Life, Death, and Self-Preservation." M.A. thesis, University of California at Los Angeles, 1995.

Wright, Robert E. "Local Church Emergence and Mission Decline: The Historiography of the Catholic Church in the Southwest during the Spanish and Mexican Period." *U.S. Catholic Historian* 9 (winter/spring 1990): 27–48.

Yohn, Susan M. *A Contest of Faiths: Missionary Women and Pluralism in the American Southwest*. Ithaca: Cornell University Press, 1995.

Contributors

GILBERT R. CADENA is professor and chair of the Ethnic and Women's Studies Department at California State Polytechnic University, Pomona. He is coeditor of *Old Masks, New Faces: Religion and Latino Identity* (Bildner Center for Western Hemisphere Studies, 1995) and has served as board member of the Program for the Analysis of Religion Among Latinas/os (PARAL). His research interests include liberation theology, religious leadership, and Chicanos in the Catholic Church.

KAREN MARY DAVALOS is assistant professor of Chicana/o Studies at Loyola Marymount University. She is author of *Exhibiting Mestizaje: Mexican (American) Museums in the Diaspora* (University of New Mexico Press, 2001) and articles on Chicana/o museums, religion, race and gender, and Chicano/a anthropology. Her current research explores the cultural codes and values that Latino and African American youth employ to resist racism. She is also the chair of Mujeres Activas en Letras y Cambio Social (MALCS).

ORLANDO O. ESPÍN is professor of theology and director of the Center for the Study of Latino/a Catholicism at the University of San Diego. He is author of *The Faith of the People* (Orbis, 1997), coeditor of *From the Heart of our People: Latino/a Explorations in Catholic Systematic Theology* (Orbis, 1999), past president of the Academy of Catholic Hispanic Theologians of the United States (ACHTUS), and the founding editor of the *Journal of*

Hispanic/Latino Theology. Espín is an internationally known scholar of Latino popular Catholicism.

Roberto S. Goizueta is professor of theology at Boston College. He has served as president of the Academy of Catholic Hispanic Theologians of the United States (ACHTUS) and as associate editor of the *Journal of Hispanic/Latino Theology*. Goizueta is also the author of *Caminemos con Jesús: Toward a Hispanic/Latino Theology of Accompaniment* (Orbis, 1995) and coeditor of *Theology: Expanding the Borders* (Twenty-Third Publications, 1998).

Luis D. León is assistant professor of religious studies at Arizona State University. His publications include *La Llorona's Children: Religion, Life, and Death in the Borderlands* (University of California Press, 2002), which looks at the ways Chicana and Chicano practitioners shape and reformulate religious traditions in response to their "borderlands" experience, and the forthcoming *César Chávez and the Religion of Revolution* (University of California Press).

Timothy Matovina is associate professor of theology and director of the Cushwa Center for the Study of American Catholicism at the University of Notre Dame. He has worked with Latino communities in academic and community settings for the past two decades and has published widely on Latino theology, history, and faith expressions. His recent books include *Tejano Religion and Ethnicity* (University of Texas Press, 1995), *Beyond Borders* (Orbis, 2000), and, with Gerald E. Poyo, ¡*Presente! U.S. Latino Catholics from Colonial Origins to the Present* (Orbis, 2000).

Lara Medina is assistant professor of religious studies at California State University, Northridge. She is currently at work on *Las Hermanas: Chicana/Latina Religious-Political Activism* (forthcoming from Temple University Press). Her previous research and publications focus on Chicana spirituality and ritual, U.S. Latino/a theology, and Chicano religious history.

Gary Riebe-Estrella, SVD, is associate professor of practical theology and Hispanic ministry at Catholic Theological Union in Chicago, where he currently serves as vice-president and academic dean. His publications have focused on the cultural underpinnings of Latino Catholicism and on a culturally responsible formation of Latino candidates for ministry. He is a past president of the Academy of Catholic Hispanic Theologians of the United States (ACHTUS) and a renowned conference speaker on topics related to Latino Catholicism and Hispanic ministry.

Index

References to illustrations are printed in italic type.

altars, 13, 25, 104; *altarcitos*, 56–58, 83–84, 93; *ofrendas*, 9, 70–71, 80–81, 83–85, 90, 93; sacred presence, 15, 56–57, 90; *Via Crucis*, 56–58, *59*. *See also* material culture; symbols

Americanization. *See* U.S. Catholicism

Anzaldúa, Gloria, 13, 117, 155n. 21

architecture of domination, 14, 21, 23–24; capitalism, 42, 44, 47, 62–63, 66; institutionalized, 43–45, 47, 59–64; patriarchy, 42, 51–52, 67; physical realities, 42, 47, 64, 66; racism, 42, 51, 59–60, 65–66; residential segregation, 43, 59, 66; resistance to, 45, 51–52, 54, 60–68, 129; white privilege, 59–60, 65; white public space, 65–67, 129. *See also* domination; racism

Asociación Nacional de los Vasallos de Cristo Rey. *See* pious societies

assimilation, 3–5, 24, 40; pressure for, 8, 23, 87–88, 91, 153n. 2; resistance to, 5, 25–26, 46. *See also* immigration; Mexicans and Mexican Americans

Aztecs. *See* Nahuas

Aztlán Cultural Arts Foundation. *See* community organizations

Benítez, Tomás. *See* Self Help Graphics (SHG)

Bruce-Novoa, Juan, 35

calaveras (skulls). See *Día de los Muertos* (Day of the Dead)

capitalism. *See* architecture of domination; *curanderismo*; domination; economic conditions

Catholic Tradition, 1–3, 5–7, 49, 120, 169n. 2, 170n. 14; development of, 2–3, 5, 7; memory and continuity, 7, 141–43, 147; and Mexican traditions, 140–41, 144, 146, 151–52; textual sources of, 142, 145, 147–50. *See also* development of doctrine; popular Catholicism

Chávez, César, 71, 85, 92

Chicago: demographics, 42–45; government policies, 43–45, 47, 62–64, 66, 68, 128; inequality, 42–44, 46–47, 64; Mexicans and Mexican Americans, 42, 44, 59, 62, 161n. 3; neighborhoods, 43–45, 47–48, 97; racism, 42–43, 66. *See also* Pilsen

Chicanos/as, 153n. 2. *See also* Mexicans and Mexican Americans; political struggle

Claretians, 26–32; educating laity, 26–27, 29–32, 39; and Mexican traditions, 32, 38–39, 136; and pious societies, 29–32, 38. *See also* clergy; Hispanic ministry; San Fernando Cathedral

clergy, 21, 25–35, 75, 87, 145–47, 170nn. 10, 16; conflicts with laity, 1, 6–7, 10, 14, 28, 49, 59–60, 91–93, 151; Dolores Mission, 70–71, 74, 78, 81, 87, 93; educating laity, 26–27, 29; in exile, 26, 32–35; and Mexican traditions, 7, 10, 12, 18, 32–35, 37–39, 92–93, 110, 136, 139–40, 151–52; San Fernando Cathedral, 10, 18, 21–22, 25–35, 37–39, 135–36; St. Vitus, 46, 59–60. *See also* Hispanic ministry; popular Catholicism

communio sanctorum (communion of saints). *See* saints

community, 4, 130–35; awareness of, 42, 48, 74, 151; family, 4, 12–13, 45–46, 57–58, 85, 106, 121–22, 134, 138, 149; leaders, 7, 44, 48, 52; Mexican American, 5, 12–14, 22, 28–29, 43–44, 48, 60–61, 70, 101, 114, 121–23, 127, 130–35, 149; support of, 28–29, 47, 49, 82, 152; unity, 48, 56, 64–65, 67, 85–86, 93–94, 131, 133, 138, 149, 151, 162n. 23. *See also* community organizations; identity; Mexicans and Mexican Americans; pious societies

community organizations, 27–32, 36–39, 44, 52; Aztlán Cultural Arts Foundation, 74, 77; *mutualistas*, 24–25, 43; in Pilsen, 45, 52, 60, 62, 163n. 23; pious societies, 27–32, 34, 37–39, 135; Proyecto Pastoral, 78–81; in San Antonio, 23–25, 27–32, 34, 36–39; Spanish Coalition for Jobs, Inc., 45, 52. *See also* pious societies

conquests, 100, 107; Spanish, 8, 13, 74–76, 86, 88, 91, 131; U.S., 3–4, 8, 26, 35–36, 86, 91. *See also* Iberian Catholicism; *mestizaje; segundo mestizaje;* U.S. Catholicism

lo cotidiano (daily life). *See* development of doctrine

Cristero Rebellion. *See* immigration

Cristo Rey (Christ the King), 27–28, 30–32; Asociación Nacional de los Vasallos de Cristo Rey, 27–28, 30–31; and Mexican nationalism, 27–28, 30. *See also* pious societies

curanderismo, 13–15; acceptance of belief, 7, 10, 106–10, 114, 116, 136, 141; believers' worldview, 100–101, 113–14, 123, 126, 138; *botanicas*, 9, 14, 96, 97–99, 102–5, 107, 113–16, 118; and capitalism, 96, 105, 107, 110, 114–16, 122; and Catholic

doctrine, 7, 13, 95, 100, 106–10, 113–14, 116–17, 152; *don*, 101, 115–16; Hortencia, 95, 97–100, 104–5, 109–18, 123, 126, 136, 152; indigenous belief, 10, 95–96, 98, 100–102; *limpias*, 101–2, 107–8, 111–12; material culture, 9–10, 102–5, 110–11, 115; roles of *curandera*, 99–101, 104, 110, 112, 117; saints, 15, 104–5, 113–14; *susto*, 101–2, 113; treatments, 104–8, 110–12; urban context, 10, 14, 95–97, 106, 115; and Western medicine, 100, 112; the whole person, 13, 101, 112, 138; and women, 99, 106–7. *See also* popular Catholicism

death, 120, 130–35; Iberian Catholicism, 75, 132; indigenous belief, 74–75, 86, 132; Mexican American worldview, 12–13, 70, 86–87, 90–91, 120, 127–28, 130–35, 137. See also *Día de los Muertos* (Day of the Dead); symbolic worldview

demographics, 45, 167n. 10; Chicago, 43–44; San Antonio, 19–20; San Fernando Cathedral, 20–21; U.S. Catholics, 2, 5. *See also* urbanization

development of doctrine, 2–3, 136–52; *lo cotidiano*, 10, 47, 67, 136–38, 143, 145–46, 148, 152; culture, 5, 7, 92, 96–97, 114, 140–41, 143–44, 147–49; discernment, 7, 39, 49–50, 120, 139, 147–52; gradualism, 5, 10, 14, 144–45; liberation theology, 136–38; *sensus fidelium*, 39, 49–50, 99, 109–11, 116–17, 120, 145–50, 170n. 14. *See also* Catholic Tradition; popular Catholicism; religious poetics

Día de los Muertos (Day of the Dead), 7, 9, 13, 121–22, 128, 146; acceptance of devotion, 7, 10, 91–93, 141, 151; *calaveras*, 69, 71, 77, 81, 82, 90; concept of death, 13, 70, 86–87, 90, 124, 128, 130–32, 135; cultural reclamation, 77, 86–89, 91, 94; history of, 71–72, 75–76; and indigenous belief, 9, 13, 69, 72, 75–77, 81–83, 85–88, 91, 94, 132, 134; material culture, 9–10, 69–71, 74, 77–85, 90; memory, 71–72, 78, 81, 85–86, 89–91, 94, 131, 134, 151; *ofrendas*, 69, 70–71, 73, 80–81, 83–85, 90, 93; poetry, 82–83, 89–91, 94; preparation for, 72, 75, 77–81, 93–94; as resistance, 72–73, 82–83, 85–90, 94, 132, 151; *Todos los Santos*, 75–76, 91, 93. *See also* death; popular Catholicism

Díaz-Stevens, Ana María, 14

Dolan, Jay P., 3